WAKETH THE WATCHMAN?

WAKETH THE WATCHMAN?

THE MILITARY AND THE JFK ASSASSINATION

HAROLD WEISBERG

EDITED BY
GERALD GINOCCHIO AND DENNIS MACDONALD

Skyhorse Publishing

Skyhorse Publishing books may be purchased in bulk at special discounts for sales promotion, corporate gifts, fund-raising, or educational purposes. Special editions can also be created to specifications. For details, contact the Special Sales Department, Skyhorse Publishing, 307 Fifth Avenue, 4th Floor, New York, NY 10016 or info@skyhorsepublishing.com.

Visit our website at www.skyhorsepublishing.com.

10 9 8 7 6 5 4 3 2 1

Library of Congress Cataloging-in-Publication Data is available on file.

Cover design by David Ter-Avanesyan
Cover photo credit: National Archives

Print ISBN: 978-1-5107-8671-4
Ebook ISBN: 978-1-5107-8672-1

Printed in the United States of America

Remarks Prepared for Delivery at the Trade Mart in Dallas, Texas, November 22, 1963 [Undelivered]

We in this country, in this generation, are—by destiny rather than choice—the watchmen on the walls of world freedom. We ask, therefore, that we may be worthy of our power and responsibility, that we may exercise our strength with wisdom and restraint, and that we may achieve in our time and for all time the ancient vision of "peace on earth, good will toward men." That must always be our goal, and the righteousness of our cause must always underlie our strength. For as was written long ago: "except the Lord keep the city, the watchman waketh but in vain."

—President John F. Kennedy
November 22, 1963

CONTENTS

EDITORS' INTRODUCTION

Harold Weisberg was without peer in his knowledge of the factual evidence related to the assassination of President John F. Kennedy. His *Whitewash*, the first book critical of the Warren Commission, was published just a few months after the release of the *Warren Report* and its twenty-six-volume appendix of hearings and exhibits. On the basis of a meticulous, factual, and logical dissection of the government's own evidence, Weisberg demonstrated that the alleged "lone-nut" assassin, Lee Harvey Oswald, fired no shots and that the assassination was the end product of a conspiracy.[1] *Whitewash* was followed by several books as he probed deeper into the government's case and how it conducted its investigation.[2] When he encountered roadblocks to obtaining information, as he often did, he turned to the courts using the newly-enacted Freedom of Information Act (FOIA) to obtain documents that the Warren Commission and other federal agencies had unjustifiably withheld. It was in the context of one of his many FOIA cases (CA75-226) that the Justice Department itself declared in court that Weisberg knew more about the JFK assassination than anyone in the FBI.

Through many years of painstaking work, Weisberg steadfastly refused to speculate on the identity of the real assassins. Among the major findings of his research was that the government, with all its resources and expertise, had not really investigated the crime itself, but was content to pin the blame on the dead Oswald. This meant that the official investigation would provide no leads that could be followed in trying to identify the real assassins. It would certainly not help matters that the media shirked its responsibility by failing to even raise questions about the Warren Commission's work and the basis of its conclusions.

Nor did it object to the commission's conduct of its hearings in absolute secrecy, as it has done in cases of far less significance. In praising the *Warren Report* on its release, months before the release of evidence on which it was supposedly based, the media was complicit in the government's deception, a complicity that for the most part continues to this very day. The critical work of investigating the president's murder was left to individuals without the vast resources of the government and the media. Unfortunately, many concocted conspiracy theories with little or no real evidence, a practice which Weisberg was quick to point out only further confused, misled, and misinformed the public, thereby reducing whatever pressure that might have been brought to bear on the government to be honest about the assassination and its official investigation, provide its evidence to the public, and conduct a real investigation, however belatedly.

Government stonewalling was not the only obstacle Weisberg faced in pursuing his work; he was also severely hampered by several life-threatening illnesses that for years made it virtually impossible for him to use the fruits of all those FOIA lawsuits—the thousands of pages of Warren Commission, FBI, CIA, and Secret Service documents stored in the basement of his home.[3] He decided that the best use of his remaining years would be to make a record for history, which resulted in producing numerous unedited, unpublished manuscripts,[4] among which is *Waketh the Watchman?* Knowing his time was limited and wanting to get as much down on paper as he could, Weisberg was not—and could not be—concerned with producing a polished product. Nonetheless, the record he left is impressive.

Waketh the Watchman? represents a departure from his earlier work in that it is more speculative, but his speculation about who was behind the assassination of President Kennedy is grounded in fact. Weisberg adopts the lawyers' approach of building a circumstantial case based on answers to three basic questions: who had the **motive**; who had the **means**; and who had the **opportunity** to carry out the assassination. He presents a solid case implicating the upper echelon of the military in the Pentagon and Joint Chiefs of Staff, but it is important to note, as Weisberg makes clear, this is not an indictment of the military as a whole. It also needs to be said, as Weisberg does, that as strong as his circumstantial case is, it is not proof, and certainly not "proof beyond a reasonable doubt." He concedes that we will probably never know who the actual gunmen were, or who gave the orders to assassinate the president, but that does not mean Weisberg's effort is without value. *Waketh the Watchman?* gives direction to further investigation, and more importantly, highlights significant institutional failures which we must acknowledge and correct for the sake of the viability of this country going forward.

Weisberg's ability to put together this case, as well as his other work, is a testament to his remarkable memory and intriguing and educational life experiences,[5] which prepared him well to undertake this work. He began writing for newspapers when he was still in high school and later became the Washington correspondent for *Click* magazine, investigating and exposing Nazi cartels, among other things. For a time in the 1930s, he was an investigator and editor for the U.S. Senate Civil Liberties Committee. Weisberg also worked for the Justice Department on the famous "Bloody Harlan" prosecution. He was a soldier in World War II, and was tapped to become an intelligence analyst for the OSS, the forerunner of the CIA. In all these various experiences, Weisberg honed his skills as an investigator and intelligence analyst who, as he puts it, developed a knack for seeing and understanding the significance of the obvious. This is a skill which he puts to good use in this book, as he did in all of his work.[6] Through all this work, he was supported by his wife, Lillian, acknowledging that without her none of this would have been possible.

As editors, we approached our task first and foremost with care to keep Weisberg's voice and argument intact. Our purpose was to make his rough draft into a publishable work that brings out his argument with clarity. To accomplish this task, we reorganized some chapters; corrected occasional grammatical errors; deleted some unnecessary material; added explanatory footnotes, some appendices, and a selected bibliography; and supplied necessary citations. We also took the liberty of slightly modifying his original title, *Waketh the Watchman? Our Strangelovian*[7] *Military and the Kennedy Assassination*, as we explain below. Our hope, finally, is that our editing succeeds in making *Waketh the Watchman?* accessible to the general public.

We first met Harold Weisberg in 1971 when we were undergraduate students at the University of Wisconsin at Stevens Point. Weisberg was the main speaker at a Symposium on the JFK Assassination at the university, which we helped organize. Then, as young sociology professors in the early 1980s interested in teaching courses on the JFK assassination, we reached out to Mr. Weisberg who generously offered his time and advice and unfettered access to the thousands of pages of government documents on both the JFK and King assassinations. Our relationship with Mr. Weisberg over the next roughly twenty years grew to the point where we considered him a friend as well as a mentor. Through countless letters and occasional visits with him at his home in Frederick, Maryland, he inspired and assisted us in the writing and lecturing we have done over the years on the Kennedy assassination.

It is partly because of our special relationship with Mr. Weisberg, as well as a familiarity with his published and unpublished work on the JFK assassination, that we felt qualified to undertake the editing of this unpublished work. Of all the unpublished manuscripts which Weisberg wrote to make a record for history, we believe this one especially deserves a wider audience. So, it is with a deep sense of obligation to the truth and respect for the legacy of commitment to the truth that distinguished the life and work of Harold Weisberg (1913–2002) that we present *Waketh the Watchman? The Military and the Kennedy Assassination*.

Finally, we feel honored to have played a small part in assisting Mr. Weisberg in fulfilling those "promises to keep" that Robert Frost spoke of so eloquently in "Stopping by Woods on a Snowy Evening," the last lines of which Mr. Weisberg frequently invoked:

The woods are lovely, dark and deep,
But I have promises to keep,
And miles to go before I sleep,
And miles to go before I sleep.

CHAPTER 1

THE JFK ASSASSINATION AND ITS INVESTIGATION: HISTORICAL CONTEXT

One of the by-products of the "Cold War" between the US and the USSR was the emergence of the national security state in which the institutional order comes to be dominated by considerations of national defense.[1] Two of its key features are the widespread cloaking of government policies and actions in a veil of official secrecy and the increased militarization of society and its institutions. Both served to undermine the free and democratic foundation of American society. "National security" became a rationale for withholding from the public knowledge necessary for the exercise of the rights and the obligations of citizens in a democratic society.[2] And it became a rationale for military and intelligence agencies to pursue their own policies instead of those of duly elected officials accountable to the electorate.

"National Security" and Official Secrecy

During the Cold War, withholding information from the American people was an everyday occurrence. Aside from seeking to preserve the mystique of secrecy, the agencies were intent on withholding from the American people information that was very well known to the USSR and other foreign governments. The courts were largely complicit; no claim of official secrecy was too ridiculous for them to accept, however irrational, preposterous, outrageous or incredible, as long as "national security" was allegedly at stake.

Through my years of efforts to rescue from oblivion official records on the assassinations of John F. Kennedy and Martin Luther King, records that belong to the people as a matter of law, I have come to know how the "national security" excuse is misused to maintain official secrecy, even when the "national security" claim is absurd on its face. In one of my Freedom of Information Act (FOIA) cases, the FBI released among other items a newspaper clipping. The clipping included the well-known name of one of its agents which the FBI redacted a dozen times from that single story! How redacting the name could protect national security when it had already been published is difficult to fathom. And yet, the clever clerk who perpetrated that outrage was rewarded with a promotion to special agent! In another example, the CIA withheld even the name of a hotel and claimed that, too, was required as a matter of "national security," because the hotel name would reveal to the local government the name of the city in which the CIA was working. In fact, the CIA was working there with the knowledge of the local government. In yet another case, the FBI claimed that maintaining the secrecy of its source was essential to "national security," that to release it would threaten international relations and might even lead to war. However, the source—the Royal Canadian Mounted Police (RCMP)—had already been disclosed by the FBI in previously released records. It also substituted for withheld records slip sheets indicating that the RCMP was its source. Yet, to protect its source in the interest of national security, it withheld dozens of documents. Neither the FBI nor the CIA ever displayed institutional embarrassment about the preposterous claims they made in order to keep information secret when there was no justification for doing so.

When many of the documents withheld on the grounds of "national security" were eventually disclosed, it became obvious that there had been no rational justification for withholding them, that their disclosure in no way threatened the nation's security. Instead, it appears that there are two basic motives behind this misuse of the national security justification. The first amounts to plain stonewalling, making lawsuits more costly and time-consuming for those legitimately seeking information from their government. The second is to avoid the possibility of official embarrassment over the information itself.

In 1994, hundreds of thousands of previously withheld records were disclosed, in compliance with the 1992 JFK Records law,[3] records kept secret for thirty years with no legal justification. When the records had to be disclosed, it became obvious that they were withheld on the basis of lies, in some cases rising to the level of perjury. Their disclosure did no harm of any kind to any proper government activity or function.

The work of the Warren Commission provides an excellent example of the harms caused by the misuse of official secrecy. Without it, the Warren Report on the assassination of President Kennedy could never have been issued. The commission would not have dared! It is only because the commission took testimony in secret that its conclusions could seem viable. Had it been known that in taking testimony the commission did not seek the truth, it would have been a major scandal. With the secrecy lifted, it became evident that much of the testimony it took directly contradicted the commission's conclusions. This is also true of the commission's unpublished documentation; it says and means the exact opposite of what the commission said. (see Appendix 1 for a few examples.) In this case, the secrecy concealed the failure of the commission to seriously investigate the president's murder and ensured that whoever was responsible for it got away with it.

The contradictions between the commission's own evidence and its report are so obvious that by mid-February 1965, I was able to complete my first book, *Whitewash*, refuting the report using only the commission's own evidence. That report had only been made public at the end of September 1964! In the almost three decades since, not a single error has been attributed to that book by all the official agencies that examined it closely seeking to find fault. Of the hundreds of people named in the book, not a single one has written or phoned to complain of unfair treatment or of error.

"National Security" and Militarization

In addition to the cult of secrecy that emerged, the new understanding of "national security" requirements resulted in an ever-greater role for the military in society. Two major aspects of this are the usurpation by the military and intelligence agencies of the powers of elected officials to set US policy, particularly foreign policy, and the devotion of an ever-increasing share of resources to military spending, both directly, such as weapons systems, and indirectly, such as aspects of the space program.

As the military became more important, it encroached more and more on the authority to set national policy, an authority granted by the Constitution to the president and Congress. The military leaders seemed to believe that in so doing, it was following the path of patriotism, serving the national interest and providing for "national security." In fact, as it quietly assumed an ever-greater role, usurping civilian authority, even that of the elected president, it subverted our most basic principles.

The "founding fathers," the most brilliant of the world's political thinkers in my view, regarded excessive power in the hands of the military as dangerous and contrary to the maintenance of a free and democratic society. In the *Federalist Papers* (No. 25), Alexander Hamilton, in arguing that the common defense would be best served by a national army rather than state armies, warned that the people have the most to fear from those they see as their trusted protectors:

> For it is a truth, which the experience of the ages has attested, that the people are commonly more in danger when the means of injuring their rights are in the possession of those of whom they entertain the least suspicion.[4]

Of what we have been permitted to piece together of the assassination of President John F. Kennedy, despite the official secrecy in which the Warren Commission's fraud of an investigation was conducted, Hamilton's prescient words have become frighteningly significant.

A good example is provided in Arthur Schlesinger's *A Thousand Days.* In his account of a conference Kennedy had with his military experts about the morass in which they were bogging us down in Southeast Asia, he notes their desire to wrest control over decision making from the president through their insistence that he agree in advance to every step they might decide is necessary, even dropping nuclear weapons on Hanoi or Peking.

> The President was appalled at the sketchy nature of American military planning for Laos—the lack of detail and the unanswered questions. One day they suggested sending troops into two airstrips in Pathet Lao territory; they could land a thousand troops a day, and there were 5000 enemy guerrillas nearby. Kennedy, after interrogation, discovered that the airstrips could only be used by day and that it would take a week or so for troops to reach them overland. He then asked what would happen if the Pathet Lao allowed the troops to land for two days and then attacked. The military did not seem to have thought of that.
>
> For all their differences, the military left a predominant impression that they did not want ground troops at all unless they could send at least 140,000 men equipped with tactical nuclear weapons. By now the Pentagon was developing what would become its standard line in Southeast Asia—unrelenting opposition to limited intervention except on the impossible condition that the President agree in advance to every further step they deemed sequential, including, on occasion, nuclear bombing of Hanoi and even Peking. At one National Security Council meeting General Lemnitzer outlined the processes by which each American action would provoke a Chinese counteraction, provoking in turn an even more drastic American response. He concluded: "If we are given the right to use nuclear weapons, we can guarantee victory." The President sat glumly rubbing his upper molar, saying nothing. After a moment someone said, "Mr. President, perhaps you would have the General explain to us what he means by victory." Kennedy grunted and dismissed the meeting. Later he said, "Since he couldn't think of any further escalation, he would have to promise us victory."
>
> The Chiefs had their own way of reacting to the Cuban fiasco. It soon began to look to the White House as if they were taking care

> to build a record which would permit them to say that, whatever the President did, he acted against their advice. This had not yet been identified as a tactic, however, and in April 1961 their opposition to limited intervention had a powerful effect.[5]

The Joint Chiefs of Staff seemed to understand the Constitution as giving the military the responsibility for deciding between war and peace, not the Congress at the request of the president. They had planned to provoke China so that China would have to react. That would have led to a stronger United States reaction until we would be dropping nuclear bombs. Of course, had they dropped, the destruction would not have been limited to that distant side of the world, but would have set the entire world afire in the deadliest of fires resulting in fatalities thousands of miles from the immediate flames. The slaughter would have exceeded anything in history. While the military had ample civilian support for its policy of policing the world, our Constitution denies to the military any such authority.

If they could drop nuclear bombs wherever they chose, General Lyman Lemnitzer, Chairman of the Joint Chiefs of Staff, said, they "can guarantee victory." But what kind of "victory" can there be once all the world's nuclear bombs are set off? "Victory" for us at home with nuclear bombs killing us by the millions and ruining the lives of even more?

So, long before the existence of such terrible weapons of unimaginable power, Hamilton was so very right in saying that the people have most to fear from those they believe they have least to fear, their defenders, the military. The US Constitution prohibits military control over matters of war and peace. Yet, for all practical purposes, the military achieved such control and used it exactly as the founders feared.

The simple dedication to Arthur Schlesinger's book, *A Thousand Days*, reads, "In memory of John Fitzgerald Kennedy." This is directly followed by a thought-provoking quotation from Hemingway:

> If people bring so much courage to this world the world has to kill them to break them, so of course it kills them. The world breaks every one and afterward many are strong at the broken places. But

> those that will not break it kills. It kills the very good and the very gentle and the very brave impartially.[6]

How pertinent when Kennedy's policy was the opposite of the military's. As he made clear in his eloquent commencement address at American University in the summer of 1963, he wanted not the world afire but the world at peace, "But those that will not break it kills." Apt as Schlesinger regarded this simple truth when he began his masterful book with it, there is now, as this book reflects, even more cause to consider it as an accurate account of what happened.

Another example of the military's efforts to manipulate policy and undermine presidential authority is its use of body-counts in Vietnam. Some time after Schlesinger's book appeared I was visiting my friend, the late Steve Barber, then the Washington correspondent for the conservative London *Daily Telegraph.* Steve had been in Vietnam and had reported on that war for some time. He was the first to confirm to me the obvious and fairly widespread belief that the body-count figures of enemy killed that the military reported were fraudulent. Steve told me that whatever they did or did not report, all reporters in Vietnam were aware of this.

In those days, government agencies regarded opposition to the government's obviously wrong Vietnam policies, policies that followed the military's agenda, as worse than criminal. Had it not been pursuing its own agenda, military advisors would have counseled the president to avoid involvement there. To further its own agenda, the military created situations that would and did lead to a wider war deepening our involvement. These actions were pursued despite the military's knowledge that even if they could conquer a country, they could not conquer a people who resisted conquest. In all that followed, the deliberate dishonesty of the military is a central consideration. The war, in fact, led to tremendous loss of life, more than fifty eight thousand Americans and more than three million Vietnamese on both sides died. Millions more were maimed. The social, economic, and environmental costs were enormous.

In addition to the military, various intelligence agencies were involved in undermining the Constitution in relation to the war. I was involved in one of the earliest protests of our actions in Vietnam. I was one of a group of writers and editors who added our signatures to an ad protesting our government's actions and policies in Vietnam. The CIA added copies of our ad to its files, one for each signer. Several of these names were marked indicating the agency's special interest in some of the participants. I remember only two, me and pediatrician Doctor Benjamin Spock. That was in 1966, after I had published *Whitewash*. Under our form of government, intelligence agencies have no business spying on and monitoring what Americans say and believe. Nonetheless, they did spy on us and the anti-war movement generally, compiling secret files on many who held views not approved by the government.

Complicit Media

Another casualty of the Cold War and the national security state was the media, which abdicated its critical role in a democratic society of informing the people and keeping the government honest. I recall that without exception the major media supported this wrongful policy and military activity, this undeclared war. In general, it reported the military's lies as established truth. It criticized and defamed those citizens who spoke out against that war and those policies. It reported as fact those fraudulent body count figures of casualties on the other side and military successes on our side. In this the media deceived and misled us all, including the president who was given those very same figures. The inevitable result intended by the military and amplified by the media was that the president was led to believe that the war was going favorably for us when the exact opposite was true.

As Steve Barber and I were talking about American policy in Vietnam, I told him that it was the military's policy to get us into a war with China, recalling the aforementioned quote from Schlesinger. He could not believe that, if true, it was public knowledge. I suggested that he look up Lemnitzer in the index of Schlesinger's book. He did and he was stunned. "How could I have missed that?" he asked. That he could and did reflects the problem faced by even honest reporters: The volume of information available to them is overwhelming. They cannot possibly keep up with all they should know.

Whatever the reason for the media's failure, Schlesinger's story went unreported. This is also true of what I will quote from Schlesinger later regarding Kennedy's instructions to Averell Harriman about nuclear treaty negotiations with Moscow. Yet both contain essential information that should be known to American citizens and their representatives in Congress whose authority it is to determine how much and on what the government spends.

In recent years, the media has on many matters, especially foreign policy, been virtually an arm of government in supporting policies that depart from the American tradition and violate our laws, international agreements, and treaties. Vietnam was one example. Before that it was Korea. Very few Americans, including a new generation of reporters, are aware that the direct causes of each of those costly wars was our refusal to permit the elections that had been agreed upon in international settlements after World War II. We fought those wars because the sides that obviously would have won those elections were not the side we favored. We talked about free elections, but that was Cold War talk. We believed in free elections where "our" side would win.

In each case the presidents involved were persuaded by the military to enact these policies. And in each case and all similar cases, politicians and the media promoted these policies that violated international law, our treaty commitments, and our own Constitution. This included most significantly fighting wars that under our Constitution can only be authorized by Congressional declarations of war. The consequence is that since World War II, we have been in varying degrees and in innumerable places engaged in de facto war almost continuously, without any declaration of war by Congress.

Revising History

Like all presidents, John Kennedy inherited the policies of his predecessor, particularly with respect to Cuba, Vietnam, and relations with the Soviet Union. And like most, he depended upon his military advisors, particularly in war situations. In the early days of his presidency, his policies reflect this.

In recent years, a minor industry has sprung up dedicated to rewriting the history of the thousand days of Kennedy's presidency. It has served to undermine the public's affection for him and his policies. In these revisionist accounts, he is portrayed as an entirely different man and an entirely different president than he was and than he wanted to be. Some of this results from a failure to understand that there were really two quite different President Kennedys. The presidency changed Kennedy in extraordinary ways. Those two weeks in October 1962, when his decisions might determine whether the world would be incinerated or not, convinced him that we needed to find ways to step back from the brink.

In the Cuba Missile Crisis,[7] Khrushchev had given Kennedy that decision to make.[8] Despite the urgings of most of his civilian advisors and all of his military advisors, Kennedy made the right decision. As a consequence, the world did not go up in a nuclear holocaust and, haltingly, detente began.

When he realized how close the world had come to an unprecedented disaster he became what was generally referred to as a "dove." Despite fearing defeat in the Congress, he began nuclear detente by initiating the limited test-ban agreement with the Soviet Union. He realized that the first step in preventing a nuclear disaster was to stop expanding the nuclear arsenal.

Twisted Priorities

Thirty years later, we are pressing the rest of the world to forego the acquisition of nuclear weapons. As I write this, the newspapers are holding forth the possibility of war with North Korea over the nuclear issue. While we lead the world in the push to prevent the proliferation of nuclear weapons, we spend a fortune designing and manufacturing new nuclear weapons of our own, which given the disintegration of the Soviet Union, there seems to be no rational need for, if ever there was. The military insists that we need them and the military gets what it wants, whether or not it is genuinely needed and whether or not it good for us or the world. For Senators and Representatives, failure to support these programs is political suicide; what the military wants, the military gets.

Spending vast sums on nuclear weapons and other unnecessary military programs means a lack of funding to address our most pressing needs. We cannot afford to adequately address such problems as crime, unemployment, homelessness, failing schools, and unsafe roads and bridges.

The consequences for the political and economic health of our country are enormous. Those countries that do not waste their wealth on unneeded military supplies, equipment, and bases, improve their schools and prepare their young people to be more productive and competitive.

The distribution of military spending has much to do with ongoing political and popular support for wasteful military production. Military installations and production facilities are crucial to the economies of most states. Members of Congress, therefore, vote against such unneeded and wasteful military appropriations at their political peril. Of course, unless and until that production can be replaced by production that meets our real needs, ending it would create massive unemployment. There is now no substitute for those military related jobs, because since World War II there has been no planning for peacetime, non-military production.

Under the most military-minded of recent administrations, those of Ronald Reagan and George H. W. Bush, the national debt climbed to four times what was accumulated under all previous administrations. While condemning mythical "welfare queens" who allegedly drove Cadillacs to pick up their welfare checks, Reagan lavished the national treasure on what the military did not need, want, and, in some cases, did not even work. He did this with such extravagance that a common hammer was billed to the government for as much as many earn in a week, all the while cutting to the bone funding for those most in need.

Our national policy was largely one of cutting as much as possible from basic needs while wasting billions on those who finance political campaigns through their ownership of the means of military production and those who profit from it, all the while neglecting the education of our young and so many other societal needs.

Countries that did not manufacture all these missiles and warheads and all the planes that could not perform as intended, that did not deny real and existing needs in favor of adventures in space, prospered. Their young received better educations than ours, preparing them to do what economic growth and efficient production requires. Their infant mortality rate declined while ours climbed. They were able to provide excellent medical care for all while many of our people have none at all. The effort at health-care reform during the Clinton administration in 1994 was defeated. What the rest of the developed world had, we could not afford.

Yet, in that same year, we sent our 64th shuttle into space. The September 1994 mission was to study "the sun's corona, or outer atmosphere, to gather information about solar wind," which "can disrupt radio communications." According to the report in the *Washington Post*, a special "$7 million clip-on jet pack" was developed for that project so that repairs could be made in space without the astronauts being tethered to the space station.[9]

That money was not available for doing something about the air we breathe that makes so many ill, killing some. The fortune required to send that shuttle into space to test that clip-on jet pack could not be spent on bridges on earth that are in danger of crumbling or have been closed as unsafe, nor could it be spent on the repairs so many essential highways need; those funds having been devoted to the military and to exciting, but hardly essential, adventures in space.

There are published reports that the military is developing aircraft capable of flying at Mach 7—seven times the speed of sound—and an SR-75 "Penetrator" plane, a replacement for the S-71 Blackbird spy plane, that can fly at three and a half times the speed of sound.

After the collapse of the Soviet Union and the end of the Cold War, the need for such disproportionate spending on the military is, at least, highly questionable.[10]

The Cold War may be over in some respects, but the structures and principles it built and maintained are alive and well, and may be so in part as a result of the assassination of a president who attempted to change course.

It is time to rethink the course our country has taken. Our priorities as a nation have been distorted. We need to restore our sense of values, of what is important, and focus on the genuine needs of the nation. And we must reconnect with the principles on which the nation was founded.

In the chapters that follow, these themes will be explored in their relation to the Kennedy presidency and the assassination. Had the assassination of President Kennedy been the act of a "lone nut," its historical context would be of no great significance. Because it was a conspiracy, as demonstrated by the government's own evidence, the distortion of our basic institutions and fundamental principles by the Cold War ideology must be explored in trying to understand why the president was overthrown and why no serious effort was made to identify the conspirators. The official secrecy, the interference of the military and intelligence agencies in policy setting, the militarization of our institutions, and the complicity of the media all need to be considered.

CHAPTER 2

VIETNAM: "DECEPTION, INTRIGUE, AND THE STRUGGLE FOR POWER"

Following the Cuba Missile Crisis, John Kennedy set about trying to change these self-destructive national policies. He made this clear in his June 1963 American University commencement address, the so-called "Peace Speech," in sending Averill Harriman to negotiate the limited nuclear test-ban agreement with the Soviet Union, and in his attempts to cancel wasteful and destructive military production. And, despite what the revisionists tell us, Kennedy had decided to withdraw US forces from Vietnam, but only after the 1964 election, realizing that doing so before would cost him the election and any hope of ending our involvement. His actions and intentions regarding Vietnam are a matter of record as is his insistence that he would never send combat troops there. This is the real meaning of his changed policy.

The military and its political allies, however, made every effort to frustrate his plans.

During the first week of June 1968, I conducted the interviews for a then popular radio program, "Authors' Roundtable," at the annual convention of the American Booksellers Association at the Shoreham Hotel, in Washington. One of those I interviewed was retired Army General

James Gavin, widely known as Kennedy's intellectual general, who had just published a book. I asked him about Kennedy's reported intention of getting us out of Vietnam. What Gavin told me has since become public knowledge and is recorded in the then secret National Security Action Memorandum (NSAM) 263. Gavin said that Kennedy had ordered the withdrawal of one thousand of our "advisers" in Vietnam by the end of 1963 and had decided to get the US out entirely after the election. Gavin also told me, and I am confident these are close to his exact words, that Kennedy was calling some of the generals in and telling them, "Vietnam is a political problem," and asking, "What can I do to convince you that political problems are not susceptible of military solutions?"

Gavin's account is confirmed by Kenneth P. O'Donnell and David F. Powers, the two men who, outside his family, were closest to Kennedy from the time he first ran for the House of Representatives. O'Donnell was the president's appointments secretary, the one who controls access to the president, and also the staff administrator. Like Powers, he was Kennedy's confidant and frequent companion. They had a closer personal relationship with the president than anyone other than his brother Robert. Powers served many roles but in fact he was "a guy that President Kennedy liked to have around him as much as possible." Press Secretary Pierre Salinger described O'Donnell as the most powerful and influential man Kennedy had in the White House. O'Donnell and Powers's 1972 book, "*Johnny, We Hardly Knew Ye,*" is a first-person account of their time in the White House. Toward the end of the book, in discussing Kennedy and Vietnam, they explain his view.

> The president had viewed Vietnam as a political problem, rather than a military crisis, and he had hoped that the fighting between Diem's Saigon government and the Communist Viet Cong could be stopped by political compromising on both sides to work out a truce and a settlement such as he and Averell Harriman had effected in Laos in 1961 with Khrushchev's help. Such a solution became impossible because Diem's fanatical brother and sister-in-law, the Nhus, persecuting and terrorizing non-Communist political enemies and carrying on religious warfare against nonpolitical

> Buddhists, had turned the Saigon regime into a police state with no popular support.[1]

While it may be suspected that because of their closeness to Kennedy, O'Donnell and Powers might be biased, there is virtually nothing that I quote here or later that does not have confirmation in other sources. That they loved the man does not in itself make their book dishonest or inaccurate.

One of the best books on Kennedy and Vietnam, in my view, is John Newman's 1992 book, *JFK and Vietnam*. When Newman wrote it, he was a major in Army intelligence and for twenty-five years was an academic who studied and taught Asian history. He had access to official records, particularly those of the Army, and to innumerable people who had first-hand knowledge. The book's subtitle, "Deception, Intrigue, and the Struggle for Power," is descriptive of its contents.

Newman's book is an excellent record of one of the most significant and tragic episodes in our history. Impressively researched, with excellent sources, and well organized, it is an exceptional achievement that makes a complicated history accessible. More than that, it presents a solid and irrefutable case of the military's most deliberate dishonesty, deception, manipulation, contrivance, and overt mendacity for the sole purpose of undoing the president's explicit national policy on Vietnam. The military did the exact opposite of what he wanted and ordered. It provoked situations and manufactured statistics that limited his options to only those favored by the military. Almost within minutes of his assassination, the policy statement he had drafted in his NSAM 263 was transformed into precisely the opposite of what he intended. Instead of the beginning of the US pullout from Vietnam, it became in LBJ's NSAM 273, a significant escalation of the war.[2]

The efforts by military officials to undermine the president's policy had begun just a few days before the assassination at a conference in Hawaii organized in part to work out the implementation of NSAM 263. As Newman indicates in quoting from *The Pentagon Papers*, Kennedy's order to withdraw troops was turned into "essentially an accounting exercise" consisting mostly "of the normal turnover cycle." Newman details what was to have happened, the units from which those thousand men were to have come and how it was to be negated, the details being handled by a couple of clerks.[3]

In his chapter, "The Drums after Dallas," Newman details the changes made in NSAM 273 after Kennedy was assassinated, changes that made it the exact opposite of what he wanted.[4] In particular, the original restricted actions against North Vietnam to South Vietnamese forces in keeping with Kennedy's insistence against introducing US combat forces to Vietnam. The revision strikes that section. As Newman points out, NSAM 273 was a significant escalation of the war.[5] The changes made possible by what became known as "The Gulf of Tonkin incident," an incident created by the military for the purpose of expanding the war. "The dam broke when NSAM 273 was rewritten four days after Kennedy's assassination."[6]

The final sentences of the chapter sum up the radical turnaround in American policy on Vietnam following the murder of President Kennedy.

> . . . While Kennedy had told O'Donnell in the spring of 1963 that he could not pull out of Vietnam until he was reelected, "So we had better make damned sure I am reelected." At a White House reception on Christmas eve, a month after he succeeded to the presidency, Lyndon Johnson told the Joint Chiefs: "Just let me get elected, and then you can have your war."[7]

It would undoubtedly be a mistake—and a very big mistake—to believe that all of the many in the military who were involved in this deliberate subversion of our system of government understood it that way at all. They likely believed they were acting in the interest of the country's "national security." I do not doubt that in their minds they were patriots, carrying out what they understood as their responsibilities. But they were wrong in what they did, wrong in how they did it, and wrong in why they did it.

The military usurped presidential authority, and the consequences were disastrous for the United States, its allies, and Vietnam. This happened because the military violated the Constitution that clearly gives to the president and Congress the right and responsibility to determine national policy, not the military. That the policy was changed around entirely from withdrawal to escalation as soon as Kennedy was assassinated—completed, wrapped up—signed and sealed within four days—inevitably points fingers of suspicion at the military.

To the nation's great cost and everlasting shame, by Kennedy's assassination, the military got what he was denying it.

It also got us a major defeat in a war, the war the military wanted and got.

This account of the early history of the war in Vietnam, particularly with respect of Kennedy's responsibility, is disputed by those generously referred to as "revisionists." They do not merely "revise" our history to correct error or misunderstanding; they rewrite it to give it an entirely different meaning. They rewrite it to hold President Kennedy responsible for our initial involvement in Vietnam and for the catastrophic consequences of the military's policies that began with Eisenhower and were implemented by the Johnson and Nixon administrations.

The distortions of this history began with the efforts to give an entirely different meaning to the disaster of the Bay of Pigs invasion of Cuba and to shift responsibility for it. Cubans who had fled when Castro's revolution succeeded in throwing out the Batista dictatorship invaded the island in an effort to overthrow the Castro regime. Batista's was the last in a long line of dictatorships that country suffered beginning when the United States went to war with Spain at the turn of the century. Whether or not, as many Cubans believed, they were about to free themselves from the Spanish yoke, the fact is that those military dictatorships were all with United States support and resulted in United States interests taking control of that poor country's economy. The country was still so poor after more than a half century of United States domination that when Castro defeated the Batista dictatorship, with Batista and his gang finding refuge in the United States, most Cubans had no shoes and could not read and write. The unsuccessful invasion at the Bay of Pigs was in fact what Kennedy inherited from the Eisenhower administration. What Kennedy also inherited from the Eisenhower administration, and what also constrained his ability to set

United States policy, was the unusual act of the outgoing Eisenhower administration in breaking relations with Cuba just before Kennedy's inauguration. That decision, by tradition, would be the decision of the incoming administration, not the outgoing one.

A little-known part of the history was reported by Watergater E. Howard Hunt in his 1974 book, *Undercover: Memoirs of An American Secret Agent.* In it he says of Richard Nixon, Eisenhower's vice president and the man Kennedy defeated to become president, "Secretly, . . . he was the White House action officer for our [CIA] covert project." If that invasion had succeeded, Hunt writes, "I was to fly there with the provisional government" he and the CIA had handpicked to take over.[8] Hunt, of the extreme political right, was also to write the constitution for the government of which he was to be the political guide.

Referring to a meeting Kennedy later had with General Douglas MacArthur, O'Donnell and Powers say:

> The president later gave us a rundown of MacArthur's remarks. He was extremely critical of the military advice that the president was getting from the Pentagon, blaming it on the military leadership of the previous ten years which, he said, had advanced the wrong officers. "You were lucky to have the mistake happen in a place like Cuba, where the strategic cost was not too great," he said about the Bay of Pigs, and urged the president not to listen too carefully to advisers who favored a military buildup in Vietnam.[9]

Later in their book, where they deal with Vietnam, the advice of both of these authorities is repeated in slightly different words:

> Charles de Gaulle sent word that we could expect no military help from France under any circumstances. He explained to Kennedy later in Paris that he would support the United States in a total war against Russia, but after his own bitter experience of fighting in Southeast Asia during the early 1950s, he wanted no part of warfare in that area of the world. "You should stay out of there, too," he added emphatically.[10]

and,

> MacArthur remarked privately to the president, he was lucky to have learned so much about the value of his military advice from an operation like the Bay of Pigs disaster, where the strategic cost was small.[11]

Kennedy assumed full responsibility for the Bay of Pigs military fiasco that had been wished on him by the Eisenhower/Nixon administration and which he confronted soon after he was sworn in, when there wasn't a thing, he could do about it with all those Cuban invaders armed and trained in Guatemala. Kennedy's full acceptance of responsibility was well received. He did not say a word about having inherited a project of the previous administration which had arranged it so that he would have no real choice. I have more on this later.

O'Donnell and Powers also say at the same point in their book:

> President Kennedy first began to have doubts about our military effort in Vietnam in 1961 when both General Douglas MacArthur and General Charles de Gaulle warned him that the Asian mainland was no place to be fighting a non-nuclear land war. There was no end to Asian manpower, MacArthur told the president, and even if we poured a million American infantry soldiers into that continent, we would still find ourselves outnumbered on every side. De Gaulle said the same thing in Paris that spring, pointing out that the French had shown us the hopelessness of trying to fight in that country.[12]

Nonetheless, regardless of this excellent advice from men with the experience to know what they spoke about, the president did get advice from his government as well, much of it unhelpful. As O'Donnell and Powers explain early in their book, during much of Kennedy's presidency, the urgency of the threat of nuclear war with the Soviet Union over Berlin and the missile crisis in Cuba overshadowed Southeast Asia. When he turned his attention to Vietnam in late 1962, he received conflicting reports from his observers in Saigon. A marine general said the war was going fine and the Diem government was strong and popular. But a State Department man reported that the Diem government was on the verge of collapse. The president responded, "Were you two gentlemen in the same country?"[13]

In December of 1962, Kennedy met with the Senate Majority Leader Mike Mansfield, for whom he had considerable respect. They write that Mansfield, having just returned from a trip to Southeast Asia, warned against sending more troops and urged US withdrawal. Mansfield was emphatic against sending more military reinforcements, which would lead Americans to dominate the combat in a civil war that was not our war. He felt it would also hurt US prestige in Asia. The president observed later: "I got angry with Mike for disagreeing with our policy so completely, and I got angry with myself because I found myself agreeing with him."[14]

This man Kennedy so "deeply respected," the Senate majority leader, kept pressing the same wise counsel on him. Mansfield again criticized our military involvement in Vietnam in the Spring of 1963 in front of the Congressional leadership at a White House breakfast. This annoyed and embarrassed the president. Later, in a private discussion with Mansfield, the president admitted he now agreed with him on the need for a complete military withdrawal from Vietnam. But Kennedy said he could not do it until after he was reelected, because if he did it now, there would be a conservative outcry which would hurt his chances of being reelected.[15]

As these two who were so close to Kennedy continue their first-person account, they relate Kennedy's instruction to McNamara to announce the troop withdrawals, plans which were not altered even with the killing of Diem and Nhu. On October 2, Kennedy asked Defense Secretary McNamara to announce to the press the immediate withdrawal of one thousand soldiers and to say that we would probably withdraw all American forces from Vietnam by the end of 1965. But in his on-the-record statement to the press, McNamara said that in his judgment "the major part of the US military task" in Vietnam could be "completed by the end of 1965." The assassination of Diem and Nhu on November 1, just prior to his fateful trip to Texas, only made Kennedy more determined to pull out of Vietnam.[16]

The military, as Newman made so clear, had its own agenda and said, even to the commander in chief, what suited its purpose without regard for truth.

"Up until the time of his death," O'Donnell and Powers say, "he was determined to limit American military assistance to Vietnam to technicians, helicopter pilots and Green Beret advisers—no combat troops and no bombers."[17]

But as Kennedy told O'Donnell and others the month before he was assassinated, "They keep telling me to send combat troops over there. That means sending draftees, . . . I'll never send draftees over there to fight." The month before, Kennedy told Walter Cronkite of CBS News,

> "It is their war," . . . "They are the ones who have to win it or lose it. We can help them, we can send them equipment, we can send our men out there as advisers . . . but in the final analysis it is their people and their government who have to win or lose this struggle. All we can do is help."[18]

In discussing a November 1961 conference Kennedy had with those he had sent to Vietnam to learn and report to him what the situation there actually was, Richard Reeves says that Kennedy "was not willing to send in US combat troops." Reeves quotes from notes taken by Vice President Lyndon Johnson's military aide, Colonel Howard Burris: "He questioned the wisdom of involvement in Viet Nam. . . . The president said that he could even make a rather strong case against intervening in an area 10,000 miles away against 16,000 guerrillas with a native army of 200,000, where millions had been spent for years with no success." While he approved many of the recommendations made by Taylor and McNamara, Reeves reports that Kennedy rejected "the first option, a $75 million Air Force plan to kill everything green over 32,000 square miles of South Vietnam, almost half the country."[19] He approved instead a more limited use of defoliants. What a way to "save" an agricultural country and its people—by ending the capacity of half of it to grow food—and showering them with carcinogens at the same time!

As Reeves continues on the next page, we get another glimpse of what the president was up against in his military advisors.

> At the end of the long meeting, after hearing General Lemnitzer argue again that communism must be stopped in Vietnam or it would engulf most of Asia, Kennedy said again that he was not sure he could justify sending troops around the globe to Vietnam while there was a Communist government ninety miles offshore in Cuba. "Mr. President," Lemnitzer said, "speaking for the Joint Chiefs, we feel we should go into Cuba, too."[20]

Kennedy got a very different picture of the situation when he used trusted civilians to learn the actualities.

> As a check on his tough guys, Kennedy also told John Kenneth Galbraith to take a look at Vietnam on his way back to his ambassador's post in India. Galbraith could write reports as fast, as colorful, and as certain as Rostow's.[21] He did not disappoint, cabling the president on November 21 that troops were not the problem. Diem had "a comparatively well-equipped army with paramilitary formations numbering a quarter million men . . . facing a maximum of fifteen to eighteen thousand lightly armed men. If this were equality, the United States would hardly be safe from the Sioux. . . .[22]

Meanwhile, he was resisting pressure to bomb North Vietnam. If Kennedy had listened to the Lemnitzers, he would have been invading Cuba and Vietnam simultaneously, on opposite sides of the world.

O'Donnell and Powers conclude what they write at this point about JFK and his determination to get us out of Vietnam after the coming election:

> The president's order to reduce the American military personnel in Vietnam by one thousand men before the end of 1963 was still in effect on the day before he went to Texas. A few days after his death, during the mourning, the order was quietly rescinded.[23]

The since-disclosed NSAM 263 and 273 to which they refer was at the time of their writing still denied the American people as a requirement of "national security."

In addition to Mansfield, Kennedy revealed his plans to several others vigorously opposed to our involvement in Vietnam, including Senator Wayne Morse and the generals to whom he spoke, like Gavin.

CHAPTER 3

CUBA: THE BAY OF PIGS

From the time of the assassination and particularly after the highly touted Warren Report was so widely disbelieved, there have been many theories of the assassination as a conspiracy. However, there is virtually nothing in the official evidence that in and of itself is proof of who conspired, nor is there lead material so solid that all other possibilities are eliminated. But, as has been obvious since my first book, the official facts do prove that there was a conspiracy.

Theorizing about a crime is as proper as theorizing about anything else as a means of thinking it through, of trying to understand it, of deciding about areas of research and inquiry. However, presenting unproven theories as fact, which the authors of most of the books on the subject do, is deceptive, misleading, and misinforms trusting readers; and it rewrites our tragic history while giving aid and comfort to official miscreants.

Analyzing what is known, particularly what is established as fact, cannot by itself pinpoint the conspiring assassins. Along with knowledge of the official evidence, however, it can eliminate many of the theories advanced by those I refer to in my lengthy book manuscript as *Inside the JFK Assassination Industry*.[1]

The first of the theorized conspiracies to get much attention were of official inspiration because they came from leaks by officials in Texas and Washington. Both of these conspiracy theories irrationally blamed the left; one argued that the Soviets did it, the other that Castro did it.

When a US president is killed, his successor is known. In our system of government, the president will be succeeded by the vice president. It made no sense at all for the Soviets or Castro to have the known "dove" Kennedy killed only to have him replaced by the known "hawk" Johnson. Khrushchev and Kennedy had been groping toward detente since they settled the Cuba Missile Crisis. In this effort, they exchanged some forty letters, and each took affirmative steps toward detente. Khrushchev wanted peace as much as Kennedy, and he needed it ever so much more. His country was far from recovered from the unprecedented devastation visited upon it by Hitler. In that war it lost more than 20 million people and much of its industry. Its standard of living was low compared to other major countries. Even before the war it had a poor industrial base which the war reduced significantly.

The solution to the Cuba Missile Crisis was an insurance policy Castro could not get from any other country or combination of countries. Kennedy guaranteed Cuba's sovereignty to a greater extent than O'Donnell and Powers detail later in their book. He assured Cuba not only against any American invasion but that it would not be invaded by any country.

Not only was this more protection than Khrushchev could give Cuba, but also at the very time of the assassination, Kennedy was negotiating with Castro in an effort to reach a *modus vivendi*, and he was doing that on two different levels: through both diplomatic and informal channels. On the diplomatic level it was with our William Attwood and the Cuban ambassador at the United Nations.[2] Informally, it was through the noted French correspondent Jean Daniel. Daniel had interviewed Kennedy just before his trip to Dallas. Kennedy asked him to feel Castro out about settling their differences and to come back and report to him after his scheduled interview with Castro. As it happened, Daniel was with Castro when they got word of Kennedy's assassination. From Daniel's description of Castro's appearance even more than from his spontaneous words, there is no doubt that Castro was completely surprised and terribly upset by the news, which he described as very bad news for the world. Daniel also wrote a series of articles about this for *The New Republic*.[3]

Thus, it makes no sense at all that the left would kill Kennedy to get Johnson; Khrushchev and Castro each had reasons for preferring Kennedy to Johnson.

The anti-Castro Cubans were always suspected by many, in part because of their anger over their misguided belief that he had let them down at the Bay of Pigs and in part because so many of them were so very violent in their speech and actions.

Another of the early conspiracy theories is that the Vietnamese did it to avenge the killing of Diem and his brother Ngo Dinh Nhu, who directed the terror by which they had remained in power. Some theorized that Nhu's "dragon lady" wife was behind it for her revenge. That Kennedy did not order or cause those killings, but rather did nothing to prevent them—they were carried out by Diem's own army—does not rule out the dragon-lady theory. However, there is nothing but suspicion; no fact or evidence supports that theory. Nor can it be made to dovetail with what is known about the facts of the crime, and its coverup and its whitewashing.

One of the early theories, not nearly as often expressed, is that our own military was behind the assassination. The reason given is that the military violently disagreed with Kennedy's policies, resented the restraints he imposed upon it, and his effort to reduce military appropriations. But I know of no proof that there was such a conspiracy. Nonetheless, there is ample reason to ask the question, as I do in *Never Again!* "Was There a Military Conspiracy?" This is true also of the several variants of the military-conspiracy belief.

One formulation is that it was by the "military-industrial complex," which Eisenhower described in his farewell address. From the time he described this complex, I have thought of it as the military-industrial-intelligence complex. There are intelligence agencies that are not organically part of the military, like the CIA and the National Security Agency (NSA). There are also military intelligence agencies that are almost never mentioned in these theories, like the Office of Naval Intelligence (ONI).

I have never believed that the CIA as an institution was behind the assassination, but there are variants of that theory. One is that self-starters from the Cuban component of the CIA was behind it. Another that it was self-starters who had worked in the Vietnam or Southeast Asian area.

When I was asked about these theories years ago, and I've not been asked about them in years, I also suggested that any such self-starters could have contrived to make it look like the other was responsible. That there could have been some kind of intelligence involvement which coincided with the fairly widespread belief that Oswald had had some connection to intelligence agencies.

While some motive can be attributed to each of these suspected groups and not unreasonably to some others,[4] from the available evidence, by which I mean official evidence, and from the public record, a stronger and more credible case for motive can be attributed to the military or the military-industrial-intelligence complex.

The record of the military in the assassination inquiry is set forth in my *Never Again!* Here, I used what was in the public domain to address motive. Did the military, any part or parts of it, with or without the industrial complex or intelligence agencies being involved, have motive for wanting Kennedy killed, which also means for preferring Johnson to be president? If so, what was the motive or motives, or what could they have been?

As we shall see, each branch of the military can be said to have had some motive, some perhaps more than others. But it was the Navy that was involved in the so-called investigation of the crime. To refer to its record on the autopsy as merely abominable is to praise it. And then, too, Oswald had been a Marine, and Marines are part of the Navy.

It can be argued, not without reason, that much of the motive that can be attributed to the military can also be attributed to the industry that supplies it, considering the fact that in most instances it could not survive without the tax money it gets through the military. However, on the basis of what is known, this is but a supposition. I know of no fact to support this supposition, however justified.

The most obvious basis for suspecting the military is the breadth and depth of its very strong disagreements with President Kennedy's policies. In its simplest formulation, he was strongly, determinedly for peace, peace throughout the world. He had a record of seeking peace with Khrushchev and Castro and of wanting it in Southeast Asia. The military was not for peace, and it regarded Cuba and the Soviet Union as enemies with whom in its belief we were virtually at war anyway.

The military exists for war. Whether a war of defense only or not, it exists to be able to fight wars. Without wars there are few promotions, fewer successful careers. This does not mean that as a result the military is always looking for a war to start so the careers of those near the top can prosper and that those of lower rank can advance. Nor does it mean that in all instances this is not in varying degrees true. This may be reflected in the attitude of some but not of others. But it is an obvious fact that without war, careers do not prosper as much and opportunities for advancement are not as plentiful. Moreover, the more soldiers and the more equipment, the better the chances of flourishing careers and promotions. And since World War II, the possibility of cushy jobs after retirement in those military related industries has been important to retirees of higher rank. When actual wars are not happening, promoting the threat of war can serve much the same purpose.

It was not only in the Bay of Pigs fiasco and in Vietnam that the military did not get what it wanted from President Kennedy. It was also vehemently opposed to his handling of the October 1962 Cuba Missile Crisis.

We continued to provoke Cuba. Innocent Cuban fishermen on the high seas got arrested and were taken to Key West. We were forced to turn them and their boats loose because they had done nothing wrong. There were projects to assassinate Castro, only a few of which got to be known. One almost succeeded. I was told of it by Douglas Lethbridge, a man who knew Castro from their boyhood and who worked for him until he defected. Lethbridge told me that if Castro had not switched jeeps after a rest stop, he would have been killed when the jeep in which he had been riding was hit with a rocket.

Of the serious efforts to foment an uprising to overthrow Castro, the best-known of them disclosed later was Operation Mongoose.[5] Of the attempts to assassinate Castro, perhaps the most infamous is one for which the CIA used the mafia leaders, Sam "Momo" Giancana and Johnny Roselli.

Castro once disclosed his knowledge of some two dozen such plots to Members of Congress and then, later, to the House Select Committee on Assassinations. Cuba's ambassador to the United Nations also disclosed some of what Castro knew. I have copies of the official texts of some of those UN transcripts in which he reported United States' efforts to overthrow his government. Castro knew about these in part because the Miami Cuban refugee community leaked like a sieve and his intelligence agents picked it all up. I do not recall seeing this reported by our media.

Similarly, in Vietnam, there were no secrets for the Vietcong opposition who had thoroughly penetrated the government we had imposed on South Vietnam and its military. It also learned of military operations from its wide network of support from peasants in the villages to the upper echelons of the military and government. There were few secrets kept from it.

Essentially, secrecy regarding what we were up to in Cuba and Vietnam was for the purpose of keeping the American people in the dark. Many of these secrets eventually came to light, but long after the fact. Some of this was in books, which did contain considerable detail. Of the books I have read on the subject, I rely considerably on the O'Donnell and Powers's book because of O'Donnell's closeness to the president, whose trust he had and to whom the president spoke candidly. I also draw heavily on Robert Kennedy's *Thirteen Days*. Robert Kennedy was with the president when others were not. He understood him and the workings of his mind better than others did. Not only is the closeness and trust of their relationship the opposite of disqualifying, Robert Kennedy's writing is confirmed by that of others not limited to O'Donnell and Powers.

He wrote his *Thirteen Days* about the Cuba Missile Crisis. He was a key participant in what was known as the Executive Committee of the National Security Council, or "Ex Comm," from whom the president sought advice and who presented possible responses to Khrushchev. The fact is that at the moment of greatest crisis, it was Robert Kennedy who made the suggestion that became the solution to that crisis that, had it not been resolved, would likely have led to nuclear war. Most of the others on the Ex Comm were for an immediate attack on Cuba, and some of them never changed their beliefs.

Deeply troubling is the fact that despite the number of these books and the importance of what they report, what they report is for all practical purposes still secret from so many Americans. They got scant attention in the major media. With regard to Vietnam, this led to disaster for that country and its people. With regard to Cuba, innocent Cubans, not Castro, suffered and continue to suffer, while pretty much the rest of the world condemns us for what we did and continue to do. The unseen costs to us are great, but the greatest cost was narrowly averted with the president's acceptance of his brother's proposed solution, one that had originated with Khrushchev, was modified by Robert Kennedy, and then accepted by Khrushchev.

All of this and more like it throughout the world, of which our people know so extraordinarily little, underscores at once the wisdom, if not the prescience, of our Founding Fathers in their belief in the importance of freedom to think and to speak, embodied in the First Amendment, and of the great hazard to democratic society from official secrecy.

The First Amendment assures the press of freedom from the government's control, but it does not assure us of a free press. It protects the press from the government, but it does not protect the people from restrictions imposed by the press itself on what it reports. If this were not true, what I write would not be virtually entirely unknown to the people. Almost all the information I use is available to everyone.

Among the costs of these institutional failures, one of the most significant is disenchantment with both the government and the media by the people who, while lacking facts and details, know that something is gravely wrong. This is amply reflected in the more than twenty thousand letters and innumerable phone calls I've received from those who are strangers, people who thank me for my work.

This relates back to Hamilton's warning about the military, in particular with regard to both Cuba and Vietnam. And this would also include the CIA in the military-industrial-intelligence modification of Eisenhower's warning.

From the very first, the military wanted to attack Cuba. The flyboy generals never stopped wanting to drop bombs, *even after the crisis was resolved*! Most of the civilian members of that Ex Comm supported the military in its aching to start a war that, with the Soviet Union required by treaty to go to Cuba's defense, could have meant World War III and a terrible nuclear holocaust. One of these civilians who wanted to attack Cuba was Dean Acheson. As Secretary of State, he was the actual author of what was called the Truman Doctrine that was the official beginning of the Cold War. When a peaceful resolution of the Cuba Missile Crisis was in the offing, Acheson retired to his farm to brood over his failure to get that war started. He did not return to any Ex Comm conferences.

It was the president who provided the restraint, supported by his brother and a few others on the Ex Comm. And it was the incompleteness of the rocket launchers in Cuba that provided the time.

Most of the books published later are in substantial agreement on the facts. The first accounts were in the Schlesinger book quoted above and in Theodore Sorensen's, also published in 1965. In his *Kennedy*, Sorensen's first words, under a photograph of the president, are from John Buchan's *Pilgrim's Way*, on the death of Raymond Asquith,

"He will stand to those of us who are left as an incarnation of the spirit of the land he loved."

Many of the letters to me reflect the sense of this quotation despite the efforts of revisionists and the major attention given them by the media. Even a boy of ten concluded the letter he wrote me in August 1994 saying, "He left us something."

That "something" he left us began with the admiration and respect he earned for his acceptance of full responsibility for the tragic fiasco of the Bay of Pigs, although he had, in fact, inherited that and his other major problem in Southeast Asia from the Eisenhower administration. Eisenhower had not truthfully or fully informed him of the actualities of these two time-bombs that had been fused for him by the military. In each of these dangerous legacies, his options were severely limited by them, as was their intent.

On the Friday after the election, he flew to his father's seaside estate in Florida for a few weeks of rest and recuperation from the strain of the campaign. While he was there, CIA Director Allen Dulles briefed him on the Nixon-Eisenhower/Joint Chiefs of Staff/CIA proxy invasion of Cuba they had planned, staffed, and trained. That briefing was far from complete. It put the best face on that ugly beast that, as we shall see and as Kennedy belatedly came to realize, had been put together to fail, with that failure intended to get us involved in a war in Cuba to get rid of Castro.

On Thursday, January 19, the day before his inauguration, with his Secretaries of Defense, State, and Treasury, he went to the White House for a final briefing. Of the trouble spots, Eisenhower barely mentions Cuba. As O'Donnell and Powers report it:

> Eisenhower urged him to keep on supporting this plan to overthrow Castro. But Eisenhower talked mostly about Laos, which he regarded as the most dangerous spot in Southeast Asia. He mentioned South Vietnam only as one of the nations that would fall into the hands of the Communists if the United States failed to maintain the anti-Communist regime in Laos. Kennedy was astonished to hear Eisenhower telling him that American combat troops might have to fight alone in Laos if we could not persuade our allies to help us defend that government. Kennedy told us later, 'There he sat, telling me to get ready to put ground forces in Asia, the thing he himself had been carefully avoiding for the last eight years. And he was very calm about it. I was finding out that things were really just as bad as I had said they were during the campaign."[6]

O'Donnell does not report here or elsewhere, when, if he ever did, Kennedy realized that he was to be the chief cop in the United States' policing the world.

The successful attempt to control Kennedy and what he could and could not do as president and as this chief cop of the world, had begun earlier. A CIA internal memo released in 1993 under the 1992 law that required, but did not result in, full disclosure of all records in any way related to the assassination (thoughtfully sent me by Anna Marie Kuhns-Walko) spells this out. As disclosed, the names of CIA employees and components are withheld, for all the world as though they are not well known to all the world's spookeries. The real and obvious reason is to protect those who engaged in the gross improprieties reported:

> that [name of the employee withheld] has established a new and (according to him) productive channel to President-Elect Kennedy, through George Smathers. According to [employee name withheld]

> Smaters (sic) conversations with the President-Elect have led [name withheld] now to take the position that he should not go along with the Department of State and have the dictator step down. It appears that Mr. Kennedy may take a considerably more conservative position than many people in the Department and in the 'fun house.'[7] (see Appendix 3)

The "fun house" is the CIA. What is meant by this "considerably more conservative position" on Castro may be ambiguous, but there is no ambiguity in the statement that Kennedy "should not go along with the Department of State and have the dictator step down." Because it is obvious that the State Department did not want Castro to continue to rule Cuba, the CIA is saying that we will get rid of him in the only other possible way, by throwing him out through war. Good, clean fun in the "fun house!" What "fun" that was when it happened, "enjoying" the built-in failure that Kennedy later realized was part of the JCS/CIA-Eisenhower/Nixon devious plot he inherited.

When O'Donnell was among those with Kennedy in the White House the night he learned of the defeat and capture of the CIA's proxy army of invaders, he describes Kennedy's decision as "one of his most courageous moments." He offers the not unbiased, but not easily refuted, opinion that:

> Any other President of the United States, especially one who had been in office for only three months, might have tried to save himself from such a humiliation by sending Marines and jet fighters to beat back Castro's defending forces and to rescue the outnumbered invaders. Kennedy had made up his mind not to involve any American troops or combat planes. . . . When the reports of failure came from the beachheads, he refused to give his military advisers, who had accepted his earlier order against any American participation in the invasion, but now argued that we had to change the plan and send American reinforcements to beat Castro and save the prestige of the United States, Kennedy firmly disagreed. . . . 'I'll take the defeat,' he said that night to his generals and admirals, 'and I'll take all the blame for it.'[8]

Then they recall that the planning for this invasion, under Dulles at the CIA and his deputy, Richard Bissell, was "with the knowledge and approval of the Joint Chiefs of Staff."[9]

The president told O'Donnell and the others with him that sad night, "that the plan was so advanced when he came into office in January that it seemed almost impossible to cancel it. The brigade of fourteen hundred . . . were fully armed and ready to go into action. If we decided now to call the whole thing off, I don't know if we could go down there (to Guatemala) and take the guns away from them."[10]

Kennedy was also under pressure from the president of Guatemala who wanted those armed men out by the end of the month. There was also pressure from the report that the Soviet Union was supplying Cuba with MiG jets, the Cuban pilots for which had been trained in Czechoslovakia. The invasion, then, should take place before the MiGs could be used against it. So, Kennedy, "with some reluctance," agreed to the invasion on Monday, April 17. But he did that only "after the CIA and the Joint Chiefs of Staff accepted his strict restrictions that no American forces could take part in the invasion."[11] All the Joint Chiefs favored the invasion.

Four days before the invasion, O'Donnell and Powers write,

> The president showed me a message that he had received that morning from a Marine Corps colonel who had just made an inspection of the Cuban Brigade at its camp in Guatemala. The message glowed with approval. The colonel was confident that the Cubans in the task force were highly capable of carrying out their combat mission and going from there to overthrow Castro. It was this impressive message from the colonel, Kennedy told me, that finally prompted him to go ahead.[12]

At his press conference following his acceptance of full responsibility, Kennedy used an oft-quoted sentence, saying that "victory has a hundred fathers and defeat is an orphan." In public he continued to assume full responsibility, but:

> in private talks with a few of us . . . he pointed out the big flaw in the military plan for the operation. He wondered why the Joint Chiefs

> of Staff and the CIA had expected the small landing force of fourteen hundred to survive in Cuba without help and reinforcements from one of only two possible sources—either from inside the island, from internal uprisings, sabotage and armed attacks on the Cuban forces by underground revolutionists timed to coordinate with the landings, or from outside military support by American troops and air cover. When the Joint Chiefs of Staff and the CIA agreed to the president's strict ruling against American military participation in the assault, he assumed that plans had been set for widespread uprising against the Castro government inside Cuba.[13]

But when Kennedy began to get the details he "was shocked to discover that there had been no plans for a coordinated revolt in Cuba."

> . . . (T)he CIA officers who were working in Guatemala with the leaders of the invasion force assured them that they would be getting strong American military support. . . .
>
> The absence of any preparations for an organized uprising in Cuba, and the assurances of military support given to the rebels in the landing force, led President Kennedy to a bitter conclusion: the Joint Chiefs of Staff and the CIA must have been assuming all along that the president would become so worried at the last minute about the loss of his prestige that he would drop his restriction against the use of U.S. forces and send the Marines and the Navy jets into action.
>
> How else, the president asked us, could the Joint Chiefs approve such a plan? . . . "They were sure I'd give them the go-ahead . . ." he said one day to Dave Powers. "They couldn't believe that a new President like me wouldn't panic and try to save face. Well, they had me figured all wrong."[14]

This makes it clear that the military-industrial-intelligence complex had its own agenda, its own "national" policies and that they were the exact opposite of those of the president, the sole American with the Constitutional right and obligation to set national policy and implement it in conjunction with elected representatives in Congress. It is clear also that they had violated the strict orders of the president, the one, and the only one, with the Constitutional authority to give such orders—the Constitution they had sworn to uphold.

They regarded the president as an obstruction, as an impediment to what they believed was in the nation's best interest. Convinced of their omniscience, the Constitution itself was an impediment to them, so they violated it knowingly, deliberately, believing they knew better than the president, Constitution, and the Founding Fathers.

They wanted war, not peace, and if that required subversion, so be it. With their betrayal of the Constitution, their violations of our international obligations, including to the United Nations and to treaties, were relatively minor in comparison, but *only* in comparison. In this alone they made us into an international outlaw. And neither the respected pundits, the sages in Congress, nor the major media informed the people about it.

CHAPTER 4

CUBA: THE MISSILE CRISIS

The military-industrial-intelligence complex neither learned from nor was content with its ignominious failure at the Bay of Pigs. They were determined to oust Fidel Castro because they considered him a dictator. They had a very different attitude toward the many military dictators of the right, some of whom they educated at military colleges and helped attain power and keep it, regardless of their anti-democratic nature or the terror they visited upon their people. This was especially true in Latin America, Central America in particular, the same part of the world as Castro's Cuba.

Our military-industrial-intelligence complex seemed to have no problem with these right-wing dictators, regardless of the deaths they caused. In Guatemala, where we overthrew the democratically elected government and installed a murderous military dictatorship, the people killed there exceeded American deaths in Vietnam. And nobody talks about that or about the other tyrannies we installed in other Latin American countries.

The continuing efforts to oust Castro included efforts to kill him. After John and Robert Kennedy were murdered, the story was put out that they were behind these plots. Not only was there no evidence of this, the existing evidence is to the contrary, as discussed below.

The best-known of those failed plots to kill Castro was the CIA's attempt to get the Mafia to do it. This led to one of the many popular theories of the JFK assassination, the "kickback" theory—that Castro had

JFK killed in retaliation. As noted above, no major media explained the irrationality of this.

The CIA had given the impression that the Kennedys ordered the Mafia-assassination scheme that it had cooked up. It knew that to be false, as its records (which I have) make absolutely beyond question. Its lie, however, got extensive attention, while the truth has yet to be reported. The proof I have is from a Department of Justice file which I got only by accident, the CIA having decided that it does not have to provide me with any information under FOIA when I am not in a position to contest their denials.

Robert Kennedy forced the CIA to check its files on the plot and report the results to him. On May 15, 1962, Lawrence R. Houston, CIA general counsel, forwarded the memo I cite to Robert Kennedy in response to his request of four days earlier. The envelope stamped "TOP SECRET" held a May 14 memo by Sheffield Edwards, the CIA's Director of Security. The memo is three single-spaced pages. Only two copies were made of it. (see Appendix 4)

As the document makes clear, this loony assassination idea had originated with CIA deputy security director Richard Bissell of Bay of Pigs infamy. No higher authority than Edwards is cited as approving the project. The key sentence reads,

> Knowledge of this project during its life was kept to a total of six persons and never became a part of the project current at the time for the invasion of Cuba and there were no memoranda on the project nor were there any written documents or agreements. The project was orally approved by the said senior officials of the Agency. (see Appendix 4)

All six were CIA officials. That is to say, it was 100 percent "fun house stuff," with the fun enhanced by falsely laying responsibility for it on the assassinated Kennedy brothers. With this unsuccessful plot publicly exposed, what purpose was served classifying this memo "Top Secret?" The only purpose served in hiding this from the public was to preserve the CIA lie of blaming the Kennedys for its own plot to assassinate Castro. This was just one of a series of its failed and misbegotten attempts at what was once, before the national security state and the CIA, anathema to all traditional American beliefs.

How publicly was it known?

One of the Mafia kingpins it asked to get Castro killed, Chicago's Sam "Momo" Giancana, believed that a famous singer of the day, Phyllis McGuire of the McGuire Sisters, was cheating on him with Dan Rowan, of the Rowan and Martin comedy team. So, Robert Maheu, Howard Hughes's chief of security and a private investigator who was organizing the plot for the CIA, was asked by Giancana to repay the favor by checking out that report. Maheu got a Miami wiretapping and bugging outfit to undertake the chore. Its operative, James Balletti, did such an amateurish job in McGuire's hotel room that he was caught in the act by the maid. When Balletti was picked up by the police and the sheriff was brought into it, the plot became public. I have a large FBI file on it.

The CIA's improper use of this high classification on public information was solely for the purpose of hiding its exclusive responsibility behind the lie of protecting "national security."

What led to the Cuba Missile Crisis of 1962 was Castro's accurate information about plans for another invasion of Cuba. That it was accurate became apparent at the most recent of the little-reported series of conferences between participants of both sides. That one, at the Cubans' invitation, was in Cuba. The transcripts have been published. They include Castro's extemporaneous accounting of some of those failed United States—that is, CIA—attempts to assassinate him.[1] Former Secretary of Defense Robert McNamara, who was on the Ex Comm, acknowledged the correctness of Castro's citation of Operation Mongoose, but said that the United States had not really intended to invade Cuba or to kill him.

Castro, of course, would have assumed that the information was correct. Fearing attack from the US, Castro reminded Khrushchev that he had given his word that he would defend Cuba. Newspapers did report that Raul Castro and Che Guevara had gone to Moscow in the middle of 1962 to ask for help.

The Soviet Union had no way to protect Cuba against a United States invasion. Actions the Soviets could have taken would only have contributed to the slaughter of Cubans and the invaders, but Cuba would have been destroyed. With no way to defend Cuba and with the reputation of the USSR and the value of its word at stake, Khrushchev sent missiles to Cuba, but withheld any authority to use them. As it turned out, whatever had been in anyone's mind, it was exactly as I had concluded at the time; they were sent there not to be used but to be removed at the appropriate time.[2] No effort was made to camouflage the missiles; they were not hidden from aerial cameras.

The official story is that those missiles were first photographed by a U-2 plane on Sunday, October 14, 1962, when the president was campaigning for New York Congressional candidates. Tuesday morning, October 16, he was shown the enlargements of the pictures of the missile installations still under construction. The Ex Comm deliberated about what should be done. O'Donnell and Powers provide this account of those deliberations and the crisis that followed:

> As late as the following Sunday, the day before the president appeared on television to announce the blockade and demand the removal of the missiles, he was still fighting opposition from Air Force leaders who were still urging an air strike. Undoubtedly, if the president had had to make a firm decision within twenty-four hours after the discovery of the missiles, he would have been under severe pressure to order a surprise attack on Cuba from the air, which would have had to be followed by an invasion. But the grace of a few more days that was given to him to consider other tactics allowed him time to work out the blockade plan, a strong and dramatic action against Khrushchev, but still a delaying move that enabled the Soviet leader to back away from the brink before the shots were fired.[3]

President Kennedy, well aware of the fact that if he made a single mistake the world could be involved in an immediate nuclear war, somehow resisted the enormous pressures on him to start that war. These calls for immediate action came largely but not entirely from his military advisers. Some advisers, especially Robert Kennedy, urged a more cautious approach.

In his short introduction to Robert Kennedy's *Thirteen Days*, Secretary of Defense Robert McNamara strongly condemns the dangerous approach urged by the military while praising Robert Kennedy's strong opposition to it:

> On the basic policy question of whether to force the missiles out by massive air and ground attack or by the far less risky application of a maritime quarantine, he strongly supported the quarantine.
>
> He did so because he saw that the air and ground strikes favored by so many would have brought death to thousands of innocent Cuban civilians and to thousands of U.S. military personnel. He saw, too, that such attacks ran the risk of triggering the launch of nuclear weapons from Cuba against the U.S. and the risk of Soviet retaliatory attacks on Berlin or other vulnerable points on the periphery of NATO.
>
> And he opposed a massive surprise attack by a large country on a small country because he believed such an attack to be inhuman, contrary to our traditions and ideals, and an act of brutality for which the world would never forgive us.
>
> He understood then as now that above all else a U.S. president must, while defending our vital interests, prevent the confrontations between nuclear powers which can lead to nuclear holocaust.
>
> His objective was to force the missiles out of Cuba without war. That objective was accomplished.[4]

In describing the JCS demand for war, Robert Kennedy noted they were unanimous in calling for immediate military action. Curtis LeMay in particular argued strongly that a military attack was essential, and he assured Kennedy there would be no reaction. A skeptical Kennedy responded, "They, no more than we, can let these things go without doing something. They can't, after all their statements, permit us to take out their missiles, kill a lot of Russians, and then do nothing. If they don't take action in Cuba, they certainly will in Berlin."[5]

While the JCS seem not to have discussed our potential casualties in an invasion, they never stopped urging one. They appear also not to have acknowledged that the Soviets would use their nuclear missiles. As Robert Kennedy writes, the president reminded the Ex Comm of this:

> The president turned to us all: "We are going to have to face the fact that, if we do invade, by the time we get to these sites, after a very bloody fight, they will be pointed at us. And we must further accept the possibility that when military hostilities first begin, those missiles will be fired."
>
> John McCone [CIA Director] said everyone should understand that an invasion was going to be a much more serious undertaking than most people had previously realized. "They have a hell of a lot of equipment," he said. And it will be damn tough to shoot them out of those hills, as we learned so clearly in Korea.[6]

It seems extraordinary that the president could and did withstand the push toward war from his own military, even as the military deliberately did the opposite of what he had ordered. When he learned that we had a spy ship "very close to the coast of Cuba," as Robert Kennedy put it in *Thirteen Days*, "he ordered it further out to sea, where it would be less vulnerable to attack."[7] Why was it "very close to the coast of Cuba?" Was it to provoke an attack that would start the shooting war the military wanted?

In the opinion of at least one of the Joint Chiefs, a nuclear first strike would be legitimate, particularly when the USSR would launch one against us. As Robert Kennedy said in *Thirteen Days*,

> One member of the Joint Chiefs of Staff, for example, argued that we could use nuclear weapons, on the basis that our adversaries would use theirs against us in an attack. I thought, as I listened, of the many times that I had heard the military take positions which, if wrong, had the advantage that no one would be around at the end to know.
>
> The president made his decision that afternoon in favor of the blockade.[8]

This was at that Saturday afternoon meeting. But the president had already made his decision prior to that meeting.

This is what Robert Kennedy said about the JCS and what they would have begun with:

> Later, Secretary McNamara, although he told the president he disagreed with the Joint Chiefs and favored a blockade rather than an attack, informed him that the necessary planes, men, and ammunition were being deployed and that we would be ready to move with the necessary air bombardments on Tuesday, October 23, if that was to be the decision. The plans called for an initial attack, consisting of five hundred sorties, striking all military targets, including the missile sites, airfields, ports, and gun emplacements.

But that was only the beginning. When the president spoke to the nation,

> . . . he emphasized that the blockade was the initial step. He had ordered the Pentagon to make all the preparations necessary for further military action. Secretary McNamara, in a confidential report, had listed the requirements: 250,000 men, 2,000 air sorties against the various targets in Cuba, and 90,000 Marines and Airborne in the invasion force. One estimate of American casualties put the expected figure over 25,000. The president gave his approval for these preparations.[9]

This assumes that the Russians under attack would not have used their small tactical nuclear weapons and that we would not use ours. Perhaps McNamara did not know then that the Russian forces were so armed. But he did learn it at the Havana conference, the transcript of which is in *Cuba on the Brink*, and the possibilities disturbed him greatly even thirty years later.[10]

The president was patient with those he consulted in the Congress just before he spoke to the nation. As Robert Kennedy says in *Thirteen Days*,

> The president, after listening to the frequently emotional criticism, explained that he would take whatever steps were necessary

> to protect the security of the United States, but that he did not feel greater military action was warranted initially. Because it was possible that the matter could be resolved without a devastating war, he had decided on the course he had outlined. Perhaps in the end, he said, direct military action would be necessary, but that course should not be followed lightly. In the meantime, he assured them, he had taken measures to prepare our military forces and place them in a position to move.
>
> He reminded them that once an attack began our adversaries could respond with a missile barrage from which many millions of Americans would be killed. That was a gamble he was not willing to take until he had finally and forcefully exhausted all other possibilities. He told them this was an extremely hazardous undertaking and that everyone should understand the risks involved.[11]

If the Air Force had gotten its way, World War III would have been all but inevitable. What President Kennedy was able to resolve peacefully would have instead resulted in a terrible loss of life and what else can hardly be imagined.

Within the Ex Comm, Robert Kennedy was part of a small minority that wanted to avoid starting a war. He recommended a blockade that would be called a "quarantine" because a blockade is an act of war. In arguing with Dean Acheson, he said with some vehemence, "We are not going to make my brother the Tojo of the 1960s," referring to the Japanese surprise attack on Pearl Harbor.[12]

Among the president's reasons for opposing an air strike is the fact that it would not destroy all the missile bases and, if nothing else, the killing of the Russians at those sites would almost certainly have started a war. Then we would have had to follow up with an invasion of Cuba, which he did not want. He preferred the "quarantine" because that gave Khrushchev an out.

General Curtis LeMay, then the Air Force Chief of Staff, never stopped arguing with great vehemence for an immediate air strike. As noted above, the president asked LeMay, "How will the Russians respond?" The president was astounded with LeMay's reply that they would not do a thing.

"Is that what you really think?" he asked LeMay. "Are you telling me that they'll let us bomb their missiles and kill a lot of Russians and then do nothing? If they don't do anything in Cuba, they'll certainly do something in Berlin."[13] Reeves provides a virtually identical account.[14]

O'Donnell and Powers write, "After the meeting the president said to me, 'Can you imagine LeMay saying a thing like that? These brass hats have one great advantage in their favor. If we listen to them and do what they want us to do, none of us will be alive later to tell them that they were wrong."[15] The president had made his mind up. He told O'Donnell that the "quarantine" had the advantages of being a strong opening move by the United States that had the least possibility of starting a shooting war, but he wanted a majority of the Ex Comm to agree. When O'Donnell asked him, "What if you cannot get a consensus" from the Ex Comm the president replied, "I'll make my decision anyway. I'm the one who has the responsibility, so we'll do what I want to do." O'Donnell and Powers then write, "He told me a story about Abraham Lincoln at his cabinet meeting saying 'All in favor vote "aye." The whole cabinet voted aye. Lincoln voted no, and then announced that the no's had it.'"[16]

In an effort to make things appear to be normal, Kennedy continued his public political activities with appearances around the country. When they were in Chicago, Pierre Salinger, who, like most of the White House staff, was out of the loop and unaware of what was going on, told the president that Robert S. Allen and Paul Scott were about to publish a column about an invasion of Cuba. *Chicago Sun-Times* reporter Carleton Kent was asking about a report on a planned parachute jump in Cuba. As O'Donnell and Powers write, "the security cover on the missile crisis had been amazingly tight" until then. "We had managed to keep Salinger in the dark, but it became obvious in Chicago that we would not be able to keep him there much longer. I could see that the president was silently cursing the Joint Chiefs of Staff," the most likely leakers. Kennedy had O'Donnell call Kent and tell him "that report is all wrong" and have McNamara ask Allen and Scott not to print their column.[17]

The secrecy held a bit longer, but "Security was beginning to fall apart" and "there was still considerable opposition among the military people to the blockade."[18]

"That Saturday afternoon," the end of the week before Kennedy did go public, "we had a meeting of the Ex Comm . . . where the President announced his decision to put the blockade into effect during the following week. . . ."[19]

One of the ongoing problems raised at that Ex Comm meeting was the missiles that we had in Turkey. How would we react to the Soviet complaint that they were only doing what we had been doing on their border for years? O'Donnell and Powers explain that over the past year the president had repeatedly ordered those Jupiter missiles removed from Turkey. "I wouldn't mind so much if the damned things were serving any useful purpose. They should have been taken out of there back in the Eisenhower administration."[20]

When Adlai Stevenson reported that both the *New York Times* and the *Washington Post* had learned about the crisis, JFK himself phoned both papers asking them to hold off until Monday night, when he would be speaking. On Sunday, O'Donnell and Powers write,

> Kennedy gave the Air Force generals one last chance to argue for immediate bombing of the missile sites. Again, he ruled against an air strike after General Walter C. Sweeney, commander of the Tactical Air Force, admitted that it would be impossible to take out all the missile sites in one blow. It had to be all or nothing, the president said, because we had no way of knowing which sites, if any, were operational . . . We might miss or overlook a few operational sites, which could immediately open fire on the United States.[21]

Clearly, the Air Force was fully aware that an airstrike on those missiles could lead to nuclear bombs being fired at this country from only ninety miles away. Yet, they were determined to bomb the missile sites, considering no other alternative.

After the "quarantine" was put into effect, O'Donnell and Powers write, "If shooting started at the blockade line, a nuclear war could quickly follow." Shortly after the blockade went into effect, the White House received two reports of Soviet ships being escorted by a submarine.

The president asked, "What do we do now?" McNamara replied that our carrier *Essex*, which was nearby "would send a sonar signal to the submarine, ordering it to come to the surface and identify itself. If the submarine refused to surface and stop, a small explosive would be dropped by a helicopter from the *Essex*."

While they were horrified that nuclear war could be so close,

> . . . a messenger came into the room and handed a note to John McCone [CIA director], who read it quickly and said, "Mr. President, we have a preliminary report which indicates that some of the Russian ships are stopping." The preliminary report was then verified and a Naval Intelligence officer came into the meeting with a full report that twenty Russian ships had come to a stop before reaching the blockade line, which Kennedy had announced in his Monday night speech. Some of them were standing still in the water and others had turned around and were heading back toward Europe. Dean Rusk, who was sitting beside the president, said quietly, "We're eyeball to eyeball, and I think the other fellow just blinked."[22]

The military and its Ex Comm allies, a majority at the beginning of that harrowing week that could have ended with the world aflame, were wrong and the president and his brother with the few others of the Ex Comm minority were right. They had both avoided nuclear war and laid the basis for resolving the crisis peacefully. But that did not satisfy the military. It lusted for war without regard for the consequences more horrible than anything in human history, devastation that could make the terrible atom bombing of Hiroshima and Nagasaki look like minor disturbances: There was bitter disappointment among high-ranking Naval officers in the Pentagon that Soviet vessels failed to make a run through the blockade. They had been looking forward eagerly to sinking or capturing a few Russian submarines. President Kennedy sent strict orders to the Essex and to Admiral George W. Anderson that none of the Soviet ships and submarines outside the blockade interception zone were to be stopped, boarded or harassed in any way. The president was concerned that Khrushchev was probably already taking enough criticism from his rivals in the Kremlin.[23]

The Navy was not content. The president, the highest authority in the nation, its commander in chief, had given orders, but the Navy had its own ideas:

> That night McNamara, with his deputy secretary, Roswell Gilpatric, visited the Navy's Flag Plot, or command center in the Pentagon, where the blockade operation was being directed, to make sure that the President's orders were being observed. He found Admiral Anderson himself in the room, watching a single American vessel that was shown on the plotting board to be standing alone far outside of the interception zone. McNamara asked what the ship was doing out there. Anderson explained that it was watching a Soviet submarine.
>
> The Secretary of Defense pointed out to the admiral that the president was anxious not to bother any Soviet ships needlessly, that the Russians must be allowed to retreat or to stand outside the blockade zone with no humiliation. Anderson informed the Secretary that the Navy needed no advice on how to manage a blockade, and suggested that the Secretary could leave the room. A few months later Anderson retired from the Navy, at president Kennedy's suggestion, to become our Ambassador to Portugal.[24]

That a career Navy man of this highest rank did not regard himself or the Navy as under civilian control and said so reflects the long-time attitude of some in the military. Anderson and the Navy were in deliberate violation of the explicit orders of the president, their commander in chief.

In both its attitude and record, the military high command under Kennedy— LeMay, Lemnitzer, and others—did the exact opposite of what the highest authority in the land had ordered. They apparently believed that the "supreme power" belonged to them, not the president.

Then the groping for a settlement began. Khrushchev, going outside his diplomatic channels, sent a personal message to President Kennedy. He followed that with a personal letter. He would remove his missiles if the United States would promise not to invade Cuba. When he did not get a prompt reply to that, he sent a stronger proposal publicly, one that he knew Kennedy could not accept; if we removed our missiles from his border, those in Turkey, he would take his back from Cuba. O'Donnell and Powers write:

> It was obvious that Khrushchev had written this letter himself, probably without consulting anybody in the Kremlin, and that he intended it to be received, like his previous personal letters to Kennedy, as a man-to-man expression of his feelings rather than as an official communication. The letter was never made public in the Soviet Union and, out of respect for Khrushchev, Kennedy did not allow it to be published in the United States, although some brief excerpts and paraphrases of certain passages did appear after the president's death. When the president showed me the letter that Friday night after he read it for the first of many times, I was deeply moved by Khrushchev's anguished fear that he had provoked Kennedy into a fighting mood and a readiness for war. He pleaded with Kennedy not to lose his "self-control" and begged him not to let "the two of us pull on the ends of the rope in which you have tied the knot of war because the more the two of us pull, the tighter the knot will be tied. . . . Let us not only relax the forces pulling on the ends of the rope, let us take measures to untie that knot. We are ready for this."[25]

Khrushchev's second proposal "was stern and demanding," O'Donnell and Powers say. It "amounted to a blackmailing trade instead of the reasonable exchange of the peaceful guarantee that Khrushchev had asked in this first letter" to which there had been no response.[26] Writing of the president's reaction, they continue:

> I found him not so much upset by Khrushchev's change in attitude as exasperated because the Jupiter missiles were still in Turkey, where the Russians could use them in a face-saving barter, several months after their removal had been ordered by the president. "Just

> to set the record straight," the president said to me, "will you find out when was the last time I asked to have those damned missiles taken out of Turkey? Not the last five times I asked for their removal, just the date of the last time." I went to my office and called Bromley Smith in Bundy's office and asked him to check the file. Sure enough, the President had ordered the removal of the Jupiter missiles in August, two months before the Soviet ballistic missile sites were discovered in Cuba.[27]

The military had its own agenda again defying the commander in chief.

In *Thirteen Days*, Robert Kennedy writes that after receipt of Khrushchev's second letter the Ex Comm believed there was confusion within the USSR, perhaps even that Khrushchev had been overthrown. Robert Kennedy also wrote about the confusion in which he was involved:

> The change in the language and tenor of the letters from Khrushchev indicated confusion within the Soviet Union; but there was confusion among us as well. At that moment, not knowing exactly what to suggest, some recommended writing to Khrushchev and asking him to clarify his two letters. There was no clear course of action. Yet we realized that, as we sat there, the work was proceeding on the missile sites in Cuba, and we now had the additional consideration that if we destroyed these sites and began an invasion, the door was clearly open for the Soviet Union to take reciprocal action against Turkey.
>
> The NATO countries were supporting our position and recommending that the U.S. be firm; but, President Kennedy said, they did not realize the full implications for them. If we carried out an air strike against Cuba and the Soviet Union answered by attacking Turkey, all NATO was going to be involved. Then, immediately, the president would have to decide whether he would use nuclear weapons against the Soviet Union, and all mankind would be threatened.
>
> The Joint Chiefs of Staff joined the meeting and recommended their solution. It had the attraction of being a very simple next

> step—an air strike on Monday, followed shortly afterward by an invasion.[28]

Robert Kennedy then suggested the simple solution of accepting Khrushchev's first offer and ignoring the second. On the same day our U-2 was shot down over Cuba, he wrote, "There was the realization that the Soviet Union and Cuba apparently were preparing to do battle. And there was the feeling that the noose was tightening on all of us, the Americans, too, and that bridges to escape were crumbling."[29] Whether this realization controlled or inspired their actions, he does not say. He then describes the president pulling everyone back from the brink.

> "How can we send any more U-2 pilots into this area tomorrow unless we take out all of the SAM sites?" the president asked. "We are now in an entirely new ball game."
>
> At first, there was almost unanimous agreement that we had to attack early the next morning with bombers and fighters and destroy the SAM sites. But again the president pulled everyone back. "It isn't the first step that concerns me," he said, "but both sides escalating to the fourth and fifth step—and we don't go to the sixth because there is no one around to do so. We must remind ourselves we are embarking on a very hazardous course."[30]

Of course, "there is no one around" because all have been incinerated in the nuclear holocaust the military denied would ever happen.

While the Ex Comm was deliberating, they got the report of a U-2 plane flying into Siberia. It had been intercepted by Soviet fighter planes but not shot down. "The president had expressly banned" such flights during the crisis. Again, by refusing to follow the commander in chief's orders, the military had almost engulfed the world in nuclear war. It was then that Robert Kennedy "suggested ignoring the second Khrushchev letter . . . and writing instead a reply to Khrushchev's first private letter . . . The president immediately agreed to the idea and sent Bobby and Ted Sorensen into another room to work on such a reply."[31]

When Khrushchev accepted the response prepared by Robert Kennedy and Sorensen, the crisis was over. Mankind was saved from the greatest of nuclear disasters. But the military was not happy that the resolution was entirely peaceful. As O'Donnell and Powers report, "We learned later that one of our military leaders said, when hearing about Khrushchev's willingness to remove the missiles, 'Does this mean our air strike has to be called off? Why can't we attack on Tuesday anyway?'"[32]

As Reeves reports, former Secretary of State Dean Acheson wrote to the president to "congratulate you on your leadership, firmness and judgment over the past tough week. . . ." Privately, though, he had considered the strategy "reckless" and the triumph, "Plain dumb luck." When President Kennedy invited the Chiefs in a few days later to thank them, Reeves reports, General Curtis LeMay looked at his commander in chief and said there was no reason for thanks. "We lost! We ought to just go in there today and knock 'em off!"[33]

To LeMay, successfully preventing a possible nuclear war was a defeat. As he said, "We lost!"

Not the country. Not the world either. Only war lost. Peace won.

In these descriptions of the missile crisis, President Kennedy comes across as a solid leader—clear eyed, intelligent, steady, in control. In this unprecedented crisis, he was able to control himself and those around him and prevent the greatest of world tragedies. Thirty-two years after this missile crisis, this is confirmed with the unexpected release of a contemporaneous record, a short tape made during "the crucial hours" early in that crisis, just a few hours before Kennedy's announcement to the American people. According to the *New York Daily News* story disclosing the existence of the tape, Kennedy remained "cool" throughout the crisis, from his first knowledge of the presence of Soviet missiles in Cuba, despite his awareness of the alternatives and the terrible potential for nuclear catastrophe. Columnist Bill Bell quotes Sheldon Stern, archivist at the John F. Kennedy Library, as stating of the tape, "There is absolutely no Cold War rhetoric. The discussion is calm, unemotional, rational and businesslike." The alternatives discussed, quoting Stern, were "bombing the missile sites, pressuring the Soviet Union to remove them, or, in effect striking a deal with Moscow to remove them in return for some U.S. gesture." In Bell's opinion, "the most striking sentence" reflects Kennedy's intent, "'The question really is,' said Kennedy, 'what action do you take which lessens the chance of a nuclear exchange, which obviously is the final failure?'"[34]

Bell's list of those who participated in this discussion does not include a single officer of any military service.[35] This may account for the absence of "any Cold War rhetoric" and calm discussion in which the alternatives were clearly stated, including the ultimate solution. Kennedy regarded what the military was pushing for as a "nuclear exchange," as "the final failure," that he was determined to avoid.

With the secrecy that has become a way of life in our nation, what should be known so decision-makers and the people can understand and benefit from it is often not available to them. It is kept secret for no apparent legitimate reason and certainly not from a "national security" need, but, in fact, contrary to that need. There can be little information more important in the modern world in the nuclear era than what relates to decisions about war and peace.

Not only was there enormous pressure from the military for JFK to order an attack on Cuba during the 1962 missile crisis, but also intense political pressure for him to take us into war. While some of this pressure was from political friends of the military, some was from more unlikely sources.

On December 21, 1994, the Associated Press carried a story I did not see reported on television or hear on radio news. The edition of the *Washington Post* that reaches Frederick did not carry it. It was in our local paper, the *Frederick News-Post*, the next morning. Oddly for a newspaper story, the source is not indicated. I assume the source was the Kennedy library, part of The National Archives. The *News-Post* ran the story across the top of the second page of its news section, with this headline: "Hill leaders urged JFK to invade in Cuba missile crisis." According to the story, Senator Richard Russell, chairman of the Senate Armed Services Committee, advised the president to take strong military action. Russell is quoted as saying, "We've got to take a chance somewhere, sometime, if we're going to retain our position as a great world power." Kennedy assured Russell that military preparations were being made, but shortly after his conversation with Russell he went on television to announce a blockade against ships bound for Cuba with offensive weapons. He had learned only hours earlier that a US strike would be less than 100 percent effective against the missiles, opening the door to a possible devastating retaliation, and a ground invasion would take months to organize. Senator J. William Fulbright, chairman of the Senate Foreign Relations Committee, criticized the blockade as the worst of all possible solutions because it might require attacking Russian ships. He advocated "an invasion, and an all-out one, as quickly as possible." "An attack on a Russian ship," he argued, "is really an act of war against Russia. It is not an act of war against Russia to attack Cuba." Kennedy countered that with eight thousand Soviet military advisers there an American invasion would provoke a Soviet response, that they would not stand by as an American invasion force was built up with designs on Cuba. So Kennedy resisted these calls for a strong military response.[36]

Russell is an excellent illustration of how the military buys political support with the tax money, the peoples' money it spends. On the armed-forces committee before he became its chairman, he was important to the military, and the military spent vast sums in Georgia. That was politically important to Russell, as it was also for the military. It was only natural that Russell's view was usually that of the military and it was only natural for the military to look out for Russell's political interest and for him to come to think sometimes as the military did.

Fulbright, however, was considered a dove, not a hawk. Yet he, as well as many others on the Hill, adopted the hawkish military position in that crisis.

These tapes that had been kept secret for so long confirm the statements of those above-quoted participants, that JFK had an understanding most of his advisers, with the exception of his brother, did not have. His was the best and correct judgement, the sound judgement that presidents are supposed to possess, though rarely do.

For years President Kennedy was berated by his political enemies. After his death, political opponents accused him of the wrong decisions regarding Cuba and Khrushchev. Under Ronald Reagan, the opposite kind of president, strong efforts were made to nullify the agreement Kennedy made with Khrushchev. The political perspective from which these tremendous pressures for war originated persisted and continues to, with nuclear catastrophe continuing to threaten our existence.

That the major media gave this important story little attention reflects the continuing failure of the major media to provide the information the people need for our system to work. Playing this story down is consistent with the revisionism that has set in. This story reflects favorably on JFK and on his judgement and his exceptional ability to somehow maintain control over the situation that made unprecedented war almost inevitable. This story presents him as a great and exceptional leader who in the time of unprecedented crisis made the correct decisions against overwhelming odds.

That such a crisis will again befall us seems, sadly, highly likely. Our failure to pursue what John F. Kennedy and Nikita Khrushchev started leaves the world today even closer to nuclear Armageddon. If we fail to learn the lessons of the history of this crisis, of how close we came, saved only by the sanity of a few, a similarly peaceful outcome is unlikely.

CHAPTER 5

"AND WE CALL OURSELVES THE HUMAN RACE"

What is truly amazing and I believe of enormous significance is that although the Soviet crews in Cuba were well aware of United States overflights, they permitted them to continue throughout the crisis. That the Cuban anti-aircraft crews also made no effort to shoot down any of ours is, in a sense, of even more significance because those overflights, each and every one of them, were an act of war against Cuba. This is not mentioned at all by O'Donnell and Powers. Robert Kennedy mentioned it frequently, but without indicating the meaning and significance of it.

Among Robert Kennedy's references to them is that the "photography taken on Wednesday, the 17th of October, showed several other installations with at least sixteen and possibly thirty-two missiles of over a thousand-mile range."[1] "Other" referred to those depicted in earlier aerial photographs. He wrote of the Tuesday of the following week that, "The U-2s and low-flying planes had returned the previous day with their film, and throughout the evening it was analyzed—by now in such volume that the film alone was more than twenty-five miles long."[2]

As his account of the crisis continues, "On the night of Thursday, October 25, our aerial photography revealed that work on the missile sites was proceeding at an extraordinarily rapid pace. By the following evening, October 26, it was clear that the IL-28 bombers were also being rapidly uncrated and assembled."[3] While these are not all references to the entirely unimpeded overflights, they leave it without question that neither the Soviets nor the Cubans had any interest in discouraging or preventing the photographs of what was going on. This leads to the belief that they wanted the United States to know, and that cannot be without meaning.

I believe that it confirms my contemporaneous analysis for *Tiger to Ride*, that Khrushchev needed Kennedy to know for Kennedy to have his own "tiger to ride," the decision on whether there would be war or peace, peace meaning a peaceful settlement of the problem. Khrushchev could not survive without a settlement of it.

As Robert Kennedy wrote in *Thirteen Days* about the beginning of the second week of the crisis,

> John McCone reported to our committee that as yet there had been no general alert of the Soviet forces in Cuba or around the globe. No extraordinary military action of any kind had been reported. In Cuba, the Russians were not permitting anyone other than Russian technical and military personnel to enter the missile bases. He also reported that they were beginning to camouflage the missile sites. It was never clear why they waited until that late date to do so.[4]

And this, it should be remembered, was several years after the Russians had the radar and the weaponry to shoot down the Gary Powers U-2 flight, which our government believed was flying so high over the USSR that they did not have that capability.

If they had been ordered to try to hide what they were doing, the Russian technicians would have made that effort. If they had been ordered to destroy any intruding United States aircraft, they would have done that too, as they did when it served their purposes.

All those many flights, the U-2s up high and the other planes much lower, continued without any molestation, with not even a threat, until it served Khrushchev's interest to force the issue, to get Kennedy to reach his decision after almost two weeks of indecision. Then, on the morning of Saturday, October 27, Air Force U-2 pilot Rudolf Anderson was shot down. That was the day after Khrushchev's first proposal was given in a hurry informally to the United States. Khrushchev had Aleksandr Fomin of the embassy, a man reputed to be the Soviet Union's chief spook in Washington, give it verbally to then ABC News correspondent John Scali. That evening, the actual Khrushchev letter was handed to the president. That was his offer to remove his missiles from Cuba in return for the United States promise not to invade Cuba.

Khrushchev got neither a response nor any indication that he would be getting one until he raised the stakes again with the public proposal he knew would not be acceptable, to remove his missiles if we took ours out of Turkey where they were on his border.

Khrushchev had reason to interpret no retaliation for shooting Anderson down to mean that Kennedy did not want war. Where the USSR had even more reason for shooting down a U-2 when it crossed into its territory in Siberia, he had his fighter jets merely escort it out of Soviet airspace. Had Khrushchev wanted war or just wanted to show he was a real tough guy, he could have and would have shot down that U-2. That was a signal to Kennedy that Khrushchev did not want to escalate the crisis, which meant he wanted a peaceful resolution. That he had the Anderson U-2 shot down the day after Kennedy had his proposal was still another signal to Kennedy to make his decision quickly, which is what happened.

Despite the persistent vigorous efforts of our military, history's most terrible war was averted and detente was begun. Kennedy's public efforts to get the people behind peace and detente were enunciated in his speech at Washington's American University in June of 1963. O'Donnell and Powers write,

> Kennedy referred to the American University address as 'the peace speech,' because it was an appeal for a lasting peace between the United States and the Soviet Union, directed at Khrushchev, who had hinted that such a new message from the president might help bring a favorable reaction to Kennedy's proposal for a nuclear atmospheric test ban treaty. 'It is an ironic but accurate fact,' President Kennedy said in his appeal to the Russians, 'that the two strongest powers are the two most in danger of devastation. All we have built, all we have

> worked for, would be destroyed in the first twenty-four hours. For we are both devoting to weapons massive sums of money that could be better devoted to combating ignorance, poverty and disease. We are both caught up in a vicious and dangerous cycle in which suspicion on one side breeds suspicion on the other, and new weapons beget counter weapons. . . . If we cannot now end our differences, we can at least make the world safe for diversity. For in the final analysis, our most basic common link is that we all inhabit this small planet. We all breathe the same air. We all cherish our children's future. And we are all mortal.' The American University speech brought an immediate thaw in our relationship with the Soviets.[5]

There is nothing the military did or said during this crisis that reflects any real appreciation of or concern for the fact "that the two strongest powers are the two most in danger of devastation." And aside from having its own policy contrary to the stated policy of the nation, as articulated by the president, it also violated his orders, those of its commander in chief, in that also risking a nuclear holocaust. But despite that, he managed to preserve the peace in this part of the world anyway.

He never knew how much more difficult this had been made for him by the military and the CIA, how much more dangerous the military and the CIA made what could have led to the greatest disaster in the history of the world.

As I wrote earlier in noting that the perceptive and experienced British reporter Steve Barber had missed the significance of what he had read in Schlesinger's book, that our military planned to get us into a land war in China, there is much too much for the best reporters not to miss something from time to time. But then all reporters, columnists, editorial writers and those contributing articles for use on op-ed pages also missed it.

They also missed the story that the military had reasons to believe much earlier that the Soviet Union had missiles in Cuba capable of carrying nuclear warheads for a thousand miles or so. In all I have read, I recall no reference by anyone suggesting that the president was given this information. There is every reason to believe that the military kept it secret from him, from their commander in chief.

Elie Abel, an experienced reporter who became dean of the prestigious Columbia University School of Journalism, also did not spell it out in his book, *The Missile Crisis*. Early in his book, Abel notes:

> Colonel John Ralph Wright, Jr., of the Defense Intelligence Agency had studied the results of the September overflights with meticulous care. He was struck by the placement of SAMs, in an oddly trapezoidal pattern, near the Cuban town of San Cristobal. This configuration roused Colonel Wright's suspicion. It resembled the placement of missile installations photographed repeatedly by pilots like Gary Powers over the Soviet Union. The colonel suggested to his boss, General Joseph Carroll, that San Cristobal might be worth a closer look. Thus a look at San Cristobal became part of the flight plan for the next U-2 sortie.[6]

Three pages later Abel has this footnote:

> In June 1963, Colonel Wright's crucial contribution was acknowledged with the award of an Oak Leaf Cluster to the Legion of Merit he had received ten years earlier. The citation reads, in part: 'He performed a unique service to his country by single-handedly analyzing a series of intelligence reports concerning the activities of the Soviet Union in Cuba and, by his analysis, pinpointing the location of the first medium-range ballistic missiles deployed by the USSR in the Western hemisphere. His analysis led him to aircraft the exact location which was photographed on 14 October, 1962, and revealed the existence of those missiles in Cuba.[7]

What "struck" Wright is that the pattern of SAMs photographed in Cuba was known to have only a single purpose, to protect Soviet "missile installations." This had only two possible meanings: that there were Soviet missiles there capable of raining nuclear destruction on much of the eastern half of the United States, or there soon would be.

And yet the president was not informed of this! It was kept secret from him and, from all that has been reported by and from Ex Comm, from every member of it other than the military, who said not a word about it. And that Ex Comm was composed of the most important people in our government tasked with making the most important recommendation of their lives.

Not only was this kept secret—this positive proof that there were or soon would be those Soviet missiles capable of carrying nuclear bombs over the United States—nothing was done to immediately obtain proof that the missiles were in fact there. What was much more important was bureaucratic in-fighting between the Air Force and the CIA. And then the weather turned bad. Here is how Abel continues:

> There was more delay due to cloud cover over the target area. The U-2 loses effectiveness when the sky is 25 percent or more overcast. In addition, a day or two was lost while new Strategic Air Command pilots were checked out on a U-2 built to CIA specifications. McNamara had suggested the shift to McCone in view of the greatly accelerated flight schedule. There was for the first time real danger of losing planes as well as pilots. In that situation, McNamara urged, Air Force regulars ought to take over. Some CIA people took this hard. General Carter, in McCone's month-long absence, had appealed to the White House, arguing that intelligence was properly the CIA's business and that it had its own control center to go with the planes, the trained pilots, and the experience. McGeorge Bundy dismissed the appeal.
>
> By October 14, the skies over Cuba cleared, the CIA had choked down its bitter pill and two Air Force pilots, thoroughly familiar by now with the CIA version of the U-2, had climbed into their borrowed flying machines. Both were Air Force majors—Rudolf Anderson, Jr. of Spartanburg, South Carolina, and Richard S. Heyser of Battle Creek, Michigan. . . .
>
> As they entered the air space of western Cuba that Sunday, forewarned of possible ground fire, they were agreeably surprised to encounter none. They made their planned sweep of suspect areas, with San Cristobal at the top of the list. They then flew home, skidding in safely with wings folded down at the tips to prevent looping. Their film magazines were quickly unloaded and transferred

> to a waiting jet for the flight to Washington. For Anderson and Heyser it had been an uneventful mission.[8]

Once again, when the Soviets and Cubans could have shot down the U-2s they did not, permitting them to make the full photographic record the United States soon used with such effectiveness by the president in his address to the nation and by Adlai Stevenson at the United Nations. Again, this means that the Soviets wanted us to have the proof it never made any effort to hide, the proof that would force the issue, and give Kennedy his own "tiger to ride" with the choice of war or peace, of what the United States had made so virtually important to the USSR, that is, of invading or not invading Cuba.

At that same point, Abel also reports that McCone had earlier warned that the Soviets might install such missiles in Cuba, before Wright developed the proof on September 5.[9] To put this more bluntly, the military had every reason to believe not later than September 5 that Soviet missiles either were already in Cuba or soon would be there and it said not a word to the president until October 16!

Information like *this* should be withheld from the *president*? From the country, for that matter? Why? Other than to make war more likely, war that could have begun with a nuclear attack on the United States if Khrushchev had had that intention. And for the five and a half weeks—39 days—when there were no U-2 overflights there was no information on the state of readiness of this missile installation! What purpose was or could have been served by this secrecy, this omnipresent curse of so much secrecy, with the ultimate in disasters possible?

The Soviets knew it had those missiles there, ready to fire or not, but there. The military secrecy withheld nothing from the Soviet Union. And as we have seen, it made no effort to disguise what it was doing. So there was nothing to be gained by not letting the Soviets know that we knew when it did all but place ads in the *New York Times* and the *Washington Post* to let it be known! All that this incredible secrecy did was to make a situation of extraordinary, unprecedented danger to us and to the world infinitely more dangerous, making the likelihood of a totally unnecessary war ever greater.

Consistent with this astounding secrecy, the military waited almost a year to honor Wright for his "crucial contribution" that consisted of "pinpointing the location of the first medium-range ballistic missiles deployed by the USSR in the western hemisphere."[10]

This language alone makes it clear that the military knew on September 5 that there were Soviet missile installations in Cuba but pretended it did not know this until October 14 and then notified the president on October 16. All it got on October 14 was confirmation of what it already knew and pictures to show and inflame the world with. For those thirty-nine days, the military denied the president any opportunity to defuse this dangerous situation. But this horror was not entirely without some good coming to the military from it. The Air Force did win its bureaucratic fight with the CIA, even if that fight wasted the only days U-2s could have flown over Cuba and learned more.

Throughout, I have in various ways referred to the entirely unprecedented situation our youngest president faced with proliferation of nuclear weaponry on both sides and its greatly increased destructive power. It was ever so much greater than the unimaginable destructiveness of the two atom bombs President Truman had dropped on Hiroshima and Nagasaki, the totality and extent of the destructiveness which shook the world as it had never before been shaken. Khrushchev did indeed give Kennedy his own "tiger to ride" in the Cuba Missile Crisis. How Kennedy managed to keep firm and calm control over himself and his emotions when confronted with such a momentous decision, and to at the same time have prevented what could have set the world afire as it had never been before, is not really dealt with in anything I recall reading. This, too, must be without precedent in world history. There are, I believe, very few individuals who could have maintained that kind of self-control and control over the forces inside his own government, with all their great power and influence, over so many men who were so determined that he make the decision that it is now without any rational question would have been the most terribly wrong decision. That he was able to is a little-noted and never really explained extraordinary accomplishment. That we have and know the world as it now is, I believe, is entirely because he was able to do what for most political leaders would have been quite impossible. And that on his part Khrushchev took no such irreversible step earns him the world's respect and appreciation.

However much we as Americans may be unwilling to face it, this was the inevitable consequence of our long-time meddling in the affairs of other countries where we had no business meddling. This is what we faced, in its most extreme and dangerous form, when we did this with Cuba after Castro took power and after the Bay of Pigs invasion (which was really our invasion by proxy, an act of war in itself), when Khrushchev promised to come to Cuba's defense. Once Castro learned of the United States continuing with such efforts, particularly in Operation Mongoose, and then when Castro publicly sent his brother Raul and Che Guevara to Moscow to ask the Soviets to meet the obligation they had assumed, Khrushchev's hand was forced.

Because there was and is no way in which Cuba could be defended from a US invasion, Khrushchev chose this way of defending Cuba. He did that very dangerously and successfully; and in doing it the way he did, he passed the buck back to President Kennedy. Considering the pressures and challenges these two men faced, as utterly unlike as they were, they managed to keep it from becoming the most terrible event in man's recorded history, which is an extraordinary tribute to both of them.

They then started groping toward peace. Each was the captive of his own domestic situation. Each also was awesomely aware of the consequences of failure from what they had just been through. Each had his own hardliners to survive (as, in the end, neither did) and try to control. We know not as much as we should of those unhappy with Khrushchev. We have seen and will soon see more of those who opposed Kennedy and what they not only were capable of, but also what they planned.

Kennedy's assassination and his successor's opting for the opposite policies made it inevitable that those Soviet forces would come to believe that they could not have Khrushchev, who had become the counterpart of Kennedy's dovishness, confront the hawk, Johnson. Without personal injury to him, they kicked Khrushchev out and allowed him to live the rest of his natural life in peace, even to write his memoirs.

What Kennedy knew at the time of the Cuba Missile Crisis is in part reflected above, but he faced an even more frightening prospect considering the heinous possibilities that were fixed by the military and in place. It is easy to believe that he was convinced he was dealing with madmen, real life Strangeloves, from what he knew before the missile crisis.

Historian Richard Reeves, who has a clear anti-Kennedy record, provides an unintended extra dimension to this unprecedented and exceptional Kennedy–Khrushchev accomplishment. He gives us an even more harrowing account of what could have happened had Kennedy made the wrong decision in 1962, the decision all of his military and many—initially most—of his civilian advisers were so determined that he make.

Three months into his presidency, Kennedy began to understand his military and its means of creating policy with the disastrous national humiliation of the Bay of Pigs. The humiliation was that of the nation, not of the president alone. His principled assumption of all responsibility increased his popularity considerably. In five more months, he learned that the military believed it had the constitutional prerogative to make national policy, not the elected president.

He then learned that the military had arranged to take from him any control over where it dropped those most terrible of all weapons of destruction, nuclear bombs. The sole option the military allowed the president in its concept—*any* president because presidents come and go—was deciding when those nuclear bombs would be launched. Where they would go and how many would be dropped, he could have nothing to do with! Richard Reeves describes this in his, *President Kennedy: Profile of Power*:

> It was only then, on September 13, 1961, after eight months in office, that Kennedy finally sat down for a two-hour briefing on the United States' most guarded secret, the plan for nuclear war. It was officially called SIOP-62—Single Integrated Operational Plan for Fiscal Year 1962. The military did not volunteer its own information and plans when it had reason to believe that presidents might change them. What presidents didn't know couldn't hurt the military, or so reasoned generals and admirals who saw presidents come and go. Kennedy knew the general outlines of the SIOP, which had been described to him by Bundy as "a massive, total, comprehensive, obliterating strategic attack . . . on everything Red." Once a

> president said yes to touching a nuclear button, his power shifted to the military. The chain of command was a gigantic and deadly snake with a life of its own if the commander in chief opened the cage.

Chairman of the Joint Chiefs of Staff Lemnitzer did the briefing in which he detailed the number of nuclear warheads to be deployed in the event of an attack, also noting that some portion of the Soviet long-range nuclear force would strike the United States. He ended his presentation by emphasizing once the attack was launched there would be no "effective mechanism for rapid rework of the plan . . ." Reeves continues,

> Kennedy was tapping his front teeth with the fingernail of his thumb for the last twenty minutes of Lemnitzer's show, a sign to those who knew him that he was either bored or furious. And there was nothing boring about the plan.
>
> "Why do we hit all those targets in China, General?" Kennedy asked. The Chinese had no missiles, no nuclear delivery systems.
>
> "It's in the plan, Mr. President," said the general.
>
> Kennedy was gripping the arms of his chair so tightly that his knuckles showed white. As he walked out of the room with Dean Rusk, he said: "And we call ourselves the human race."[11]

Reeves has twelve source notes for these two pages, which include the SIOP itself.

What this actually says and means is that the military created the situation in which it was in charge, not any president. One of the means by which it was able to create this situation was keeping what it was doing secret from the president. If in 1962 President Kennedy had decided it was necessary to drop a single nuclear bomb, the military, being in charge and assuming it knew better than any president, would begin by dropping more than a thousand of them on more than 3,700 targets, and that within a quarter of an hour of getting any permission to drop a single one. It would then decide when to start the destruction of much of the world and all the people there. Hiroshima and Nagasaki were child's play compared with SIOP-62, tin-soldier stuff to what Lemnitzer laid out to Kennedy. And nothing could be done about it.

All it permitted the president—*any* president —was the decision to drop a single nuclear bomb, if in fact they let him decide that.

If a single bomb was authorized, it was not only China, but Albania—little Albania, no threat to anyone—they were going to wipe out. As Reeves says in one of his source notes, when Secretary of Defense McNamara was first briefed on the SIOP the month after the Kennedy administration was sworn in, General Thomas Power told him, "Well, Mr. Secretary, I hope you don't have any friends or relations in Albania because we are going to have to wipe it out."[12]

Not only did the military give the president to understand that it would do whatever it damned well pleased, including wiping out much of the populated area of the entire world, it made it clear that once the president, who had no control over it once he decided that a single bomb was to be dropped, would be held responsible for what the military did and he did not authorize it to do.

The military's plan, which neither he nor any other president had anything to do with, could not be changed. They would "wipe out" much of Europe and Asia. How much worry and trouble therefore, how much greater his unknown distress, when confronted with the next year's Cuba Missile Crisis!

Presidents do come and go, as Reeves says, but not the JCS. They seldom change; they remain clones of Dr. Strangelove. As R. Jeffrey Smith reported in the *Washington Post* of September 22, 1994, President Clinton accepted the Pentagon recommendation to make no changes in basic nuclear policy. It put off further nuclear-arms reductions with Russia and preserved the right[13] to first-use of nuclear weapons.[14]

This meant continuing to keep almost 500 nuclear weapons in Europe, improving those for our nuclear submarines and preserving its plan for destroying about 2,500 targets in Russia from the existing arsenal of 6,000 strategic nuclear weapons.

Under Clinton, the scope of this review was scaled down, so less of the existing policy was reviewed. One of the officials who urged more cuts told Smith that the civilians were afraid of the military. And to make it all easier, Secretary of State Warren Christopher and Clinton's National Security adviser Anthony Lake were not involved in this review of nuclear policy for the coming decade.

How much *had* the danger from Russia increased *after the USSR had come apart*? In an adjoining story, the *Post* reported that "The central command for Russia's strategic nuclear missile forces had its power cut off for failing to pay its electric bills" for quite some time. The same thing happened to the Russian's "mammoth nuclear shipbuilding facility." Its power station was closed down for non-payment of bills.[15] This *increased* the danger to the United States?

There is no reference to Albania or China in Smith's story. That there can be 2500 targets in Russia, as distinguished from the entire USSR, can account for the report of a reduction of about 1200 targets under this plan for the decade. It seems like a rather large number of remaining individual targets. Whether or not the other countries of SIOP-62, countries earlier unidentified and those identified such as Albania and China, are within the same plan, or the "anything Red," in national security adviser McGeorge Bundy's interpretation of SIOP-62, Smith does not go into.

As Smith's story also points out, when this study was prepared, the "key work (was) turned over to the military officers and Bush administration holdovers." Consequently, the SIOP-62 plan remains the national policy and the destruction under it may well be greater because of the increasing destructive power of nuclear bombs more than twenty years later. This is to be the country's nuclear policy for at least the decade ahead.

This is also to say that despite the end of the Cold War and the dissolution of the USSR, the United States nuclear destruction policy continues just as it was. It does not require a new Cold War; it requires only an understanding of the military and its mind and policies. According to the military, we needed the enormous expenditures for all those nuclear warheads and the means of delivering them, plus the magnitude of the problems associated with merely making and possessing them and in the end having to dispose of them, all those warheads that were sufficient to destroy the world many times over, because of the Cold War.

Now that there is no Cold War, it is claimed that we still need them and the policy of needing and retaining them for at least the coming decade, with improvement in some and the manufacture of still new ones when the country is so broke it cannot keep all its schools and libraries open; can't provide medical care and homes for the sick and homeless; can't provide enough police for the streets or jails to hold criminals, among all the other real needs the country without question has because of the nuclear needs of the Cold War even when the Cold War is over.

Does it make sense? Of course it makes sense to the military! And there is no John Kennedy to hear of all this and remark, "And we call ourselves the human race."

This SIOP-62 design for wiping out much of the world and poisoning the rest of it was intended for what was called a "preventive" war. That concept did not originate with this SIOP-62; it harkens back to the more modest and less inhumane military concepts and practices of Genghis Khan and Attila the Hun. As we here consider it, it began not later than the military plans of the first Eisenhower administration.

David Wise, an experienced Washington correspondent for the *New York Herald Tribune* and later author of political and intelligence exposé books, wrote a best-selling book in 1973 entitled, *The Politics of Lying*, which is a thorough and frightening account of government secrecy through extraordinary misuse of "national security" classification claims and of the extensive government lying that makes it possible.

Robert J. Donovan preceded Wise as that Republican newspaper's White House correspondent. When Sherman Adams, Eisenhower's top assistant, "conceived the idea of letting a journalist have access to the administration's internal papers, classified and otherwise, to write a book" promoting Eisenhower, naturally, that paper was asked for a reporter to do the writing. Donovan agreed when his stipulation of complete independence was agreed to. After clearance, Donovan took a leave of absence from the newspaper. He was then given an office in the White House, and as he told Wise, "They brought in documents in wheelbarrows and on dollies. . . . A great many were classified. . . ." Wise writes that one of the most chilling secrets Donovan learned came in conversation with Robert Cutler, Eisenhower's assistant for national security affairs. Cutler and Donovan met over dinner at the Harvard Club in New York where "Cutler cryptically disclosed that 'there had been discussions of preventive war within the councils of the government.'" Donovan recalls that he "nearly fell off my chair." He subsequently came across a Top Secret document which confirmed this. It concisely summarized the administration's philosophy of the military "New Look." Despite pressures not to disclose any of this, Donovan wrote his book, which was published in 1956 and became a national best seller.[16]

"New Look" or "preventive war" or SIOP: It is all the same thing, a surprise nuclear holocaust. It does not "prevent" war—it starts one. The difference is that in 1956 we could not begin to destroy nearly as much as what was conceived as the enemy world because we had so relatively few weapons capable of it. That is why in 1961 the SIOP was for 1963, when we could have the arsenal the military wanted to be able to destroy much of Asia and Europe with their surprise attack, as outlined in their Single Integrated Operating Plan.

The Kennedy administration also inherited this from the Eisenhower administration, as it had the involvement already begun in Southeast Asia and the Bay of Pigs scheme to force us to invade Cuba.

CHAPTER 6

CUI BONO? THE CIRCUMSTANTIAL CASE

In the summer of 1966, after I'd written my second book, *Whitewash II: The FBI-Secret Service Cover-Up*, I awakened after only a few hours of sleep with part of something I'd long wanted to say in mind. Before washing and dressing, I began banging away on the old Underwood upright which was favored in many newsrooms because it could take that pounding. Except to wash, dress and get some coffee made, I did not stop working even for breakfast, which I ate at my desk, until I'd completed the Epilogue to that book. In it, for the first time, I raised the question asked by lawyers but not by lawyers alone, "Cui bono?" Or "Who benefits?" Who benefits is always a question the answer to which should be sought.

Unanswered Questions

Even before I began writing my first book, *Whitewash: The Report on the Warren Report*, I was troubled that the media did not seem to have any interest in this and the many other obvious questions left unanswered. Shortly after the assassination I spent some time with Tom Wolfe when he was a *Washington Post* reporter. I posed some of these questions to him. He typed the list, but as far as I am aware, he did nothing more with them. I spoke to other journalists, and nobody was interested. It was clearly a story that for some reason was of no interest to the newspapers; they were toeing the official line.

When the report was out, I started working to find answers to these questions which were never addressed by the official "investigations."

My first book, based entirely on the official evidence then available, made clear beyond a shadow of a doubt that the official evidence itself proves absolutely that there was a conspiracy to kill JFK. There was a conspiracy and officialdom knew there was a conspiracy. While it was important to demonstrate that this was covered up, whitewashed, by the official investigation, it still leaves unanswered the major question: Who committed the crime?[1] I believe that insight into that question may be revealed by exploring the question, "Who benefits?"

So "who benefits?" or in the Latin of lawyers, "Cui bono?" is a question that lingers and one that I address herein. It relates most directly to motive, the first of the three elements of circumstantial evidence that are so essential in approaching a criminal investigation: motive, means, and opportunity. Who had a viable motive (who stood to benefit)? Who had the means to commit the crime? Who had the opportunity to do so? As I explore evidence relating to these questions, I do not claim what I present is proof; it is not. But it does suggest avenues that should have been investigated. The circumstantial evidence is more than sufficient to require some effort to resolve the question.

In attempting to answer these questions and develop a circumstantial case, I present evidence that is available to anyone with any interest, and certainly to the media, which apparently has no interest.

The assassination of a president is not just a murder; it is a political crime. It is in effect a coup d'état, the removal of one regime and replacement with another. In our system of government, the vice president becomes president upon the death or incapacity of the president. With the assassination of President Kennedy, Lyndon Baines Johnson became president. And with him, a predictable change in foreign and domestic policies. To answer the question of "Who benefits?" from the crime, it is first necessary to determine what the outcome, the "benefit" was. In this case, a radical reversal of Kennedy's policies, particularly in foreign affairs, was a major outcome, a "benefit" from the perspective of those so vehemently opposed to them.

As discussed in previous chapters, President Kennedy had attempted to exert control of US policy especially with respect to Vietnam, Cuba, nuclear weapons, and relations with the Soviet Union, much of which he inherited from the Eisenhower administration. His efforts to change course were met with fierce resistance from the military and intelligence communities and their allies in Congress, who had their own views of the national interest. Kennedy believed that the policies and actions favored by them were faulty and would lead to mass destruction.

The Roots of Resistance

What were the roots of their resistance and their efforts to undermine the commander in chief? I believe that the roots of this resistance lie in faulty analysis based not on a clear assessment of reality, but on ideology.

If our policy and actions in Vietnam had any rational basis, it was faulty, as generals de Gaulle and MacArthur had both warned President Kennedy. So too in the Cuba Missile Crisis, the inevitable result of our own actions pursuant to policies that if they had any rational basis, they came from still another faulty analysis. More than likely, however, it was a knee-jerk reaction based not on rational, fact-based analysis, but rather on ideology. This was the "Cold War" ideology, begun long before the war against Hitler was won. It is an enlargement of domestic political policies in this country of a powerful minority that regarded all efforts by working people to improve their lot as of Communist origin or inspiration. Earlier policies that discouraged the payment of decent living wages were now described as Communist once Karl Marx could be made the symbol of all that is evil. In the 1930s, I was part of the Senate's investigation of abuses that were attributed to the need to defeat Communism, when those who were defeated were ordinary, everyday working Americans and their families.

World War I was hardly over when Attorney General A. Mitchell Palmer and his then youthful right-hand man, J. Edgar Hoover, were forcibly deporting those they considered Communists and anarchists, of whom there were really very few; most were simply advocates of better working conditions and proponents of political beliefs the Palmers and Hoovers did not approve of. Denied access to the legal system and due process of law, they were deported by the ship load. This national shame was the beginning of Hoover's long career. Soon thereafter, he became the first director of the Federal Bureau of Investigation with a reputation as the greatest Red-Hunter of all.

Then came the so-called Un-American Activities Committee, an apt name not for what they investigated, but for what they did. Their hearings on "un-American activities" attracted enormous media attention that fixed the national mind, as Hoover had earlier and Joe McCarthy and his ilk did later.

During World War II when I was in the OSS, I recall that a few of our European echelons along with some of the Army's began a secret war against the USSR, then our ally, an ally that killed more Nazi soldiers than the rest of the allies combined. One incident I recall was the theft by the OSS of a large number of bags of Soviet Army mail. Another was an Army jeep expedition into the Soviet-held part of Austria for some espionage purpose at which they were caught.

Then there were the efforts to protect anti-Soviet Nazis and to use them against the Soviets. Among the books written about this is an excellent one by correspondent, later university journalism professor Linda Hunt, called *Secret Agenda*.[2] Among other things, she brings out the fact that our rocketry was advanced by Nazi war criminals.

We took over the Gehlen anti-Soviet Nazi intelligence operation and made it ours. General Gehlen lived out his life without punishment, as did those under him, regardless of their war crimes. Our Army even hid from the State Department captured Nazi records that identified Nazis they might want to use and to keep the USSR from using the records for prosecuting war criminals. I was once called back from leave to tell the head of State intelligence, a man dedicated to rooting out Nazi war criminals, where some of those records the army hid were stashed away, that information having passed through my hands. When Mussolini and his mistress were captured by Italian partisans who trusted us, his some twenty-five suitcases of records were microfilmed and flown to the Pentagon, where they disappeared. A French refugee economist engaged in war work for our government had the same futile experience I did in trying to locate and examine those microfilms of Mussolini's records when he was captured.

Then there were the blacklists that included some of the most prominent, talented, and devotedly democratic in the arts and sciences, as well as ordinary working people and union leaders. As a result of these massive efforts, anything that called itself anti-Communist was accepted and respected no matter how anti-democratic, irrational and even just plain silly it really was. The national mindset was fixed.

This Cold War ideology was not limited to the United States. In varying degrees, it existed in most of the developed countries. It was Winston Churchill who sounded Harry Truman's Cold War battle cry for him with his Iron Curtain speech in this country. That is the same Winston Churchill who, according to the authoritative British book, *C*,[3] ordered the redirection of British intelligence against the USSR as soon as the beachhead in France was secure.[4]

Vatican officials helped Nazi war criminals escape, as did anti-communists of many hues and colors, some with Nazi odors of their own. For them, the mantle of anti-Communism was all they needed for justification.

With the passing of time, there came to be some public admission of the fact that we started the Cold War. What was called anti-Communism and The Cold War became a national state of mind as well as a national policy that justified anything at all. It was the shibboleth for getting and keeping government jobs of all grades including, of course, the very highest. It was also the basis for recruiting into our intelligence services after World War II, resulting in some amazing examples in "intelligence" reports.

I remember a very early CIA report of the late 1940s on the small South American country of Paraguay when I was in a part of State Department intelligence and temporarily sat on the Paraguay desk of my division. Paraguay then had two major political parties. They were known by their colors, the Liberal party was the "azul" or blue party, and the Colorado Party was the party of the red color. One was more liberal and the other was more than just conservative. It was the party of the vicious, Nazi-like dictator, Higinio Morinigo. That CIA intelligence memo identified the

Colorado Party as Communist. It was a natural enough assumption, its color being red. But intelligence is not based on assumptions. It is supposed to be based upon fact. And in Paraguay the Colorado or "red" party was that of the Morinigo dictatorship.

This kind of stupid mistake that could have influenced policy was the natural consequence of recruiting that favored those of this political mindset from the Ivy League. And it lingers in our intelligence services, all of which were and remain geared to the Cold War.

Analysis is the essence of intelligence. In recent years, we have had a grim record of failed policies stemming from faulty analyses. In saying that I was able to make correct analyses of the Cuba Missile Crisis and the Gulf of Tonkin incident contemporaneously when others did not, I am not boasting but criticizing. Seeing the obvious is not cause for boasting; missing or not understanding the obvious is a legitimate cause for criticism. Cold-War blinders made those wearing them look only straight ahead, looking for the color red and looking for it so concentratedly they could not see black and white.

However, there came a time when disgrace, having followed rapidly on the heels of fiasco after fiasco, the agency was forced to take a look at itself and then speak out. More or less.

The reckoning came when one of its senior and long-time employees, Aldrich H. Ames, was caught spying and confessed to disclosing more than fifty CIA intelligence operations to the KGB. He also betrayed thirty-six United States and allied paid agents, many of whom were subsequently executed by the Soviets. He was undetected for years despite extravagantly living it up with his KGB payments. That did compel some CIA introspection and self-criticism.

Douglas J. MacEachin, a former CIA deputy director for intelligence, published a report on this that was highly critical of the agency. In an interview with *Washington Post* columnist, Walter Pincus, MacEachin "called for a new emphasis on facts and the analysis derived from them" by the CIA.[5]

That is *new*? In fact, that is what intelligence was always supposed to be—analysis based on facts—and it was until corrupted by an agency shift of focus to "dirty tricks," including overthrowing governments and assassinations. The CIA had a major component devoted to just these kinds of non-intelligence functions. It was disguised in the organizational table by being referred to as "plans" and "operations." This story-book stuff that was never of any real value grew to dominate the agency while its basic functions were neglected. These functions, grounded in dependable, fact-based analysis, the essence of intelligence, were degraded by the preoccupation with "dirty tricks."

In confessing that his people had to start all over again in the intelligence kindergarten, Pincus wrote that MacEachin also admitted that CIA failures "often came because analysts made what he called wrong judgements about the driving or 'linchpin' factors." He attributed these analysis failures to "analysts wanting to give readers [those who received their reports] forecasts and predictions without giving them the facts and analysis that led to those conclusions."[6]

An additional factor, he claimed, was that the analysts were "part of a production system for classified reports that emphasized the need for getting promoted rather than the needs of policymakers." That is to say, they reported what those who read their reports wanted to read rather than the facts, fearing the fate of the messenger killed over the message he bore.

What a remarkable confession by one of the CIA's top four, the meaning of which the *Post* did not point out, that forty-five years after Harry Truman disbanded the OSS, the CIA had to begin again from scratch. Whether that can be done without the recruitment of new people lacking the Cold War mindset is doubtful. The CIA is not staffed, as any intelligence agency should be, with impartial analysts, well-educated rather than indoctrinated.

As we have seen, those at the top of the main branches of the military are so determinedly the apotheosis of Cold Warriors that it is not likely that they, any more than those at the top in the CIA, promoted those who were not their Cold War clones. If there were any intelligence analysts who were not Cold Warriors, it is doubtful that their analysis would be heeded.

MacEachin does not, however, make any mention of the most serious weakness in our intelligence, the preconditioning mindsets that control what intelligence reports. That is the CIA's political weakness—its adherence to and contribution to the creation and perfection of national Cold War policy. Good intelligence agencies should be objective and completely independent of any political ideology.

Thus, many CIA projects that on the face seemed like successes were ultimately great disasters. They did, however, provide good public relations to the CIA and were well-received by the politicians in the White House and Congress.

One such disaster was the CIA's overthrow of the democratic government of Iran. It was only after the Iranians expelled the Shah and the new Mossadegh government nationalized the oil wells that the CIA began a campaign against that emotional nationalist, Mossadegh, who had a clear record of anti-Communism. The CIA succeeded in having this anti-Communist nationalist painted as a Communist. After it succeeded in getting Mossadegh overthrown, it put the Shah back in power. And, junior-grade Hitler that he was, the Shah created and nurtured opposition to himself and to his policies. While for a short period of time his oil policies pleased the world's major oil corporations and governments, including ours, he grew more and more unpopular. The more unpopular he grew the more we armed, trained, and equipped his police in the arts of repression and torture, as we did elsewhere in the world. The more we helped him abuse his people and siphon off the country's wealth, the more certain it became that he would be overthrown.

And who did that Shah hire for counsel and advice? The former head of the CIA, Richard Helms. When the Shah was overthrown, he was succeeded by the tyrannical fundamentalist government we now know, an exporter of international violence and terror and a menace to that part of the world so important because of its petroleum resources, as well as to other Muslim countries that did not share the Ayatollah's extremist interpretation of the Koran.

The real reason for overthrowing the Mossadegh government was not that it was Communist, which it wasn't, but because it took back ownership of the oil wells from the foreign oil corporations. The oil itself continued to be sold around the world. It was not a threat except to the oil companies who lost their profit source. Working to ensure the profitability of large corporations is not the proper function of an intelligence agency. In

Iran, the CIA could hardly have created a greater disaster in what it originally touted as a great success.

Intelligence agencies can and do hide behind secrecy. They pretend they cannot talk about their claimed great successes because all of that has to be secret in the interest of "national security." In fact, they all find ways of leaking their claims of great success. The politicized CIA has few legitimate claims of success of any real value to the nation, but it was and is quite adept at taking credit for what it had nothing to do with. Thus, at the time it leaked the text of Khrushchev's speech denouncing Stalin's terror and paranoia, the CIA gave the world the impression that it got the text of that speech by its skilled intelligence operations inside the USSR. The truth is the opposite. The CIA had nothing to do with getting the text of that speech; it was a gift from Israeli intelligence. A Polish Jew who emigrated to Israel and had a copy of that Khrushchev speech took it with him. He gave it to Israeli intelligence who then gave it to the CIA. And as clearly reported in the Israeli press, this is the truth about that greatest of CIA Cold War coups; it had nothing to do with getting it.

The real situation is that when the head of the CIA, Richard Helms, was caught in perjury, a felony, and the government that wanted to help him charged him with a lesser offense, he was praised as a patriot for his perjury to Congress by his lawyer after receiving the sentence that was hardly even a tap on the wrist. Who was his lawyer? The eminent and respected Edward Bennett Williams[7] had long been a member of the president's intelligence advisory or "oversight" board which approved the CIA's excesses, at least those of which it knew.

In the military there was not even any pretense of "oversight." Those at the top, with rare exceptions, were Cold Warriors or they would never have gotten to the top. They surrounded themselves with only those of like mind. As we have seen, they unanimously opposed their president's policies conscientiously and with determination. They were products of their respective branches of the military and the educational institutions of those branches, the Army's at West Point and Navy's Annapolis being the best known and most highly regarded, and many others for more advanced study. That all at the top in all the military services were of similar political mind could not be an accident. They were the intended product, the product that may well have believed that President Kennedy was "weak on Communism" or worse than that. They could easily have seen him as their enemy and therefore the country's enemy. And that frustrating his policies, as they did, was the apotheosis of the true patriotism.

All of those in the military top command who opposed Kennedy's policies could not have done that on the basis of impartial intelligence analysis. They, personally, were incapable of making their own impartial analyses. They could think and analyze only in Cold War terms. Their minds were captive to Cold War beliefs and doctrine, a prerequisite to success in their military careers.

No matter how much they were proven wrong in the field, as they were in Vietnam, they explained it away with the lies they had come to believe. It is important to note that they believed the lies were the truth, incredible as that may seem. They believed that their policy was grounded in true patriotism. They believed their China policy, provoking a land war with China to wipe out that bastion of Communism with nuclear weapons, was in America's national interest, even though China had no nuclear weapons, as Kennedy noted when SIOP-62 was explained to him.

Is it any wonder that so many countries would spend their limited resources to have their own nuclear arsenals?

The genuineness of their convictions and their patriotism does not legitimize their actions any more than the sincere beliefs of Iran's Ayatollah Khomeini excused his policies. Beliefs and convictions are no substitute for objective analysis. Furthermore, their efforts to undermine the president's policies, as they did with respect to Vietnam and Cuba, violates the Constitution they all swore to uphold and defend. And they violated our obligations to international organizations such as the United Nations and the Organization of American States as well as various treaties and agreements. If, as they believed, their policies were right and they were patriotic, they were convinced the president and his policies were the opposite.

One cannot dismiss the possibility that they came to regard him as the country's enemy. As we have seen, these are people capable of drastic action, who regarded it as necessary and right to lay waste to the Vietnamese countryside, preventing food production in order to "save" it. They are the ones who wanted to bomb Cuba and then invade it for the sin of doing what they had themselves done by placing missiles in Turkey, Italy, and England. What was right for them was wrong for Cuba and the USSR. And as the record shows, they really believed it.

They are the people who were not content with the victory Kennedy achieved in getting those missiles out of Cuba; a victory for a policy they opposed was no victory to them. Our military leaders were the people who wanted to bomb Cuba and sink Soviet merchant ships and submarines—*after* peace, *after* victory!

More than likely, this would have been the start of World War III—and nuclear catastrophe.

For them, true patriotism was violating orders, harassing Soviet submarines on the high seas in spite of specific presidential orders not to. And when the Secretary of Defense caught them at it, they told him more or less to go to hell, and continued doing that—in direct violation of the specific orders of their commander in chief.

These were people who, as we have also seen, had planned to take nuclear war decisions out of the hands of the commander in chief, once the president authorized the use of a single nuclear weapon. The military would then have dropped nuclear bombs on "*3,729 targets*" with more nuclear bombs in reserve that "could be fired within six hours," killing more people than had ever been killed in the history of the world and laying waste to more than three thousand cities. Cities would have been reduced to radioactive dust, farmland incapable of producing anything but crops poisoned by radiation, and millions of innocent people killed in an instant. This, to them, was the true patriotism, the true reflection of love of country. Otherwise, they would not have developed an inflexible and unchangeable plan that gave them complete control.

All these things they genuinely believed were the country's urgent need. Starting a war with the Soviet Union, laying waste to Vietnam and Cuba, and wiping out much of Europe and Asia. This is what they wanted, what they regarded as necessary for our national security. President Kennedy opposed them—successfully.

Military leaders were no less dead set against Kennedy's other quests for world peace and for the reduction in weapons of mass destruction. They saw these efforts too as a threat to the nation.

One of these efforts involved sending Averell Harriman and Carl Kaysen to Moscow to explore a limited nuclear test-ban agreement and to discuss China as the long-term danger to peace. As Schlesinger writes in *A Thousand Days*,

> Harriman and Kaysen had a final meeting with the president before the mission's departure for Moscow. Kennedy said that Harriman could go as far as he wished in exploring the possibility of a Soviet-American understanding with regard to China. Averell responded that he would more than ever need something to sweeten the package. Kennedy mentioned possible concessions. The president added, "I have some cash in the bank in West Germany and am prepared to draw on it if you think I should."[8]

Wise and astute as he was, Schlesinger must have had some compelling reason for not explaining his last sentence in this paragraph. What Harriman meant by needing "something to sweeten the package" with is obvious enough, but what Kennedy meant by his reference to "cash in the bank in West Germany" is not.

Clearly, Kennedy was not talking about cash in the literal sense, nor was he talking about trying to bribe the Soviets with cash. The "concessions" he referenced seem to be limited to either concessions regarding NATO, the anti-Soviet North Atlantic alliance that extended far inland from the Atlantic, or our relations with the West German government.

That he was prepared to compromise any part of either of these relationships to reach an understanding with the Soviets was quite significant. The military (for which NATO was also a rich source of high-level jobs and promotions) would certainly have been greatly disturbed by this and by any move toward nuclear disarmament, however small.

If the military could, in the name of national interest and patriotism, push for actions that would kill millions, is it difficult to believe that they could have regarded the killing of a single person as any less necessary, any less the demand of true patriotism, any less their duty?

In trying to solve a crime, lawyers say, look for who has "motive, means, and opportunity." Nobody had, or could have had, the motive our military leaders had, and they had the means and the opportunity as few others could have had.

Media Complicity

Those "who benefited," whoever they were, were helped enormously by the immediate failure of the media to fulfill its Constitutional role. They failed to report what they should have and, under normal conditions, would have reported. There is no question of the importance of all this; there is little in a democratic society as significant as the assassination of a president. Not only is it a crime of exceptional importance, it is in effect a coup d'état, whether intended to be or not. It removes the government chosen by the people.

When John Kennedy was gunned down, in broad daylight and on the streets of a modern American city, communications were better and more efficient than they had ever been. The media had many highly educated reporters, many with exceptional investigative skills. And the media itself, particularly television, had developed rapidly. Nonetheless, there was no real investigative reporting by the major media when John Kennedy was assassinated.

Had the owners, editors, and newspaper publishers wanted real investigative reporting on the Kennedy assassination, reporters would have dug and come up with what was readily available. But instead, we had "press release" journalism, reports based on carefully orchestrated leaks and official handouts. The thrust of these was to make it appear that Lee Harvey Oswald was not only the lone assassin, but also sought at the height of the Cold War to portray him as a "Red." By then, the country had been conditioned to hate and fear all "Reds" in every way. So, Oswald as the lone "Red" assassin became the lead in all coverage. The supposedly questioning media did not question this, accepting and reporting Oswald as the lone, unassisted "Red" assassin.

The lone Red assassin theory was contradicted by the very first hard news of evidence that came out of Dallas. That was at the official press conference of the Dallas doctors who saw and examined the president at Parkland Hospital. What they had to say made the lone assassin story impossible. There was no following up on that lead by the media.

All the reporters there heard the only doctor who examined the wound in the front of the president's neck before surgery describe it three times, in response to questions, as an entry wound. His description was confirmed by the hospital's chief of neurology.

What Dr. Malcolm Perry said, confirmed by Dr. Kemp Clark, made all the news stories, although in those I saw it was merely included without any particular attention being given to it, even after Oswald was said to be the lone assassin, firing from behind the president. Oswald, therefore, could not have fired the shot from the front causing what the doctors described repeatedly as an entry wound. No questions were asked of him when Dr. Perry turned the press conference scheduled for the day after the assassination over to Dr. Clark and then disappeared. If the obvious questions had been asked about the previous day's press conference, all of subsequent history might have been different. The story of the assassination certainly would have been.

J. Edgar Hoover, having ordained Oswald the lone assassin the previous afternoon, would have found his made-up "solution" difficult if not impossible to support. The Warren Commission might well have found it impossible to outline its report and conclusions before any real investigation at all relying almost exclusively on Hoover. (See chapter "Conclusions First" in my *Post Mortem.*) Arlen Specter, the commission's counsel in charge of that area of its work, would not have been able to get away with his single-bullet theory that is the basis of the official lone-assassin conclusion. Nor would he have been able to pressure Perry into testimony he knew was not true.

The circumstances of the publication of Dr. Clark's testimony by the Warren Commission may have resulted in reporters missing a great deal of significant material. It was a massive release of twenty-six large volumes all at once in November 1964, roughly two months after the release of the Warren Report. However, there was no great mass when I brought Clark's testimony to light in the first book on the Warren Report, *Whitewash: The Report on the Warren Report.* When it went into general distribution, I mailed copies to many newspapers and radio and TV stations and I hand-delivered copies to *The Washington Post*, *Star*, and *Daily News*, to the news services and the network Washington bureaus, and those of a number of major newspapers. The *Post* got several copies. I received so many requests for copies from people at *The New York Times* that beginning with the thirteenth I asked for payment for them.

At the *Times*, a review was assigned to its then legal reporter, Fred Graham, an experienced reporter in the Washington bureau and a lawyer. Graham indicated to me that he thought highly of the book. I was told that he had intended a favorable review but was instructed not to review it at all.

The point is not that my book was ignored, but that long before it appeared, the major media for whatever reason decided that there would be no questioning of the official assassination story. The book, which was the first to question and refute the official account of the "crime of the century," with only the official evidence itself, was completely ignored by the major media. Their job was to ask the important questions, yet they asked none.

Of the many critical questions which arose from the Warren Report, one of the most obvious and significant involves the testimony of the Parkland doctors which totally undercut the lone assassin story and the findings of the autopsy doctors at Bethesda. There is no reason to assume that what Doctor Clark testified to when he was under oath, he would not have told any inquiring reporter at the Dallas press conference the day after the assassination. As I reported his testimony in *Whitewash*, from page 23 of Volume 6 of the commission's published hearings, this is what Clark testified:

> "Dr. Perry stated that he had talked to the Bethesda Naval Hospital on two occasions that morning and that he knew what the autopsy findings had shown and that he did not wish to be questioned by the press, as he had been asked by Bethesda to confine his remarks to what he knew from having examined the president, and suggested that the major part of this press conference be conducted by me." Doctor Clark thought two others, whom he named, were witnesses to this conversation.[9]

To the best of my knowledge, Perry never retracted what he said at that first press conference. He did not when I interviewed him, as I report in *Post Mortem*. Nor do I know of any retraction by Clark. There is also ample confirmation, including official confirmation, that the chief autopsy pathologist, Navy Commander James J. Humes, phoned Perry more than the once, contrary to his testimony under oath to the commission. The call to Perry he testified to took place at some time after daylight the morning after the assassination. There is plentiful confirmation that Humes testified falsely, perjured himself, when he appeared before the commission. The autopsy radiologist, Dr. John Ebersole, testified to the medical panel of the House Select Committee on Assassinations, as I report in *Never Again!*[10] that he was in the autopsy room when Friday night, between 10:00 and 11:00, he heard Humes phone Perry.[11]

Because Humes told Perry that the autopsy was going to say the opposite of what Perry saw and knew to be true, Perry had to make himself scarce. Otherwise, he would have been involved in a great national scandal of unimaginable magnitude with the possible ruin of his career and excellent reputation, not to mention federal retaliation against Parkland Hospital. And at that time, the day after the assassination, he had every reason to believe he would be called upon to testify under oath at Oswald's trial.

If any reporter who read the Clark testimony in the commission's appended volumes or in my book remembered what he had confirmed when Perry said it, that the wound in the front of the neck was a wound of entry, he should have perceived immediately that the contradiction was fundamental and that if Clark was truthful the entire report was in jeopardy and Humes was a perjurer. Many reporters read my book. It seems that the media did not want to be embroiled in that scandal.

What a scandal that would have been, too. Beginning with the fact that the military pathologist in charge of the autopsy performed on the president perjured himself. His three assistants agreed with all that he had testified to. Added to that is the fact that he had decided (or was told) what the autopsy report would conclude before a proper autopsy examination could be made. He then told Perry so that Perry would not disagree with him publicly. Had this been reported in the media, it would have been a scandal of unprecedented magnitude.

This is, then, just one of many possible examples that illustrate that the crime of the assassination of the president went unsolved. It went unsolved because it was intended not to be solved. It was not solved because the government decided not to investigate the crime itself and then lied about it. And the media went along with that. Which is to say, the media went along with the de facto coup.

Of the many possible examples of the media not fulfilling its Constitutional role, all those examples a benefit to the assassins, this one is critical. No later than December 2, just eleven days after the assassination, the FBI had begun to leak the conclusions of the special report ordered of it by President Johnson the night of the assassination. Its five-volume report is the commission's first numbered file, CD1. Who is to say what its ruthless director had ordained the day of the assassination? The FBI said, and the commission later agreed, that all the shots were from the back of the president, where Oswald allegedly was.

Could not the media remember back less than two weeks to what they all reported, that the Dallas doctors had said one shot was from the front? It was thus impossible for Oswald who they claimed to be in back of the president. Failing to explore this made all that followed possible.

"Cui bono?"

Who benefited from the lies of the Warren Commission, from the lies of the FBI, from the complicity of the media?

Who benefitted from the assassination?

The assassins.

"Cui bono?" The assassins who got away with their coup d'état and succeeded in radically altering the course of US policy.

CHAPTER 7

THE NAVY DEMANDS THAT IT BE SUSPECT

To this point in this book, as well as in the FBI's assassination investigation and that of the Warren Commission, the Navy has received little attention. It deserves much more now, and deserved much more during the "investigation."

The Navy did make its Oswald records available to the FBI as soon as Oswald was arrested. The two-page FBI report I have on that discloses nothing of any special interest and it does not report that Oswald had any, even the lowest, security clearance.

The Navy did make its Oswald personnel records available to the commission and it sent Lieutenant-Colonel Allison G. Folsom, head of the Marine's Records Branch's personnel department, to testify.[1] He provided a written statement "by direction of the Commandant of the Marine Corps" to attest to the fact that as a Marine, Oswald was a "rather poor 'shot'."[2] It is contrary to the Warren Report's conclusions, so it was ignored.

The Navy also gave the commission a copy of the cable it sent the Moscow embassy as soon as it got word of Oswald's alleged "defection." That cable states that there was no security clearance indicated in Oswald's records, but it was possible he could have held the lowest of security clearances, "confidential."

Hiding the Evidence

But there is so much more that the Navy should have provided the commission but didn't, and still to this day keeps entirely secret. There also is what the Navy did not do either at the time of that staged "defection," in which Oswald did not defect, or at the time he was accused of assassinating the president.

On its part, the commission, meaning both its members and staff, who bragged of being only honorable men who did all they could have done as the commission's counsels, failed to demand of the Navy what they knew the Navy was withholding from them, and in effect keeping secret from the American people as well. As a result, questions about the Navy in relation to the assassination remain unasked and unanswered.

One obvious explanation is that no official wanted those questions asked or answered. Another is that the Navy had its own reasons for suppressing what the investigations needed, which the Navy knew was required for an honest and full investigation.

Oswald was a Marine; the Marines are part of the Navy. Thus, when Oswald went through the motions of defecting to the USSR, but was careful not to actually defect, the primary investigation was conducted by the Navy's Office of Naval Intelligence (ONI). What is known of its so-called investigation would get it failing grades in a phony mail-order course in private detecting.

Oswald learned to read, write, and speak Russian fluently when he was in the Marines. There is no record reflecting how he was able to do that, or of any investigation of it. He allegedly received Communist literature openly in the mail, which is handled and distributed by the Marines, and despite the open discussion of that and it being well known, he had only sensitive assignments. There was no investigation of that, either.

As I brought to light in my book, *Oswald in New Orleans*, Marines who were his friends and knew him well were never interviewed—not when he "defected" and not after he was accused of assassinating the president.[3] Not by the ONI, not by the FBI or Secret Service, and not by those so honorable men, the commission's counsels.

As noted above, when Oswald "defected" and the chief of Naval operations cabled our Moscow embassy about him, that cable stated that while

Oswald's records show no security clearance for him, he could have held the lowest security clearance, confidential. However, there was no investigation of what he could have told the Soviets. Nor was there any FBI or commission investigation of why the Navy's records were not complete or were withheld, kept secret from them.

When he was charged with being the president's assassin, the FBI examined Oswald's Navy personnel file. Its report, which says it holds everything of significance, makes no mention at all of any security clearance. They accepted this without question. But they knew Oswald held a high clearance. As I also brought to light in *Oswald in New Orleans*, it was the testimony of many of the Marines who served with him that Oswald held "at least" a "secret" clearance. Aside from the enlisted men who worked with him, the commissioned officer under whom he did his classified work, in an outfit of which the entire Marine Corps had only five and in which all held some degree of classification, ticked off those secrets with which the Marines, meaning the Navy, trusted Oswald:

> . . . we received word that he had showed up in Moscow. This necessitated a lot of change of aircraft call signs, codes, radio frequencies, radar frequencies. He had access to the location of all bases in the west coast area, all radio frequencies for all squadrons, all tactical call signs, and the relative strength of all squadrons, number and type of aircraft in a squadron, who was the commanding officer, the authentication code of entering and exiting the ADIZ, which stands for Air Defense Identification Zone.
>
> He knew the range of our radar. He knew the range of our radio. And he knew the range of the surrounding units' radio and radar . . .

Here, commission lawyer John Hart Ely interrupted to ask:

> You recall that various codes were changed. Now, at what level were these changed: Was this an action of your specific unit, or a fairly widespread action?

> Mr. Donovan: Well, I did not witness the changing in any other squadrons, but it would have to be, because the code is obviously between two or more units. Therefore, the other units had to change it. These codes are a grid, and two lines correspond. . . . There are some things which he knew on which he received instruction that there is no way of changing, such as the MPS 16 height-finding radar gear. That had recently been integrated into the Marine Corps system. It had a height-finding range far in excess of our previous equipment, and it has certain limitations. He had been schooled on those limitations. It cannot operate above a given altitude in setting—in other words, you cannot place the thing above a given terrain height. He also had been schooled on a piece of machinery called a TPX-1, which is used to transfer radio-radar and radio signals over a great distance. Radar is very susceptible to homing missiles, and this piece of equipment is used to put your radar antenna several miles away, and relay the information back to your site which you hope is relatively safe. He had been schooled on this. And that kind of stuff you cannot change.
>
> Mr. Ely: Did Oswald have any kind of clearance?
>
> Mr. Donovan: He must have had a secret clearance to work in the radar center, because that was a minimum requirement for all of us.[4]

None of this shows in any record the commission got from the Navy or from the FBI or in any of the many FBI records I obtained through FOIA that they did not give the commission. This does not reflect an investigation. It is what I described in the title of the first in my series of books, a "whitewash," and in the subtitle of my second book, a "Cover-Up."

The Marine friend of Oswald who wanted anonymity because he was afraid he would otherwise suffer retaliation, who was never spoken to by the ONI or any other official investigator, also told me that Oswald held a CRYPTO security clearance and was one of only five men in that entire outfit with that very high security clearance. A prerequisite for it was having been cleared for TOP SECRET. I was able to confirm this.

Why was it that the only man accused of killing the president, the Navy's commander in chief, held these high Navy security clearances, and the Navy kept that secret from all investigations, including its own?

When I sought Oswald information from the Navy, I drew a complete blank. Not a page did I get. So after letting a little time elapse, I made a different request, for the results of the court-martial inquest into the death of Marine PFC Martin Schrand.

Schrand was one of the five men in that outfit who got his basic and advanced radar training with Oswald and who performed the same duties inside that van he was guarding when he killed himself at Cubi Point in the Philippines. For a mere $9.65 I got the results of that inquest, which establishes the clearances required for that work. To even set foot inside that van required top security clearances.

Following my lead on this Warren Commission counsel Albert Jenner, then a candidate for the presidency of the American Bar Association, set off in excitement to obtain these records. Jenner was excited about it because a couple of those undereducated Marines, anxious to help the government, suggested to him that Oswald might have killed Schrand. The commission would have loved that, an Oswald history of violence. It got not one but two sets of those records which I got later from the Navy.

But do not look for it in the commission's report or in the twenty-six volumes of evidence of an officially estimated 10,000,000 words. In all those words, in all those twenty-seven large volumes, there is not a mention of this. Those "honorable men" kept it secret. Oswald did not kill Schrand, so what difference did it make that the man charged with killing the president of the United States held these exceptionally high security clearances as a Marine? It made no difference at all to the commission's lawyers.

Neither the Marines nor the Navy gave this information to the commission, but it received and published a great amount of information that included some of Oswald's training and assignments—without mention of these exceptionally high security clearances. But thanks to Jenner's insistence on falsely accusing Oswald in order to make him appear to be a violent man and thus more likely to have been an assassin, the commission did learn of these security clearances but conducted no investigation of them at all.

The Navy's duplicitous handling of the question of Oswald's security clearances, not to mention the commission's lack of interest in investigating this, is just one aspect of the Navy's actions and inaction following the assassination which raises legitimate questions about its possible involvement in it. More consequential, as I discuss at great length in *Never Again!* is the Navy's handling of President Kennedy's autopsy, of which those Naval officers in charge of it made an incredible mess.

The Navy's Autopsy

Then, too, what the Navy did and did not do when it had complete control over the disgraceful autopsy performed on the president, requires that the Navy be suspected.

I began going into this in great detail in *Whitewash: The Report on the Warren Report*. Then, in 1975 in *Post Mortem*, having access to some of the records that were not available at the time I wrote that first book, I was able to go into greater detail. And to this day I have not had a single complaint about what I published from or on behalf of any of the Navy medical personnel in any way involved in that autopsy. I add to these earlier writings in *Never Again!* This is not the place to repeat all of that great amount of misrepresented, *official* information. That is not only impossible, but also unnecessary for my present purpose, which is to highlight what makes the Navy suspect. What follows is from what I published earlier, which, I repeat, has never been disputed or complained about by or on behalf of the Navy medical personnel.

Navy Commander James J. Humes was the pathologist supposedly in charge of JFK's autopsy, but what he did and did not do was in fact dictated to him by his boss at that large Naval Medical Center at Bethesda, Maryland, Admiral C. B. Galloway. Humes's assistant, also a pathologist at Bethesda, was Commander J. Thornton Boswell. Neither was an accredited forensic pathologist, which is required for an autopsy in a criminal case. They did not make required examinations in that autopsy. The X-ray and photographic films taken during the autopsy were of poor quality. In addition, they were not made available to the pathologists during the autopsy and the preparation of the autopsy report. As I first indicated in *Post Mortem*, there is every reason to suspect that some film exposed during the autopsy was withheld by the Navy. Without question, the photographs and X-rays taken at Bethesda were far less than required of a competent autopsy.[5]

During the autopsy examination, all civilians were made to leave the autopsy room, and a Navy guard was posted to prevent any civilians from entering. The only exceptions were the FBI and Secret Service agents who were there throughout.

Humes testified to the commission that he knew nothing about the tracheostomy on the front of the president's neck, performed at Parkland Hospital by Dr. Malcolm Perry, until he spoke to Perry for the first time the day after the autopsy. That was false as reported above. He spoke to Perry and learned what Perry had said about that wound *during the course of the autopsy.*[6] Perry, supported by the Parkland Hospital chief of neurosurgery, Dr. Kemp Clark, had identified the wound in the front of the president's neck as a wound of entrance. I also repeat because of its significance—*they did that three times* in the course of the press conference soon after the president was pronounced dead. That press conference was taped and transcribed by the White House and was released to the media in Washington.[7] That the neck wound was identified as an entrance wound was also reported in the media. The *Washington Post*'s story, parts of which Humes used in his autopsy report, also identified that wound as one of entrance.

Humes had completed his holograph of the autopsy on Sunday, November 24, when he saw on television that Oswald had been killed. That meant there would be no trial of Oswald, no cross-examination regarding any evidence, including the autopsy report. Humes then burned that handwritten copy of the autopsy in the fireplace of his recreation room and wrote a different one. That evening in his office, Admiral Galloway directed other substantive, factual changes be made in Humes's substituted handwritten autopsy report. It then was typed at the Navy hospital. I have photographs and a xerox of the original of that replacement holograph. The commission published a xerox of it. I found the original and other hidden medical records misfiled by the commission where nobody would ever think to look for them, in what the commission sent to the Government Printing Office to be published. I also found there the original and all copies of the death certificate signed by the president's physician, Admiral George B. Burkley, hidden there along with other of his records. I published both along with other related records in *Post Mortem*.

For Oswald to have been the lone assassin, the official determination that was almost immediate and well before anything that could be called an investigation was undertaken, all the shots had to have come from the back because Oswald was supposedly behind the president when he was killed. So, the entrance wound in the front of the president's neck became an exit wound. A wound in the president's back was mislocated several inches higher, and it became the entrance wound of the alleged exit wound in the president's neck. Then, still trying to limit it to a single assassin, all the non-fatal wounds, five of them suffered by Texas Governor John B. Connally who was in the jump seat in front of the president, were also attributed to that one bullet that traversed the president's neck, and to it alone. And from that history, which was not ever to be duplicated in any of the testing done for the commission, that magical bullet emerged virtually unscathed without so much as a scratch from the many bones it allegedly struck. Yet it is said to have struck bone in smashing four inches of Connally's fifth rib, to have demolished the heavy bones in his right wrist, and to have lodged in his thigh, leaving a fragment there; then to have snuck out much later and after much travel and hid under a hospital gurney mattress said to have been the one on which Connally had been placed. But the hospital employee who found that bullet, which fell out from *under* the mattress, not only refused to so testify; he testified he'd not be able to sleep if he did.[8]

Despite no mention of it in the autopsy protocol and testimony to the contrary by the doctors, X-rays show fragments of bone in the president's spinal-column area. This was later admitted elliptically by the prosectors, and it is stated specifically in the study of the autopsy film made by the most eminent experts the Department of Justice could convene. I reproduced both of these official reports on the autopsy film in *Post Mortem*.[9] In the Department's panel's interpretation of the X-rays, under "Neck Region," they report "several small metallic fragments are present in this region." That is to say, a bullet did strike bone in the president's body, contrary to what the prosectors testified to.

I follow these reports in *Post Mortem* with a suppressed FBI picture of the front of the president's shirt that in itself destroys this official autopsy mythology.[10] That magical bullet is, in the official mythology, required to have exited through the president's shirt collar and tie. The picture reflects what the Warren Commission's ignored and misrepresented testimony says, that the bullet hole in the president's neck was *above* the shirt collar. There are no bullet holes at all in either the collar or the tie, both of which are supposed to have this magical bullet go through them!

When Humes appeared before the Warren commission, he testified to his burning of the original autopsy protocol. He also then testified that he had turned his notes in. I published a series of receipts for those notes. That the commission had them was stated by its counsel in charge of that area, Arlen Specter, who later became the senior senator from Pennsylvania. But when he was before the House Select Committee and then also under oath, Humes testified that what he burned was his notes. Receipts for those notes that I published are by the Secret Service, which received them from Admiral Burkley, and by the Admiral himself on Sunday, November 24, when they and a copy of the protocol were delivered to him. The commission had them, and memory-holed them.

Humes later said that the reason he burned his notes is that they were bloody and he did not want any improper uses made of those bloody records. By the Secret Service? The Admiral? In fact, the page of them that could not be withheld, what is known as the body chart locating wounds and marks on the body, holds the president's blood and other fluids. I held it in my hands after finding it where it was hidden. I have color pictures and a xerox of the original. I published a xerox of the original in *Post Mortem*.[11] It bears Admiral Burkley's "verification" of it in his handwriting.

Whatever the reason, Burkley personally "accepted and approved" Humes's certification that he had "destroyed by burning" the autopsy rough draft. Burkley also wrote "accepted and approved" on Humes's certification that he turned in the "autopsy notes and holograph draft" and was silent when Humes later testified that what he burned was those autopsy notes. On the next page, I printed in facsimile Admiral Galloway's covering letter to Burkley that included these notes. On the following page is the Secret Service receipt to Burkley from two days later which includes getting from Burkley the "notes of the examining doctors."[12]

Much of this has to have been well-known to many in the Navy hospital at the time, including but not limited to Admiral Galloway. And it is important to note that it was Admiral Galloway who ordered his pathologists not to do a complete autopsy, not to do what is absolutely essential in a death by gunshot, i.e., trace all bullet paths through the body. I go into all of this in detail, with new information, in *Never Again!*

There is more, much more, but this was the kind of autopsy the Navy performed on the body of its commander in chief and an indication of what Navy officers testified to that was simply not true. Why the Navy saw to it that there would not be a complete, competent autopsy and why there then was all this dishonesty about it, including false swearing by Navy officers and unanswered questions, amounts to a very serious accusation against the Navy.

Perhaps in some respects innocently, it was the Navy that arranged for the autopsy to be at its major medical installation. On the plane back from Dallas, the president's physician, Admiral Burkley, told his widow that the autopsy had to be at a military hospital for security. He then suggested to her that because the president had served in the Navy during World War II, the Navy's hospital would be appropriate. But there was no need for any special "security" for a corpse and there was no need at all for the autopsy to be at only a military hospital. The most urgent need was for the best possible forensic pathologists to perform the autopsy, considering the fact that it was part of and basic to a *murder* investigation, not a military or protocol matter.

When I wrote the Navy Hospital under the Freedom of Information Act seeking any autopsy records it had, it replied that it had none, that it had turned all its records over to the White House. This is unlikely. Under its own regulations, what the Navy did was wrong and it knew that it was wrong. It is required to keep such records for set periods of time. From what it wrote me, I simply do not believe that it did not keep even a xerox copy of anything at all. It remains to be seen whether the Navy has anything stashed away in some "Davy Jones' Locker."

Beginning with the strong and determined opposition to the president's policies that the Navy shared with the other services and their representatives on the Joint Chiefs of Staff, continuing through what the Navy has kept secret about Oswald, indicated in part above, and climaxing with its seeing to it that at best, to quote my second book in 1966, the president had an autopsy unworthy of a Bowery bum, the Navy's record demands suspicion and raises the most substantial questions about it and any possible involvement in the assassination.

How many other reasons can there be for keeping all that Oswald information secret and seeing to it that the autopsy would be as terrible and as misleading and deceptive and dishonest as it was, quintessential as an autopsy is in any murder investigation?

But it is not only the Navy hospital that claims not to have a single piece of paper on the assassination. The entire Navy, including the Marine Corps, claimed under the 1992 law requiring the disclosure of all records relating to the assassination in any way to have not a single piece of relevant paper!

Under that law, the National Archives made public its list of what had been transferred to it. It is headed, "JFK Collections Register." The first of the six columns of this register of the collections transferred to the Archives is "Agency." There is a partial description in the second column; the extent of each deposit is indicated in the next to last column. The last is "Comments." Not a piece of paper from the entire Navy is listed as given to the Archives for disclosure under the 1992 law! Not one! With all that it has, for example, on Oswald. But in fairness to the Navy, this is also true of the entire military.

Perhaps the Air Force had no records, but the Army did. I have referred to some. Its Military District of Washington D.C., which at the very least was involved with the body and its honor guard during and after the autopsy, does have some. It disclosed copies of some to others and to me years ago. But, of course, with Oswald having been in the Marines, which is part of the Navy, each has to possess and should have transferred those records to the Archives under that 1992 law.

The military is far from alone in this overt dishonesty, this deliberate and flagrant violation of the law relating to records that have any assassination connection. To cite another example, the records of the President's Committee on CIA Activities Within the United States, which was created and ceased to exist under President Gerald Ford, is represented by a deposit of three feet. It was transferred by the "Gerald R. Ford Library," which is part of the National Archives in any event. That commission was headed by Ford's pal from the Warren Commission, David Belin, who had proclaimed loudly and often that he had seen everything. With a total of only three feet to the records he saw, that is "all," as he said, that the CIA had. But we find that the CIA itself transferred but a single file—and it has to have more than this one file—titled "Lee Harvey Oswald's Personality File (201-289248)" with an extent of eighteen feet!

And in three feet, self-righteous, know-it-all Belin saw all eighteen feet?

Of the other relevant files the CIA has, only a tiny fraction of which it disclosed earlier, some concern what the agency did to interfere with critics of the official mythology and its spying on us. I have a considerable file on some of the agency's spying on me in relation to my statements regarding materials that the CIA illegally withheld from me. It did not disclose that to me, even though the 1967 law I invoked required its disclosure, and I repeated the request later under the Privacy Act when it was the law of the land. The CIA has other records, such as what it did for and told to the Warren Commission. The existence of such CIA records was disclosed by the commission. I have several hundred pages of them and that is far from all.

So, all of the government part of the military-industrial-intelligence complex is also lawless, not having given the Archives as much as a single piece of paper from the military, and the CIA having given it but a single file.

The former head of the CIA, Allen Dulles, is represented in this transfer by an unexplained one inch! The commission transcripts he was given alone are of greater extent and he had many, many other records, copies of which were given to him so he could perform his duties as a member of the Warren Commission. Yet Dulles is alone among the members, save for Gerald Ford, in being reflected in this register of the "all" that was required to be made available to the people through the National Archives.

Others deposited records elsewhere but that is not reflected in this register.

The Department of Justice, of which the FBI is a part, got on the mendacity bandwagon through several components. The Civil Division, which handles all the FOIA lawsuits filed against the government—of which I alone filed more than a dozen—gave the Archives four inches! Under "comments" is this, the entire comment: "Includes Weisberg vs. Webster case." William H. Webster was for a while the FBI's director. I filed more than one suit against the FBI, so there is more than that one lone "Webster" case file that the Civil Division has. And how about the other dozen or so of my cases the Civil Division handled? And how about its relations with Congress on the assassination, including by giving testimony on FOIA to the Senate Judiciary Committee's appropriate subcommittee?

Besides what I have in boxes, my copies of what the Civil Division has in my litigation alone, and there were many, many other such lawsuits, take up two stuffed file cabinets, each drawer of which holds two feet of paper! My copies of the part of the Civil Division's relevant records are more than twenty-four times greater than all the Civil Division gave the Archives! And it has other relevant FOIA records of which I know. It handled, for example, the Department's panel of experts who reviewed the autopsy film. It handled the litigation in which that report and the one by the prosectors that I published in *Post Mortem* and cite above, were disclosed. And I know of much more. It violated the law by not giving these documents to the Archives.

But the Department's Criminal Division is even worse—it did not give the Archives a single page! In a long-delayed and partial compliance with my request more than a decade ago, it gave me several file drawers of copies of records it has and kept secret from the Archives. That it is incomplete is certified in what I was given because it included a partial list of materials I was not given.

I have in my files relevant records from other Justice Department components such as the Office of Legal Counsel. These are not represented in this register of what was given to the Archives. For example, I have a file cabinet with records of my own and other's appeals of decisions to withhold documents contrary to the requirements of the Freedom of Information Act. The Justice Department's appeals office transferred nothing at all.

All of these components of Justice transferred a total of four inches of records.

Then there is the FBI, which has a much larger volume of records. It transferred 52.5 feet of records. This is impressive compared with others, but it is far, far from all the FBI has. Its transfer was limited to four of its relevant files. Those that it transferred it had already disclosed in 1977 and 1978. I have had them since January 1978, when a federal court ordered the FBI to give me copies of them as rapidly as it could (CA 77-2155). Files which I received from the FBI as the result of several lawsuits fill several file cabinets with relevant records, which it failed to provide to the National Archives as required by law. In short, I have a much greater volume by far of the FBI's records than what it gave the Archives, according to this supposedly complete list.

I have at least a file drawer of CIA records I got from the FBI which the CIA did not include in what it gave the Archives under the law. I also have about a file cabinet full of other CIA records not included in the registry. Then there is also the perplexing question: What in the world was the CIA doing with *eighteen feet* of records in its one "personality profile" on Lee Harvey Oswald? *Eighteen feet* of records on Oswald, and that in a single file only, the personality profile? That means, assuming jam-packed file drawers, two full file cabinets and an extra drawer of just this one file, without our knowing how much of that one file is still secret, secrecy being the fuel which keeps the CIA going.

Eighteen admitted feet in that one file, all withheld for thirty years from the people who paid for it, with not even a mention of this file to the Presidential Commission in charge of the investigation. This file and its content had to be kept secret from the official investigation, too? Not mentioned to the FBI, either?

John Newman, a retired Army intelligence major and longtime academic, saw evidence of the CIA's interest in Oswald beginning even before this 201 file, Oswald's personality profile, was authorized. That CIA interest in Oswald was by three different CIA components, each of which deals with spies: our spies, their spies, and the spies of both.

What was there about Oswald, the young Marine who said he was defecting to the USSR, that justified this initial interest by three different CIA components whose work related to spies? Or that in the end justified the simply enormous amount of money, effort, and time represented by at least eighteen feet of records on him? Does the CIA go to that much trouble and expense for all defectors, real or not?

This certainly was not some kind of spook parlor game, not what grew to at least eighteen feet of admitted records in that one file. It seems to indicate an out-of-the-ordinary interest in Oswald, with no visible explanation for the magnitude of it. Whatever the reason, it must be extraordinary. So also is the deep secrecy of it all, with it being hidden from all official assassination investigations. What in the world can there be that the CIA had to hide from the Warren Commission and the FBI?

We have no way of knowing how many more secrets the CIA is still hiding. That it was able to hide *eighteen feet of records from a single file*, when it is known to have other relevant records, does justify the belief that it does not intend to come clean and comply with the law. It may have more secrets than the Navy, judging from the extent of this one file. And the FBI also still has secrets, still has not disclosed all it has, not by far!

When the law required the deposit in the Archives of *all* government records relating to the assassination and *the entire government violates the law*, is it not necessary to wonder why? What do they all have to hide, keep secret in violation of the law, and why do they keep it secret and violate the law?

But our major interest here is in the military, and the Navy in particular. What does it have to hide that impelled it not to give the Archives even a single piece of paper? We may have to wonder why, but there is no wonder about the fact that it kept secret all it has, and that "all" has to be extensive. It is still secret after more than thirty years, and despite a 1992 law requiring its disclosure.

What the Navy still and illegally keeps secret includes its records on Oswald's security clearances and the records of its investigation to determine whether or not he should have been given those clearances.

It includes the investigation required to have been made when it was reported that Oswald had defected to the USSR. It includes the investigation required to have been made when Oswald was accused of assassinating the president.

Among many others, it includes all records in any way relating to that disgracefully bad autopsy which has been criticized from the time the Warren Report was issued in 1964. This should include, of course, records of those criticisms and of any responses to them.

There have to be some reasons for all this, and those reasons must include addressing why the Navy wants to maintain these secrets. But there can be no legitimate reasons for this secrecy in clear violation of the law.

This, still again, is the military pointing an accusatory finger at itself.

CHAPTER 8

HOW MANY LIVES DID OSWALD LEAD?

What is known about Oswald and his beliefs has been consistently misrepresented both officially and in most of the literature, particularly the literature supporting the official assassination mythology. In light of this, the lack of official attention to the Navy and the information it withheld becomes more provocative.

Almost as soon as Oswald was arrested, he was proclaimed to be a "Red." This originated in the since disbanded 112th Army Intelligence component based at San Antonio, Texas. It immediately dispersed this false information, including to the Dallas police by phone. From then on, Oswald was branded in the public mind as a "Red" or a "Marxist," both taken to be what he was widely called, a Communist. Oswald was never a Communist; he was always anti-Communist, a fact hidden in the official records and always misstated in most of the literature, in all the sycophantic literature.

Although he was a high-school dropout who never had a good record as a student, Oswald was comparatively well read, particularly in political matters. I brought much of this to light in *Whitewash*, the first book on the Warren Commission, only to have it ignored. So from the time of that first book, it was public knowledge that Oswald was an anti-Communist rather than a Communist.[1]

As a sixteen-year-old, Oswald pretended to be sympathetic to both the Young People's Socialist League of the Socialist party and the Socialist Workers party, or Trotskyites. He also wrote the Communist Party pretending sympathy with it. It will not be easy to find two political parties of people who hated each other more than the Communists and the Trotskyites. Oswald could not have been truly sympathetic to both at the same time, even less at the same time to the Socialist Party, too.

The truth is, as I wrote then, that "Oswald's hatred of the Communist Party and the Soviet Union exude from 150 consecutive pages of his notes" in the commission's appendix volume, from which I had just quoted, "as well as from other exhibits" in the commission's published record.[2]

The previous paragraph in *Whitewash* refers to the fact that Oswald, with his wife and some relatives, went to Battles Wharf, Alabama, where a cousin was in a seminary, where "he unburdened himself of his anti-Soviet feelings." He was then so anti-Soviet that a priest who was present told him he would be more effective if he restrained himself a little.

That was after he returned from the Soviet Union.

The rest of that page reads:

> . . . For example, in Exhibit 97 (pp. 422–3) he raged, "The Communist Party of the United States has betrayed itself! It has turned itself into the traditional lever of a foreign power to overthrow the government of the United States, not in the name of freedom or high ideals, but in servile conformity to the wishes of the Soviet Union . . . (the leaders) have shown themselves to be willing, gullible messengers of the Kremlin's Internationalist propaganda . . . The Soviets have committed crimes unsurpassed . . . imprisonment of their own peoples . . . mass extermination . . . the murder of history, the prostitution of art and culture. The communist movement in the U.S., personalized by the Communist Party, U.S.A., has turned itself into a 'valuable gold coin' of the Kremlin. It has failed to denounce any actions of the Soviet Government when similar actions of the U.S. Government bring pious protest." [Spelling improved.] (16H422-423)

> The report quotes some of this as well as ". . . I hate the U.S.S.R. and Socialist system. . . ." (R399).
>
> He also described himself as one with "many personal reasons to know and therefore hate and mistrust Communism. . . ." (16H442)[3]

One of Oswald's more kindly references to the Soviet leaders was that they are, "fat, stinking politicians" rather than leaders interested in helping working people.

As a boy, Oswald's favorite TV program was Herbert Philbrick's *I Led Three Lives*, as reflected in the commission's published records, including its testimony. Philbrick had become an FBI informer. The TV show was based on the book Philbrick wrote about his experiences as an informant. The TV show and the book were quite popular at the time. According to his brother's testimony before the commission, Lee Oswald never missed an episode of that show, even the reruns. As a boy, he longed to be the secret agent or a spy or at least a lionized informer like his hero, Philbrick, and even started trying to practice this craft.

Oswald's favorite book, the commission's record also shows, was, according to one of his under-educated friends in the Marines, an anti-Communist classic. This came to light in commission counsel Wesley Liebeler's questioning of Nelson Delgado. I published it in *Oswald in New Orleans*.[4] Delgado had just given Liebeler his recollection of what Oswald had told him about George Orwell's *Animal Farm*. Delgado did not remember its title:

> **Mr. Liebeler:** Did you tell the FBI about this?
> **Mr. Delgado:** Yes.
> **Mr. Liebeler:** Did they know the name of the book?
> **Mr. Delgado:** No.
> **Mr. Liebeler:** The FBI did not know the name of the book?
> **Mr. Delgado:** No.
> **Mr. Liebeler:** It is called the *Animal Farm*. It is by George Orwell.
> **Mr. Delgado:** He didn't tell me. I asked him for the thing, but he wouldn't tell me. I guess he didn't know. The *Animal Farm*. Did you read it?

Mr. Liebeler: Yes; there is only one thing that Oswald did not mention apparently and that is that the pigs took over the farm, and then they got to be just like the capitalists were before, they got fighting among themselves, and there was one big pig who did just the same thing that the capitalist had done before. Didn't Oswald tell you about that?
Mr. Delgado: No; just that the pigs and animals had revolted and made the farmer work for them. The *Animal Farm.* Is that a socialist book?
Mr. Liebeler: No.
Mr. Delgado: That is just the way you interpret it; right?
Mr. Liebeler: Yes; I think so. It is actually supposed to be quite an anti-Communist book.
Mr. Delgado: Is it really?
Mr. Liebeler: Yes.

A simply enormous amount of Oswald information was withheld on the spurious rationale of "national security." As I write this, what was required to be released under the 1992 Assassination Records Act is being examined by others. This includes what was described to me as a great volume of CIA information. But in earlier years bits and pieces were rescued from their official oblivion. I reported what the defected KGB agent Yuri Nosenko told the FBI about Oswald when it interviewed Nosenko in early 1964. Nosenko offered to testify before the Warren Commission. The CIA talked the commission out of listening to him. Here is how I brought to light some of the little then newly available information in my 1975 *Post Mortem*:

> Suppressing fact and truth was an early, major and endless problem. On the reality of Oswald, its confrontation with unwanted proof began 2/4/64 when a former KGB deputy section chief, Yuri Nosenko, defected to the CIA. Nosenko had had custody of the KGB's entire Oswald file.
>
> With his life at stake if he lied, Nosenko talked. His story checked out. There is no mention of him or what he disclosed in the report. Total suppression. I have obtained hundreds of relevant

pages, seek more and will be writing about this separately. Nosenko told the CIA (not one report from which can be found in the Commission's files) and the FBI that the Russians actually believed Oswald was a "sleeper" or "dormant" American agent and had him and his mail under surveillance all the time he was in the USSR. Despite this, Oswald did not hide his dislike of the USSR. Marina's uncle, a colonel, begged Oswald "not to be too critical of the Soviet Union when he returned to the United States."

The Commission and its witting staff had to hide all of this. Then they and the Commission's successors have perpetuated secrecy to the degree possible.

The CIA could not deny the FBI access to Nosenko. FBI agents known to have interviewed him are Maurice A. Taylor, Donald E. Walter and Alekso Popanovich, beginning 2/26. The wily Hoover, knowing it would embarrass and compromise both the CIA and the Commission, arranged without being asked for Nosenko to offer to testify, the last thing the Commission wanted, and then put it in a letter.

The CIA people involved were under James Angleton, who, with others of them, was forced out as a result of the Watergate scandals. Typical of the continuing suppression is the withholding of the paragraph from David Slawson's 3/12/64 "TOP SECRET" memo on a CIA conference: "The first topic of conversation was Yuri Nosenko, the recent Soviet defector. A general discussion was held on this problem [sic] with the CIA's recommendation being that the Commission await further developments."

"Await" is the right word. The CIA stonewalled successfully. As of October 1975 I "await" response under the law to months-old requests for declassification of what never qualified for any classification, what Nosenko told the CIA about Oswald.

Slawson's colleague in this work is Ford's Secretary of Transportation, William T. Coleman, Jr. Then they put "TOP SECRET" classification on what the FBI did not classify at all and suppressed it all from their part of the report.

It is a big secret but on 6/24/64 the Commission actually had Nosenko study some of its Oswald files. The day before it held an executive session. After not being able to get that transcript for eight years I filed suit on 9/24/75 (C.A. 75-1448). Also on 6/24 this same pair wrote and classified TOP SECRET a memo to "The Commission" that begins by justifying their not questioning Nosenko, making no mention of the prior day's events of Nosenko's willingness to testify:

> The Commission has asked us to prepare a short memorandum outlining in what respects the information obtained from Nosenko confirms or contradicts information we have from other sources.
>
> Nosenko's testimony to the FBI is the only information we have on what he knows about Lee Harvey Oswald. (Commission Documents No. 434 and 451.) Perhaps more useful information could be gained if we were to question Nosenko directly, but it is unlikely. Nosenko told the representative of the FBI who questioned him that he had given all the information on Oswald he possessed.[5]

They say Nosenko's only important knowledge was that Oswald was not a KGB agent. That he was suspected by the Russians of being an American agent was not important!

There can be no more classic example of Hoover's daring and expertise in his own special brand of "dirty tricks." His unsolicited offer of Nosenko as a witness shifted all possible Commission interest away from Hoover and reports Oswald had worked for him. Hoover put his monkey on the Commission and CIA backs. The Commission saw irreparable destruction of its whole fabrication. The CIA knew Dulles told the Commission the FBI had no agents in Russia.[6]

Whether or not Oswald ever had any connection with any intelligence operation of any kind cannot be stated with certainty from the official records not still kept secret. But from the outset, what was known of Oswald as a boy and Oswald after his return from the Soviet Union did raise questions about this possibility. As I write in my first book, Oswald's career in New Orleans after his return from the Soviet Union is consistent with what in intelligence is called establishing a cover. As I also write of him in that book:

> Even his oft-mentioned notes on Russia, widely discussed but unquoted in the press, are a narrative full of the kind of information intelligence agencies, including our own, seek about other countries, especially the Soviet Union. It includes such items as the location of an airport, the layout of a city, and all sorts of intimate details of the electronics factory in which he worked, including what it produced, its rate of production, the number of employees engaged in various pursuits and other such non-travelogue data.[7]

I use these few selections from what I published and was available to all[8] so the reader can know what was publicly available, what required no work, no days of poring over official records or travel to Washington. This gives the reader a way of evaluating other books that often got simply enormous attention and at the same time evaluate the integrity or lack of integrity by the government agencies involved in the sad pretense of an investigation of the assassination of their president.

This is not presented as proof that Oswald was some kind of agent. Rather, I use it to show that there was a solid basis for the government to investigate this. No part of the government ever did.

There is more that is highly suspicious that got little or no attention. Some of this relates back to the Navy's suppression of information it had to have, such as information on Oswald's exceptionally high security clearances the fact of which remains an official secret as I write this.

Oswald obtained his "hardship" discharge by fraud. There is no question about it at all. Yet, when he returned to the United States with money advanced to him by our government, by the State Department, the Marines, meaning the Navy, did not charge him with getting that discharge by fraud. Despite an open-and-shut case that he did.

Oswald's pocket address book had in it the name and address of the mother of the Army doctor assigned to the Moscow embassy, Captain

Alexis Davison. It is highly unlikely that Davison gave Oswald his mother's address so he could look her up if Davison, the Embassy, and Davison's fellow spies in the Embassy were not absolutely certain that Oswald was very strongly anti-Soviet.

Davison's Russian mother met his American father when she was a nurse in the anti-Communist Wrangel's White Army fighting the revolutionists around the time of World War I. His father was an American doctor with the American forces who along with forces from five other countries invaded what became the Soviet Union in an unsuccessful effort to defeat it militarily. Davison's mother was virulently anti-Soviet. Her son would not have offended her by sending her a visitor who was in favor of the Soviet Union.

Who was Captain Alexis Davison other than the doctor assigned to our Moscow embassy? He was expelled by the Soviet Union for his espionage activities there. That was in the famous Penkovsky case. My files hold even Russian newspaper accounts of this. Davison was one of those caught "servicing," as the spooks refer to it, what are called "dead drops," places in which spies like Penkovsky deposit what is to be picked up by those intelligence agents who "service" those "dead drops," like a hollow in a tree or a discarded newspaper, or a hole in a wall.

This is enough of a record of the real Oswald, not the supposed "Red" of the official mythologies, to return to the Navy and what it has kept secret, even from official investigations.

When Oswald went through the motions of defecting while being careful to not actually defect, he was seen by an attaché named Richard E. Snyder.[9] Right off the bat he told Snyder that he was going to give the Soviets all the secrets he knew about the Marines' special radar unit in which he had worked and whose secrets he really did have. On this basis alone there was at the least reason to question Oswald, and the additional need to determine whether a criminal charge of spying should be placed on him once he was back in the United States.

The Soviet Red Cross established Oswald in a job in Minsk as a noncitizen, the Soviet Union having refused him citizenship. When Oswald, who was openly anti-Soviet when he was in the Soviet Union, wanted to return to the United States, he travelled to our Moscow embassy from

Minsk. At the embassy, he made it clear that he wanted to return, but under two conditions. One was that his wife, a Soviet citizen, accompany him and be admitted to the United States. The other was that he not be prosecuted for anything.

Then there is the fact that he did obtain his discharge by fraud.

The United States was anxious to get Oswald home. The records do not indicate why but they do reflect the fact that they wanted him back. One obvious reason is to get an American citizen back. Another has to do with whether or not he gave military secrets away and if he did what those secrets were. Still another could be to learn from him what he had learned and observed in the USSR in those Cold War days.

The Soviet Union was anxious to get rid of him because he was suspected of being an American agent in place or "sleeper" agent, whether he went or he was sent there for that purpose. So, they agreed to allow their citizen, Oswald's wife Marina, and their infant daughter, to leave the USSR.

The State Department agreed to Oswald's demand that he not be prosecuted and that his wife and daughter be permitted to enter the United States. Lending him the money was not that unusual, but the lack of State Department records relating to him, including any reference to denying him a future passport, is suspicious. In fact, he did later get a passport—faster than others who applied when he did.[10]

This history indicates that the Navy had to have been consulted regarding any decision not to prosecute Oswald for fraud in his early discharge application or for disclosing military secrets. But the Navy never gave any such records to the commission; in the hundreds of thousands of pages of its records that I got from the FBI, there is not a single one relating to this. This also means that the FBI, fully aware of Oswald's record, did not demand those records of the Navy. But it is obvious that the State Department could not promise Oswald that he would not be prosecuted without having the agreement of the Department of Justice and the Navy, as it obviously did. This also is one of a number of reasons to wonder whether Oswald had some kind of connection with the Office of Naval Intelligence (ONI), the Navy's intelligence arm.

That Oswald had some connection with some agency was one of the earliest rumors about him. The first such rumor reported was that he worked for the FBI. The commission ignored that report for a month after it was first published, pretending to be unaware of it. It wasn't until Texas State Attorney General Waggoner Carr told commission General Counsel J. Lee Rankin that his Texas Court of Inquiry planned to look into it that the commission considered it. After hearing from Carr, Rankin called a special nighttime executive session of the Warren Commission that very evening. At that meeting the members let their hair down, confessed that in Rankin's words, "if it ever came out and could be established, then you would have people think that there was a conspiracy to accomplish this assassination that nothing this commission could do or anybody could dissipate."[11]

The commission's assigned duty was to investigate to establish the truth about the assassination, not to try to disprove that there had been any conspiracy to kill the president.

If the commission were to ask the FBI about it, they feared, not without cause, that the FBI, as Rankin told the members "could probably say—that it isn't our business." The FBI had already given the commission to understand before that day, January 22, 1964, that in Rankin's words, "They have found the man. There is nothing more to do . . . and we can go home and that is the end of it."[12]

Despite the commission's established policy of having "[stenographic] records of meetings," and having "called the [court] reporter in the formal way . . . ," they decided to destroy the record they were making of the executive session.[13] They believed that it had been completely destroyed. However, they overlooked the stenotypist's tape and when I sued to get it under FOIA, the National Archives abandoned its stock "national security" claim and had the tape transcribed not by that court reporter but at the Pentagon and gave it to me.

This was the first of the commission's TOP SECRET deliberations regarding the report that Oswald had worked for the FBI. It arranged in advance for there to be no court reporter at the next one two days later. There it heard from the Texas Board. But there is no transcript of that session. I interviewed two of those Texans, Dean Emeritus of the SMU law school, Robert G. Storey, and the then Dallas District Attorney, my friend Henry Wade. Both were under the impression that a stenographer was taking it all down verbatim. Instead, Rankin had a staff stenographer there pretending to do that. All that was recorded of what the Texans told him and Warren is what Rankin decided to include in a six-page memo.

The next executive session was that of January 27. Most of the members were there and this time they had a stenographic transcript. It also was classified TOP SECRET, and I also had to sue to get it. Nothing in it warranted any classification. The sole purpose of classifying it was to suppress. I published *Whitewash IV* about that transcript and in it reproduced the entire ninety-five-page transcript in facsimile. The large TOP SECRET stamps are on every page, top and bottom.

Commissioner Allen Dulles, who had headed the CIA, was asked by his fellow commissioners about official lying about such things. Dulles told them that anyone who knew about it would lie and that for him to lie would be proper, that "I wouldn't think he would tell it (the truth) under oath, no." He added that he, personally, might not even tell the Secretary of Defense the truth. With regard to the report that Oswald worked for the FBI, Dulles said, "I think under any circumstances, I think Mr. Hoover would say certainly he didn't have anything to do with this fellow, [Oswald]."[14]

But, Dulles assured them, the FBI did not run agents in the USSR. The CIA did. Whether any other agency did was not discussed.

Rankin, fully expecting the stenographic record of the session to remain forever secret, spoke frankly to the Members, "I don't see how the country is ever going to be willing to accept it if we don't satisfy them on this particular issue [of Oswald as an agent], not only with them [the FBI] but the CIA and every other agency."[15]

The commission accepted self-serving pro forma denials from the heads of the FBI and the CIA and wiped it out that way. This, of course, leaves the question still one without any meaningful answer.

Commission Member Gerald Ford, who went on to become our first unelected president, had been nominated as vice president by Watergating President Richard Nixon to succeed Spiro Agnew, who was forced to resign after being indicted for corruption. Ford stole the transcript of this session and used it in his ghost-written commercialization of the assassination, *Portrait of the Assassin.* At the Senate Judiciary hearing on his appointment as vice president, Ford swore that he had used nothing in his book that was not public. A decade later, it was still classified TOP SECRET and withheld from me; it was that "public." In addition to resorting to perjury to get the committee's approval—and all this is set forth in *Whitewash IV*, with the documentation—Ford made changes in the transcript for his own political purpose. These included buttering up Hoover and the FBI and eliminating criticism of it. In *Whitewash IV*, I follow the facsimile reproduction of that transcript with a word-for-word comparison of the actual transcript and the Ford version prepared for me by Dr. Paul Hoch, of Berkeley, California.[16]

In the two decades since that book appeared I have had not a word of criticism and not a word from or on behalf of those I write about in it.

One of the sources of this report on Oswald as agent was *Houston Post* reporter, Alonzo (Lonnie) Hudkins, who became a friend of mine after he left that paper and was working for the *Baltimore News-American*. He told me that the number the commission used, S-172, was one he and two associates made up in the belief that the FBI was tapping their phones when they were working on this story. Lonnie was open with me in all details of this business except one, the correct number. The commission avoided looking into this, going out of its way not to call Hudkins as a witness. In fact, it did not even speak to him informally. In hiding Hudkins and the Oswald-as-agent information, the commission was greatly assisted by Leon Jaworski, who later gained fame as the Watergate special prosecutor. Jaworski, a partner in a major Houston law firm and a power in Texas politics, served as counsel to the Texas Court of Inquiry into the JFK assassination where he proved himself another whitewasher, especially in intelligence matters. On that so-called Court of Inquiry, he did what the White House, which was involved in it, Commission Chair Warren, and commission counsel Rankin wanted done. He helped curtail investigations into Oswald's connections to intelligence agencies.

As Jaworski wrote Rankin early in the commission's life, he went to see the publisher of the *Houston Post* to have him lean on Hudkins to get him to prepare an affidavit denying the story. Jaworksi's friend, William P. Hobby Jr., the paper's executive vice president and executive editor, told him that Lonnie had left his employ. "Inasmuch as you have an FBI denial of the story," Jaworski wrote Commission Counsel Rankin, "is it really worth your while to follow up on Hudkins?"[17] Rankin took Jaworski's advice, so the highly significant question of Oswald's FBI/CIA connections remains unanswered.[18]

The commission knew that the number Lonnie and friends made up was phony, but its pretense of an investigation is in terms of that phony number only, never of the correct number which it in fact had. The Texans on November 24, 1964, told Rankin and Warren the actual number which Rankin included in his memo, 110669. This is not an FBI number. It is inconsistent with the FBI's system for numbering its informers. It is, however, consistent with CIA numbers and may be consistent with other agency numbering systems as well.

Given what the commission knew about Oswald's high security clearance in the Marines, it should have taken testimony from those in the Navy who had knowledge of such matters and should have questioned them vigorously, instead of attempting to suppress such knowledge to the degree possible. And this is not the only suppressed information on Oswald that required it to question the Navy.

Not only did Oswald have these exceptionally high security clearances, he openly got Russian and supposedly Communist literature in the mail. Under normal conditions this would have led to some Navy interest and inquiry. But these were other than normal conditions and there was no inquiry. Oswald also learned how to speak and write Russian when he was a Marine, i.e., when he was under the authority of the Navy. Not only did the commission fail to explain this, it failed even to investigate it.

From the records the Navy, including the Office of Naval Intelligence, gave the commission, neither the Navy nor the ONI made even a pro forma investigation of that rather exceptional thing, that it taught a high-school dropout to be fluent in Russian while he was a Marine along with giving him those high clearances and then a hardship discharge so he could go to Russia a few weeks earlier instead of waiting for his discharge. And then did not prosecute him with getting that "hardship" discharge by fraud. It also did not give the commission the records of Oswald's security check that had to exist for him to have those high clearances. Normally, just getting Russian and Communist literature would have jeopardized, and probably terminated, those high security clearances. There would, at the least, have been an ONI investigation of it.

I begin my *Never Again!* by stating and proving that there was a de facto government conspiracy not to investigate the crime itself. Those identified in the documents I use there do not include the Navy or any of the commission. But is it not obvious that the decision not to investigate the crime itself extended to the commission and to the Navy?

Whether or not Oswald was the assassin, the official mythology that is disproven by the commission's own misrepresented and ignored records, he was the *only* assassin according to the entire government. That makes anything at all about him more than merely relevant in any investigation. Any detail about the only official candidate for assassin is essential in any investigation.

Nobody knew more about Oswald than the Navy. Yet it withheld at least what I indicate herein from all, from the FBI to the commission. And that about the man who, supposedly alone and unassisted, allegedly killed the president, the commander in chief of the Navy.

It cannot be regarded as a simple bureaucratic oversight that the Navy suppressed all these significant details of Oswald's career in the Marines. That the Navy did this and has not since disclosed any of it, not even under the 1992 law that requires it, points the Navy's own accusatory finger at the Navy.

There are other details and other mysteries. For example, Oswald could not have gotten from London's Heathrow Airport, from the time stamped on his passport, to the Helsinki hotel he checked into en route to Russia by any commercial carrier. The CIA made that investigation, and the commission published its report in its appended twenty-six volumes. The investigation to learn how Oswald was able to get to Helsinki before any commercial carrier could have gotten him there was never made. The obvious possibilities include having been taken there on a military plane.

Neither the commission nor any agency made even the pretense of an investigation into all these at the very least strange and provocative things in official records. Each has its own importance, and each indicates that the government had some kind of special relationship with the man the same government says assassinated its president. That his stay in Russia was in the interest of some military agency is an unavoidable conclusion given the aborted CIA investigation of whether he could have gotten to Helsinki when he did on any commercial flight. There was no investigation to determine whether he was flown on some military plane, planes our military attaches often have at their disposal. This means that no special plane would have had to have been provided. Moreover, records are kept of all flights. So the investigation would not have been difficult. But all interest in any investigation died when the CIA learned and reported that Oswald could not have gotten from London to Helsinki by any commercial plane. In turn, this indicates that after his Marines discharge, which he got by unprosecuted fraud, he maintained some kind of connection with some arm of the military services, the Navy being the most likely.

CHAPTER 9

IS THERE ANY LIMIT ON WHAT THE CIA IS CAPABLE OF? OR DID?

What we know of the military's unlawful and unconstitutional activities, some of which are discussed in previous chapters, we know only because such activity was not always cloaked in secrecy. The cult of secrecy has, however, served to conceal most of the CIA's transgressions from the American public. We will never know about most of their unlawful activity, but we do know that the agency planned such illegal acts, including assassinations. We know this thanks to the work of the Church Committee, the first Senate investigation of intelligence activities, headed by Idaho Senator Frank Church. His fate is instructive to those who would attempt to rein in rogue intelligence agencies. He was defeated by a vicious, dishonest, and well-financed attack by the radical right.

Richard Helms was the first CIA director to go public. In a speech before the American Newspaper Publishers Association in Washington, he asked that they "trust us," assuring them that "we do not target on Americans." At that very time, as exposed by the Church Committee, the agency was engaged in "Operation Chaos," directly targeting Americans opposed to the disastrous war in Vietnam.

The CIA also intercepted the mail of Americans in Europe and other foreign countries, as that committee also exposed. It had the assistance of the FBI in that task. The FBI picked up the foreign mail at designated post offices in New York City in particular, and delivered it to the CIA. Among the mail intercepted was mine, though this is not reflected in the records disclosed to me by the FBI and the CIA in response to my requests under the Freedom of Information and the Privacy Acts. In so doing, the agencies interfered with my right to be published. In one case, Sidney Kaufman,[1] a friend from OSS days who had connections in Europe, introduced *Whitewash* to both British and German publishers. Both liked the book. Collins, the British publisher, asked John Sparrow, warden of All Souls at Oxford, to review the book. He killed it, as Kaufman later told me.

As I also learned later, German publisher Fischer AG wrote me several times about its desire to publish *Whitewash* in Germany. I never received any of Fischer's letters. When I did not respond, it mailed the manuscript back to me. That never reached me either.

In 1966, I had a fine agent in London, Gordon Harbord. I sent him the chapters of *Whitewash II* as I wrote them. I heard nothing from him. Then, after two months, I got a cable from him telling me that all my mail had reached him in one delivery. It then was too late to mean anything at all. Prior to that, Harbord had submitted *Whitewash* to Sir Leslie Frewin, a London publisher. Frewin also was enthusiastic about the book. As he later wrote me, when it too made no difference, he was literally drafting the contract for its publication when he was fed bad information about a competing book and the opinion that the British market would not support two books on that subject. There was a competing book, but it did not appear until long after *Whitewash* would have done very well in the market.

When I told my friend Steve Barber, Washington correspondent of the *London Standard*, that Sparrow had talked Collins out of publishing *Whitewash*, Steve told me, among other things about Sparrow, that he had longtime intelligence connections, especially as a recruiter.

After all the earlier books on the JFK assassination had been published in this country and after Jim Garrison was getting great international attention, Sparrow wrote a lengthy article, "After the Assassination," for *The Times Literary Supplement* of December 14, 1967. It is seven newspaper pages of small type, a long piece. It attacks all the books critical of the Warren Report in various ways, using the usual formula, the Warren Commission was right because it says it was right. The article got considerable attention here. The *New York Times*' longtime Warren supporter and biographer, Anthony Lewis, gave it a full column, for example, as did other major United States publications. The *Times* gave another full column, also by Lewis, in support of Sparrow by Lyndon Johnson intellectual in residence, John P. Roche, *the day before* Sparrow's article was published in London.

Then, of all improbable things, the Sparrow article that had already gotten such extensive attention was published here as a book when in fact it was more like a pamphlet in size and format when it appeared.[2] It was far less than the page size of a book and ever so much thinner. But it once again got considerable attention in all the media, old as it was by then. There was little likelihood of it being a commercial success, but then it was published by a publisher owned by a large defense contractor. For its purposes, the relatively slight loss the inexpensive book would have sustained was worth it.

After it appeared, I wrote Sparrow reminding him of his getting Collins not to publish *Whitewash*. In his response of March 8, 1968, he does not deny this. He does not even refer to it. In a later letter he says merely that he did not remember it.

There is little doubt about it. The CIA does target Americans, and it does so to undermine legitimate protest against government (or agency) policies and to frustrate the work of critics. The CIA issued a directive to its stations abroad to draw on all assets to have books on the Kennedy assassination disapproved and publicly criticized. (*Countering Criticism of the Warren Report: Dispatch to Chiefs, Certain Stations and Bases*, 1967) This fact was disclosed by the agency. Is this a proper function of an intelligence agency? In the United States of America?

There is other evidence that suggests CIA interference with publication of my work. In February of 1965, Ivan Obolensky, the publisher who had contracted *Whitewash* in 1964, told me he had a best seller. I was told by John Ledes, his vice president, "The salesmen have orders for 39,000 copies." This was without any advertising, from the subject matter alone. "That," Ledes added, "means a gold-plate best seller," as it did in those days.

But then that same Ledes made an overnight trip to Washington and on his return the book was cancelled, without the manuscript being returned to me and without any explanation. Who he saw in Washington he did not tell me. Obolensky did not last long as a publisher.[3]

Being secretly in the publishing business was itself another way in which the CIA controlled what could be published. Sol Rabkin, a dear friend from my days working on the Senate Civil Liberties Committee, referred me to the Frederick Praeger publishing house. He sent me to a friend of his, Mort Puner, who was Praeger's director of special projects. After Puner read the book, he predicted an initial print in hardback of fifty thousand copies, large for those days. "However," he told me, "the final word is Mr. Praeger's. He is in San Francisco. Call me after he returns next week." When I called the following week, he told me that Praeger had rejected the book, the book Puner believed would be a best seller. Praeger claimed as his reason that the company only published "established scholars." It took a few years for the real reason to surface as the Church Committee began exposing the CIA's extracurricular activities disclosed that Praeger was a CIA publisher. It planted books it wanted with him and scuttled those it didn't, including books critical of the Warren Commission.

That the government is prohibited by the First Amendment from "abridging the right of free speech, or of the press" apparently didn't apply to the CIA. Like the military, the CIA seems to believe that our Constitution and laws do not apply to it and that it knows best what the country needs. If it decides that the national interest requires that it violate the Constitution and break the laws, that is what these self-proclaimed patriots do.

Two other examples of likely interference in my right to publish involve intercepting manuscripts sent by US mail. First, the copy of the manuscript of *Whitewash II* that Harrison Salisbury, managing editor of the *New York Times*, mailed back to me in the late summer of 1966 never did reach me. The second is stranger and highly suspicious. The original copy of *Oswald in New Orleans* mailed to me from New York took three weeks to reach me. When it did, it was in a post office wrapping, the original wrapping entirely missing. With it was a note from the Washington post office telling me that the package had been received in Washington without a wrapping and that it was sent to me at the address found inside it. There was not a single damaged page of the more than two inches thick manuscript. Not one page was bent over or torn. Yet it had been received at Washington's main post office without any wrapper? The only "address" found inside the manuscript was the name of a nearby town that appeared at the end of the foreword. The post office used my full address.

There is, of course, no proof that it was the CIA that had these two manuscript copies intercepted within the United States. It could have been by the FBI on its own or the CIA's behalf. Or perhaps there is a more innocent explanation for these incidents. But in the larger context of CIA illegal interference in the lawful activities of Americans and, especially its known interference with mail, there are ample grounds for suspicion.

Aside from its direct efforts to interfere with basic American rights and to spy on those of us critical of the official assassination mythology, the CIA also used commercial services to spy on and report what critics said in public. I have copies of transcripts of public statements I made which were sent to the CIA but not addressed to it by name, but to the Washington post office box of "The Public Affairs Staff." This "Public Affairs Staff" had an account in that name at the Riggs Bank in Washington and it had that name and box number on its envelopes, which I have. Although there is no reference to the CIA, it was a part of the CIA used for spying on what Americans say and think. Two of its agents drove to the Washington office of that commercial service to pick up transcripts. One I was told had an attaché case handcuffed to his wrist! The manager of that office told me in a phone conversation that I had the CIA's "all-time track record" in its assassination related interests. I taped that conversation. I have a transcript of another conversation between him and someone in one of their offices in another city in which when told I would be there, he responded "goody, goody!" believing the CIA would want a transcript meaning more business and more money from it. I have the envelope the "Public Affairs Staff" used in mailing checks and copies of those checks. Much of the evidence of this illegal CIA spying on Americans was sent to me by strangers, Americans who did not approve of the CIA police statism.

As I report elsewhere, there is a *prima facie* case that the CIA blocked the arrangement I had made with the original *Saturday Evening Post* for the serial rights to *Whitewash*. E. Howard Hunt, later of Watergate infamy, was involved in that effort. That *Post* editor wanted to deal with me through a literary agent, which I did not have. He sent me to Maxwell Wilkinson, of Littauer & Wilkinson, literary agents. Wilkinson read and liked the book but reneged on the agreement I had already made with the *Post*, claiming that the book did not lend itself to the use of individual chapters. Later, the men's magazine *Saga* asked me for the use of one chapter standing alone, for which it told me it paid me a dollar more than it had paid Ernest Hemingway.

During the Watergate scandal, I checked Hunt through standard sources and found that for those years he gave as his address in *Who's Who* "Littauer & Wilkinson, 500 Fifth Avenue, New York City." Later, he switched his address in *Who's Who* to the address of the building in Washington that was used as a cover address by the public relations firm, The Mullen Agency. Mullen, a CIA asset or front for years, then had fancy offices only two blocks away, at 17th Street and Pennsylvania Avenue, where Hunt maintained an office. His office mate was Douglas Caddy, who then ostensibly worked for the United Fruit Company, a CIA asset as revealed in the Senate's Watergate investigation. Earlier, in Washington and other cities, The Mullen Agency had the same address as the CIA's Free Cuba Committee, again as listed in standard sources.

CIA's Director Richard Helms lied when he told the Senate Watergate committee that the CIA recommended Hunt to The Mullen Agency only after he retired from the agency. Hunt was a CIA employee when years earlier he began working at Mullen, and Helms certainly knew it. But then, as I note elsewhere, when Helms was found by the courts to be a perjurer, his lawyer, Edward Bennett Williams, praised him for that. The same Williams served on the President's Intelligence Advisory Board with oversight responsibility over the CIA and did nothing at all about its anti-American domestic activities prohibited by its charter and by the Constitution.

Another "Mullen" employee who used that same Mullen/Hunt cover address also used a Mexico City address, as did Mullen, on the same street as the office of the Mexican lawyer who was involved in laundering large illegal campaign contributions to Richard Nixon's re-election effort. This money was used for improper and illegal purposes by Nixon's former law partner, his Attorney General and campaign manager, John Mitchell. This man, whose name and address I have, disappeared from Washington when the Watergate scandal broke. None of this was ever investigated by either the Senate Committee or the Watergate Special Prosecutor, Leon Jaworski. That office did not respond when I filed a FOIA request for copies of records it had entered into evidence in court, thus making them public. It was nonresponsive when later I went there; I did not even get inside the door.

After the resignation of Spiro Agnew, who had been caught in criminal activities involving graft, Nixon nominated Gerald Ford, former Warren Commission member, to be his vice president. Shortly after that, Nixon resigned following the Watergate scandal thus avoiding impeachment. Ford thus became the first unelected president in US history. One of Ford's earliest acts as president was pardoning Nixon.

This is the same Ford who appointed a Presidential Commission to supposedly investigate CIA excesses. He chose Nelson Rockefeller to head it and his fellow Warren Commission whitewasher, commission counsel, David Belin, to head its operations. Belin was every bit as proficient in whitewashing the CIA as he was in whitewashing the Kennedy assassination.[4]

Helms's testimony that Hunt went to work for Mullen only after he retired from the CIA is perjury and it was allowed. That committee also failed to follow up on a lead that Hunt had as a New York address that of the literary agency, Littauer & Wilkinson. In a taped conversation, Hunt spoke of having in his New York office a phone with a direct line to his Washington office. He said that people who phoned him, believing that he was in New York, spoke to him when he in fact was in Washington. If the Senate Watergate Committee or Jaworski's Office of Special Watergate Prosecutor or David Belin's Ford Presidential Commission had done any investigating at all—had even looked at *Who's Who*—they would have uncovered another and a major CIA scandal that they all wanted to avoid. And if they had checked the well-known and widely published lists of fronts used by the CIA, they would have found among the CIA's foundations the Littauer Foundation with a New York City address. It could then have learned whether the Littauer of the Foundation and the Littauer that the CIA's Hunt used were in any way connected. If they had wanted to, as obviously they did not.

I had no secret leads on any of this. They were all public and all ignored by the "investigators" and the media. All of this avoidance of the obvious served to protect both Nixon and the CIA and to deny the people the full truth about their subversions of our democracy.

How obvious was this information? Besides my use of *Who's Who*, David Zitch, then a schoolboy in California, using only standard sources at his public library, sent me his tracing of the CIA's Mullen Agency, its Free Cuba Committee, and others at the addresses they shared.

The highly respected Watergate Committee and its much-honored chairman, reputed Senate Constitutional expert Sam Ervin, could have and should have exposed the lie that was Helms's assurances to the nation's publishers that the CIA did not "target" Americans when it did that in multiple thousands, as the Church Committee later exposed. That was strictly prohibited by its charter, as was all domestic activity of which we have had but the slightest glimpse. Nor does its charter authorize it to kill, either here or abroad, a practice which the Church Committee began to expose but failed to follow through. There is no question that the CIA planned assassinations and attempted them. And who plans and attempts assassinations without intending to carry them out?

While so much of what the CIA did was so very wrong, it would be a mistake to believe that they saw it that way. Like the military, they believed that they were the true patriots, doing what the country needed done; because it was in the national interest, it was right, not wrong. This, of course, is an attitude that can justify anything, including as it did, assassinations.

It further violated the law by refusing to disclose these nefarious activities, even when required by the law, specifically the Freedom of Information Act.

The point I want to emphasize is not personal. It is that when an agency runs amok in its unlawful activities, is there any point at which it stops? When in the habit of violating both the law and the Constitution, is it equally impelled to commit even greater wrongs in its convoluted thinking about what it deems as in the nation's interest?

When I used Freedom of Information Act seeking all the CIA's records on or about me, I received no response at all. Attorney Jim Lesar, who handled my FOIA lawsuits, phoned its general counsel, Lawrence Houston. Houston invited us to come see him. He did see us in his seventh-floor office near that of the Director. He then told us that the CIA had no record of my filing any such request. So I showed him the carbon copies of them. That appeared to surprise him. He said he'd look into it. That did result in my getting a small collection of the CIA's records on me, but far from all of them. It included some which I had specifically requested. These particular records were not an embarrassment to the agency. Those it withheld would have reflected poorly on the agency.

Without going into the whole story, before Pearl Harbor and the establishment of the OSS, FDR's son Jimmy was working in a predecessor agency. I was at the time the Washington correspondent for *Click* magazine and was given plans for a Nazi putsch in Santiago, Chile. The writer who had acquired the plans was in Chile where the postal service was thoroughly penetrated by the pro-Hitler Spanish Falange. He gave them to me and with the assistance of friend who was an Undersecretary of State, I was able to get them into the US in a diplomatic pouch. I gave the plans to Jimmy to give to his father. I also made that information available to the Department of Justice, where I then had a friend who headed its criminal division. FDR used that information in one of his famous "fireside" chats. The OSS inherited those records which in turn went to the CIA. Included in these would have been files relating to my involvement in this, including some type of award from the OSS Director, General William "Wild Bill" Donovan, the nature of which I have long forgotten.

What was also given to me, probably by accident, was an internal CIA Office of Security memo written when Houston had first asked for all the records on or about me. That memo states that the "Security" office had two files on me. The memo was x-ed through and not given to the CIA's General Counsel. Even though the existence of these files was disclosed to me, they were not included among those I received. Nor did anyone reviewing the records ask for those two relevant files. More than two decades later, the CIA continues to withhold at least those two "security" office files from me. This is despite the new law that requires their disclosure.

It's bad enough that those in other parts of the CIA had lied to its General Counsel in telling him they had nothing on me, which he did tell Lesar and me. But then giving the proof of the existence of these files to me and then withholding them with nobody inside the agency picking that up and asking for them is much worse. Everyone who saw that memo is culpable.

In the materials that the CIA finally gave me, there was nothing about its domestic spying on my appearances, about its interference with my mail, and its efforts to prevent publication of my work.

Simple, ordinary, everyday honesty is not a CIA virtue. Nor is complying with the law. This again raises the question of whether there is any limit to what it is capable of if it lies even to its own general counsel with the intent of violating the law.

It has no law-enforcement responsibility and is in fact prohibited from acting in such a capacity. What business is it of the CIA's what any American thinks, says, writes, or publishes?

The CIA was, in fact, compiling dossiers on Americans who were not engaged in any activity that fell under the legitimate business of the CIA. If the CIA compiled a dossier on an American writer and had at least two separate files on him, does it do so for all writers it regards as controversial or whose views do not meet with its approval? If it engages in these illegal activities—and it does —should we not question the extent of its illegalities and whether there is any limit to them?

It seems unlikely that this was limited to writers. Might not that wrongful thinking and wrongful activity extend to teachers and college professors, to lawyers who handle cases the CIA does not like, to reporters, editors? Is there any end? Is this not the manifestation of the police state, the same in principle as the Gestapo and the KGB?

Then the CIA resorted to another of its dirty tricks, a CIA specialty, to keep me from getting any more records from it. It sent me a large batch of records I had not requested and had no use for. They involved its mind-bending experiments on human beings. Under its own regulations, had I requested those records, the CIA was required to give me an estimate of cost in advance and get a partial payment from me. It did neither. They refused to accept the records back and then held that because I had not paid for the records I had not ordered, I was prohibited under its regulations from getting any more records.

I filed appeals with copies of its own regulations which it violated. These appeals were ignored and the agency has not disclosed a single page to me in the last twenty years. The only CIA records officially disclosed to me since then are copies of those it gave other agencies, like the FBI. Government FOIA regulations require that any other agency disclosing records obtain approval from the agency of origin before disclosing the records.

In denying my request for records on or about me, records which it later disclosed without allowing me copies, it deliberately violated the law. In so doing, it denied me the ability to make use of the Privacy Act to protect myself from public disclosure of CIA records which defame me. I was told by Anna Marie Kuhns-Walko that records the agency deposited in the National Archives under the President John F. Kennedy Assassination Records Collection Act of 1992 include some of these defamations. This in effect grants immunity to those who wish to misuse these records to defame me.

The Privacy Act, among other things, gives Americans the right to file corrections to files the government has on them and to have those corrections filed with the original records. The FBI's records abound with distortions and omissions that impart dishonest and defamatory meanings to many of the records it generates, with the truth frequently the exact opposite of what its contrived records suggest.

Thus, in keeping secret from me records I had formally requested under FOIA more than two decades earlier, the CIA also denied me my right to file corrections to these misleading and defamatory records. While those using those records could ignore my corrections, it would have enabled those of honest intent to know and use the truth. And if I had been able to file corrections when I asked for those records, the CIA would have been required under the Privacy Act to make my corrections available to the FBI and those within the CIA and others in government and enable them to know the truth.

My friend Ray Kurpis, of Orlando, Florida, when he was working at the new and modern Archives building on the University of Maryland campus in College Park, obtained a computer printout of what were supposedly the records on me provided by all agencies to the Archive as of the fall of 1994. The stack is about three-quarters of an inch thick but is far from complete; the CIA did not directly provide the Archives a single record on me. On the list are a few items it had given other agencies, but not a single one transferred by the CIA, not even its records of my FOIA lawsuits seeking disclosure of its records on the Kennedy assassination.

I wrote the director, R. James Woolsey, about this on October 17, 1994. My letter is long and detailed. Under both Acts I requested belated compliance with my requests going back to 1971. I reminded him of the CIA's obligation to have done that under the 1992 Act that required full disclosure of all assassination records. I ticked off proofs I have of records it has and withholds and of its intrusions into my life and work, with documented details. He did not respond. Three weeks later I mailed a copy of this unanswered letter to the new Assassination Records Review Board (ARRB) that is to see to full disclosure under the 1992 Act. Five days after that I reminded Woolsey that he had not responded as the law requires. Neither Woolsey nor any of his associates ever responded. Woolsey was forced to celebrate the Christmas season by resigning, largely due to his protection of those involved in the case of Soviet mole, Aldrich Ames. As a *New York Times* story on the resignation puts it, "the Ames case, which started out as a case of one C.I.A. officer's treason, soon became a study in C.I.A. incompetence."[5] Quitting under strong pressure is at least one honorable act that can fairly be attributed to Woolsey.

On its part, the Assassination Records Review Board (ARRB) let me know in December that it might get around to what I wrote Woolsey about sometime in the future. Maybe. After all, the CIA had only behaved like the KGB in its intrusions into my life and work on the Kennedy assassination.

The CIA is unchanged and without a complete rebuilding it will remain so. But there can be no meaningful rebuilding while it continues to be staffed by authoritarians who disregard fundamental principles of our democracy. No matter how often it preaches that it believes in and is the protector of democracy, its record is the opposite. When the CIA can be as intendedly lawless on so relatively minor a matter—though not minor to me—is there any reason to believe that it can become democratic without such a rebuilding? And if this is its record on so small a matter, should we not believe that it can justify anything at all?

The CIA has a long record of broad violations of the law and Constitution, both major and minor. This raises the question of whether its lawlessness has been much greater than what has come to light thus far and whether, considering that it did plot assassinations, it could have been involved in the assassination of its own president

For all these years, Congress has been easy on the CIA. At first it had no oversight committees. When it finally did, the supposed oversight sometimes amounted to a license to do wrong. Congress has always gone out of its way to minimize the CIA's illegalities and to shield the agency from the consequences of its actions. Thus, for example, the Senate Watergate Committee, while putting on a big and exciting show on live television, actually avoided to the greatest extent possible any real investigation.

Aside from the CIA as an institution, which no record I have seen indicates had anything to do with the assassination itself, there are its overly dedicated self-starters, such as E. Howard Hunt, and others of his ilk. What about these super-patriots who believe that whatever they believe is right and proper? Of what are they, in their genuine dedication, capable?

In saying that I have seen no record in any way involving the CIA in the JFK assassination, as distinguished from disinforming and under informing about it, I do not mean to imply that if there were CIA involvement that there would be a paper record of it. The best-known of the CIA's assassination plots which enlisted top mafia figures to get that job done had no records at all. Not a single one of any kind.

It disclosed this to me under date of February 14, 1989, with a referral back to it from the Department of Justice. On May 11, 1962, when Robert Kennedy was Attorney General, he asked it for a statement of fact regarding the aforementioned Castro assassination plot the CIA had actually attributed to the Kennedys. The CIA prepared a "memorandum for the record" on this three days later. In it, the CIA says:

> Knowledge of this project during its life was kept to a total of six persons . . . and there were no memoranda on the project nor were there any other written documents or agreements. (see Appendix 4)

Nobody outside the CIA knew and it saw to it that it had no records relating to it in any way.

The CIA's assassination plots were not limited to Castro. Castro gave a visiting Congressional delegation what he said was a list of about a dozen of them with some details. The CIA has not admitted to those plots Castro identified. So there is no way of knowing how many times the CIA plotted assassinations of foreign leaders or others. The one against Patrice Lumumba in what was then known as the Congo was officially admitted.

By ghoulish coincidence, just when JFK was assassinated, one of the CIA's officials was handing a ballpoint loaded with a deadly poison to a Cuban official who was to kill Castro with it. This CIA agent, Rolando Cubela, later confessed to the assassination attempt but Castro spared him and several other plotters from execution.

The headline of a December 26, 1975, interview of E. Howard Hunt by John M. Crewdson of the *New York Times*, reads, "Hunt Says C.I.A. Had Assassin Unit." Hunt said that in the mid-1950s he was told by agency superiors that this unit was headed by Boris T. Pash. Pash denied it. It was reported to have planned to kill other heads of State, including Egypt's. There may or may not have been others.

The question thus lingers of whether the CIA as an agency or through the actions of rogue agents, was involved in the assassination of its own head of state, a man with whose policies it was in the strongest disagreement, the man who fired its popular long-time director, Allen Dulles, who went on to serve as a member of the Warren Commission!

One of the reasons this and other questions linger is that supposed oversight was a farce. In his book, *The Politics of Lying*, David Wise wrote about this alleged oversight prior to the limited exposures of the Church Committee: He notes how the Central Intelligence Act of 1949 gave the director of the CIA power to spend money "without regard to the provisions of law and regulations relating to the expenditure of funds." It is a great myth that the CIA's classified budget and activities are carefully scrutinized by Congress. Senator John C. Stennis of Mississippi, who chaired both the five-man CIA subcommittee of the Armed Services Committee and the Armed Services Committee itself, assured the Senate that: "This agency is conducted in a splendid way, . . ." And during a debate over the CIA Stennis observed that: "You have to make up your mind that you are going to have an intelligence agency and protect it as such, and shut your eyes some and take what is coming." When Senator Fulbright asked if the reported army of thirty-six thousand in Laos had been approved, Senator Allen J. Ellender, the chief Senate watchdog over the CIA's budget, gave the following revealing response: "It never dawned on me to ask about it."[6]

When Stennis said the CIA "is conducted in a splendid way" without having called a single meeting of his "oversight" committee and another of those chairman, Senator Allen J. Ellender, "did not know anything about" the CIA's having an army of thirty-six thousand in Laos, it is obvious that there was no oversight at all. With the knowledge that there was no real oversight, there was nothing to inhibit the CIA in acting on some of its wilder notions.

At the second TOP SECRET executive session of the Warren Commission, focused on reports of Oswald's connection with intelligence agencies, Warren Commission Member John J. McCloy, who had had considerable experience with these agencies, told the other members, "I have run into some very limited mentalities both in the CIA and the FBI." At that same session, Commission Member Allen Dulles, who had steered the CIA into its Bay of Pigs fiasco which some in the CIA blamed on President Kennedy, assured the commission that perjury was right and proper for agents and for the director. When asked whether a CIA agent would tell the truth about something touchy to the CIA, Dulles said, "I wouldn't think he would tell it under oath, no." Asked "Why?" by Warren, Dulles replied, "He ought not tell it under oath. Maybe not tell it to his own government . . ." Asked if he would (as CIA director) "tell the Secretary of Defense?" Dulles said, "Well, it depends a little on the circumstances."[7]

Quite aside from whether the CIA had JFK assassinated, keeping in mind the ultra-right political beliefs and "limited mentalities" of the "Hunt-niks," there is sufficient reason to believe it possible for it to have been involved in the assassination.

The CIA blamed the Kennedys for its own dirty works, what is known in the trade as "executive actions" or "wet jobs." Helms had to know that this was false. Yet the CIA's well-practiced liar and perjurer, Richard Helms, swore to the House Select Committee on September 22 and 25, 1978, that the Kennedys were behind its plot to assassinate Castro when its own records prove the exact opposite.[8]

So, while on the record—and on this it should be remembered that there was that immediate government conspiracy not to investigate the crime itself—there is nothing to indicate that the CIA had anything to do with the assassination. At the same time, there is nothing in the CIA's record to persuade that any such involvement was not possible for it.

The CIA has always made policy, as Peter Grose, author of the favorable biography of Allen Dulles, *Gentleman Spy: The Life of Allen Dulles*, admits. David Wise, without question a subject-matter expert, concludes his *New York Times* review of the book as follows:

> "He always claimed that his duty was only that of a professional intelligence officer, leaving the policy-making to others—to his brother." [Secretary of State John Foster Dulles] That was not the whole story, of course. Mr. Grose also notes that many of the C.I.A. operations under Allen Dulles determined policy.
>
> In the end he grew weary. Not long before Dulles' death, an eager young C.I.A. recruit called on the great man at his home, hoping for inspiration. He did not find it. "Oh," Dulles said, "perhaps we have already intervened too much in the affairs of other people."[9]

The CIA's dirty works extend to creating foreign policy. Under our system of government, foreign policy is determined by the president. So, naturally, the CIA says it does not create policy but does only what it is told to do. This was the testimony of former director Richard Helms before the House Select Committee.[10] That testimony was as truthful as his word to the newspaper publishers when he told them, "Trust us. We do not target on Americans." In fact, he was convicted of not being truthful, of lying to Congress about CIA attempts to prevent Salvador Allende from becoming president of Chile.

The disastrous U-2 flight of Francis Gary Powers, shot down deep inside the Soviet Union, illustrates the CIA's policy-making and its determination that the Cold War should continue, that there be no detente. Its purpose was to undermine the Paris Summit that President Eisenhower and the USSR's Nikita Khrushchev had arranged to pursue detente and a more peaceful world.

On May 31, 1960, thirty days after the incident, the Senate Foreign Relations Committee took testimony on it, testimony that was kept secret for twelve years. I obtained a copy of a related volume when it was released in 1982. Much was expurgated, but the unexcised transcripts were to be deposited in the National Archives. The committee's volume has an understated title, "Events Incident to the Summit Conference."[11] When the committee's report critical of the whole incident was issued, fourteen of the committee's members endorsed it, one voted against it, and two issued a minority report defending that May 1 overflight. In his speech on that occasion, Committee Chairman William Fulbright (D. Arkansas) said that as a result of the U-2 affair, the international prestige of the United States, quoting the Committee's report, "had reached a new low."[12] That overflight was a violation of international law. Our U-2 flights had been violating international law for four years and could have been interpreted as acts of war. The seriousness of the offense and its offensiveness to the USSR cannot be exaggerated.

CIA Director Allen W. Dulles said that he personally selected the date of May 1, the May Day holiday in the USSR, making it an even greater insult to the Soviets. He said he acted under "the existing authority" for those flights in general but that it was only on the afternoon of the day before, April 30, that he ordered the flight for the next day. (see Appendix 5) The cover story for picking that day, the one most certain to offend the

USSR more than almost any other day, was "weather"— they had to do it that day and not later because of "weather conditions." And then, to leave no doubt at all that he wanted to give the USSR and Khrushchev the greatest possible offense, he called Khrushchev a liar for saying that the USSR had shot the plane down when it was over seventy thousand feet in the air and when he put its wreckage on display. According to Dulles, the USSR could not have shot the plane down from that altitude but did so when it was much lower and that the USSR had not recovered the wreckage.

Dulles said that Khrushchev's statement on May 5 was "as an attempt at deception." He then referred to what the USSR had put on display in Moscow in May as "photographs of a pile of junk—according to experts, pieces of an old Soviet fighter plane—possibly for the purpose of making us think that the U-2 plane had been effectively destroyed. Since the fake wreckage was quickly identified for what it was, this particular ruse had no effect." (see Appendix 5)

What the unidentified "experts," most likely Dulles's own in the CIA, referred to as "pieces of an old Soviet fighter" was in fact the Powers U-2 plane, as American reporters and anyone else who wanted to saw.

Powers, after repatriation, testified that the explosion of the missile made it impossible for him to reach the self-destruct mechanism that opened his parachute after he was clear of the plane, and that he did not take the poison the CIA gave its U-2 pilots with instruction to use it if captured.

This whole thing quite obviously was designed to wreck the summit and any beginning to the end of the Cold War. The retired General of the Armies, Dwight Eisenhower, reacted as a Cold Warrior, not as president of the United States. When Khrushchev expressed a willingness to go ahead with the summit after an apology, Eisenhower refused to apologize. It was an act of war, an invasion, a violation of their borders and international law, a recognized cause for declaring war. And to add insult to injury, we called their leader a liar.

Whatever Eisenhower's reason for refusing to issue an apology, it was his top spook, Allen Dulles, who without specific orders sent that plane on his own authority, knowing fully that it had an excellent chance of heightening rather than cooling Cold War tensions. He was pursuing the

CIA's policy, not Eisenhower's. Eisenhower had invited Khrushchev here. His coast-to-coast tour was a big success and was well received by the public. He and Ike then agreed to the summit. Those were meaningful steps in reducing tension and leading to better relations. But that was not the Dulles/CIA policy and so the Cold War got colder and the enormous costs to the world were greatly magnified.

When the CIA can do this—and it did do it!—can it be said that there is anything of which it is not capable, even an "executive action" against the president?

Ike did not fire Allen Dulles, brother of his first secretary of state, John Foster Dulles. Instead, he put him in charge of the next great fiasco, another one that resulted in a still further international reaction against the country, disgracing it then and in history, the Bay of Pigs. As discussed elsewhere in this book, the CIA again pursued its own agenda, taking the country and the world to the brink of nuclear disaster.

The CIA proudly boasts that in accord with national policy it supports democratic regimes, especially in Latin America. In fact, it has a long and consistent record of actually installing vicious, murderous dictatorships and of overthrowing democratically elected governments. David Atlee Phillips and E. Howard Hunt have written glowingly of their own roles in the CIA's overthrow of a moderately leftist elected government in Guatemala. Its crime, as seen through CIA eyes on the extreme right, was including all elements in the government and instituting a land reform program, something the United States has promoted elsewhere in the world.

As *Washington Post* columnist Mary McGrory wrote on November 6, 1994, the blood-lusting military dictatorship installed by Phillips, Hunt, and the like-minded CIA Cold Warriors was "a regime that has murdered between 150,000 and 200,000 of its citizens in recent decades."[13] McGrory was writing about the tragic case of Harvard lawyer, Jennifer Harbury, whose Guatemalan husband was among the thousands arrested by the CIA-installed regime and its successors and about whom, without American protest, those regimes claim to have no knowledge at all.

A great number of Guatemalans fled to avoid being murdered merely because they were democratic and thus regarded as enemies of the CIA's military dictatorship. Under the Reagan and Bush administration these refugees were denied refugee status in the land of the free and the home of the brave. Organizations, especially religious groups that sought to help them, were actually prosecuted by the Department of Justice. Guatemala is not the exception. It is one of the many illustrations of the fact that murder is a CIA business.

Less than a month later, Walter Pincus, one of the *Washington Post's* CIA experts, reported what the outgoing chairman (Dan Glickman of Kansas) of the House intelligence committee said about the "gap" between the CIA and presidents: "There is a serious distance between the White House and the CIA that is harmful to President Clinton, the agency and the development of foreign policy."[14] Also, the same issue reported President Clinton's decision to ask for the appropriation of an additional $25 billion dollars for the military. The Republicans were then demanding an additional $45 billion dollars for the military.

So we could "lead" the world. "Lead" or "SIOP" the world, it is the same thing, save for the number of deaths and the suffering. This enormous military expenditure diverts precious resources that could meet urgent domestic needs. With the Cold War ended and the dissolution of the Soviet Union, the military needs this fantastic added sum? Not to defend the country! The CIA continues to do what it wants to do and the SIOPified military gets whatever it wants. All other considerations are subordinate to them. This, too, is policy making by those not authorized to do so under our democratic system of government.

As I neared completion of this book, there was surprising confirmation of what I say about the CIA following its own agenda and not doing what it was created to do. It was in a statement by Stansfield Turner, the man Jimmy Carter appointed as CIA Director. It is reported in Christopher B. Daly's December 3, 1994, story in the *Washington Post* about a conference in Cambridge, Massachusetts, sponsored jointly by the CIA and Harvard University.

> Former CIA director Stansfield Turner today stunned a conference of dozens of current and former agency analysts with a blunt critique of the CIA's effectiveness—and his own—during his term in office.

> Although not listed on the program, Turner stole the spotlight. . . .
>
> Turner said the CIA "didn't do well" in foreseeing the downfall of the Shah of Iran or the collapse of the Soviet Union and had consistently failed to serve the president in its handling of its premier analytical product, the lengthy documents known as National Intelligence Estimates.
>
> These reports were not inaccurate or misleading, Turner said, but were simply "irrelevant" to the president in making policy. "If anyone is to blame, it is I," he said.

Turner continued, speaking of the enormous wastefulness and great cost of continuing to manufacture nuclear weapons when we had a vast superiority in them.

> Turner said it was important to recall that at the time U.S. forces were capable of absorbing a Soviet nuclear attack and still deliver a counter-punch that would have destroyed 70 percent of the Soviet economy.
>
> "How could we have thought we possibly needed more?" Turner asked. He said the agency should have told Carter there was no need to build more weapons, except for purely political reasons. "What it should have said to him, in my view, was simply two words: 'Too much.' We and the Soviets both have too much firepower to need any more, . . ."[15]

CHAPTER 10

WHOSE COUP?

In this country, the assassination of any president has the effect of a coup d'état, whatever the intent of an assassin or assassins. By that, we mean that the government is overthrown by force, that the positions, policies, and programs it pursued are supplanted by differing, opposing ones. This is a consequence of two unique aspects of the American political system, the rules governing presidential succession and the impact of the electoral system on the selection of candidates for vice president. In the United States, upon the death of the president, the line of succession is prescribed and inflexible and, consequently, completely predictable. The vice president becomes the president. If something were to happen to the vice president, the line of succession is also fixed with the Speaker of the House of Representatives assuming office, and so on down the line. Although not prescribed by law, the selection process for vice president has followed a fairly consistent pattern historically with presidential candidates generally urging the nomination of someone with different beliefs and positions from their own. This is a practical matter, a way to appeal to a part of the electorate to whom the presidential candidate does not appeal or not appeal as much.[1]

There are numerous examples of this in recent history. Ronald Reagan represented the ultra-right extreme of the Republican Party when he ran for president. In his first (unsuccessful) campaign, he selected Pennsylvania's liberal Republican Senator Richard Schweiker as his nominee for vice president. Politically, they could not have been more different. When he ran the second time, he chose the man who had ridiculed him during the campaign for the GOP presidential nomination, George H. W. Bush. Bush had referred to Reagan's economic proposals as "voodoo economics." To take another example, Eisenhower selected Richard Nixon, not because he liked or respected him, but because Nixon with his Red-hunting credentials could appeal to those with more extreme views.

That is the way it has typically worked, and it is the way it worked with Kennedy and Johnson. They held different views and did not even like each other. In fact, in choosing LBJ, Kennedy precipitated a major revolt among his strongest supporters, the unions, which were so influential in the important state of New York. The biggest difference between them concerned their approach to foreign policy: while Kennedy was dovish on foreign policy, Johnson was a leading hawk. This difference was even sharper by the time of the assassination.

Whoever killed President Kennedy knew with certainty that in so doing, they would radically alter the course of US policy by making the known hawk, Lyndon Johnson, president. This was as certain as night follows day.

The official mythology is that Oswald was the lone assassin. That it is, in fact, "mythology" is overwhelmingly and irrefutably proven by the official evidence itself. That official evidence also establishes beyond question that the assassination was the product of a conspiracy. Of all the many and entirely undisputed proofs of this, which I brought to light in *Whitewash*, based on official evidence only, is the little-known fact that when the country's best professional shooters tried to duplicate the shooting attributed to Oswald, not one of them could do so. A few pages later, I included a facsimile of the official Marine evaluation of Oswald as a "rather poor 'shot'."[2]

An intentionally dishonest test was carried out for the commission by the US Army at its Aberdeen Proving Grounds in Maryland. The professional shooters, all with the highest rating of "master," fired at fixed rather than moving targets with no obstruction in their way. They had all the time in the world to adjust to their shooting, not the tiny fraction of time Oswald allegedly had for his first shot through a tree of dense foliage. The rifle had been thoroughly overhauled for them, as it needed to be, with shims placed under the telescopic sight to make it work. Otherwise, it would have been off target. And instead of shooting while supposedly trying to hide from a window more than sixty feet in the air, they were on a stable platform half that height and with no obstructions of any kind. Yet with all that, not one could fire the requisite number of shots attributed to the duffer, the "rather poor 'shot,'" Lee Harvey Oswald. Not one could do the shooting within the time permitted in the official "solution." I go into this in greater detail in *Never Again!*

While there are innumerable other proofs that the official "solution" was known to be wrong and impossible at the time it was hoked up, the most comprehensible and unquestionable fact is that the best shots in the country, under vastly improved conditions and without the stress and all the obstacles that Oswald allegedly had to meet and overcome, failed to duplicate the Super-William Tell feat officially attributed to him.

There is nobody who had any experience at all with rifles like the one Oswald is said to have used who did not, at the very least, have real questions about even the possibility of that kind of shooting in that very, very short period of time, less than six seconds. After my first book was out, two young men, both twenty and members of the National Rifle Association, came to visit me and ridiculed the official solution that attributed that shooting to Oswald with that rifle. They told me that rifle was known as "Mussolini's contribution to humanitarian warfare." There are few of any rank in any of the military who did not know that the shooting attributed to Oswald was impossible. As we see above, the Commandant of the Marine Corps certified that Oswald was a lousy shot. Throughout the military it had to have been well known and understood that the official "solution" to the assassination of their commander in chief was impossible. Yet none in the military said a word about this in public. And the *official* test that proved the impossibility of the *official* solution was an Army test. So the Army in particular was aware of the truth, and remained silent.

Conspiracies do have purposes. The obvious purpose of this conspiracy was twofold. One was to get rid of Kennedy and his policies and the other to make Lyndon Johnson with his very different policies the president of the United States.

Even Lyndon Johnson, if his word is to be believed, knew there had been a conspiracy, which means that he knew he became president as the result of a conspiracy. In 1994, in the disclosure of some of Johnson's phone calls confirmed what I first brought to public attention in my 1974 book, *Whitewash IV*. In it are facsimiles of staff memos by Melvin Eisenberg and Howard Willens reporting on Chairman Earl Warren's first conference with his staff on January 20, 1964. Eisenberg left his law firm to become one of the commission's counsels. Willens was a Department of Justice lawyer who was on loan to the commission. Eisenberg states that Warren told his staff that the reason he took the job of chairman, which he knew as Chief Justice of the Supreme Court he should not have taken, was that if he did not there could be a "war that could cost 40 million lives." Willens avoids this specific language, stating instead that "the President was concerned about the international repercussions of the assassination and called upon the Chief Justice to help."[3]

If the assassination had been carried out by a lone assassin without assistance, how could that have resulted in a nuclear war that might have killed 40 million people? The statement presupposes the involvement of a nuclear power in a conspiracy to assassinate the president. It is only if the assassination was a conspiracy that it could result in a nuclear war with the USSR.

Johnson confided in trusted associates that he believed there had been a conspiracy to kill JFK. In a phone conversation with high-ranking FBI official, Hoover's assistant, Cartha DeLoach, late the night of April 3, 1967, in DeLoach's words, the president's close assistant "Marvin Watson . . . stated that the President had told him in an off moment that he was now convinced that there was a plot in connection with the assassination. Watson stated the President felt the CIA [part of the military-industrial-intelligence complex] had something to do with this plot." (see Appendix 6)

There is no question, as previously noted, that there was a conspiracy to kill President Kennedy. The only question is who conspired. In the absence of any official investigation of the crime itself, and no real investigation of the crime was made or intended to be made, we are left with only circumstantial evidence, what lawyers refer to as motive, means and opportunity. Who had or could have had the motive *and* the means *and* the opportunity. Not just motive, or the means, or the opportunity, but *all* three.

As John Kennedy himself said about the means and opportunity, anyone can kill the president if he is willing to give his life for doing it. But in the case of his own assassination, there is an extraordinary number of people, groups or organizations who may have had a motive for killing him. With most, however, what is known from the official investigation, and in many cases, despite it, meeting all three requirements limits the possibilities to very few.

If Oswald was not the assassin, and he was not and could not have been based on the official evidence itself, he was framed. Who could have known enough about him and who could have gotten away with framing him? And not just to frame him, but to exculpate themselves and, at the very least, to permit the actual shooters to escape.

Those with the capability of doing this are very, very few and almost certainly had to be in or connected to the government.

Who, for example, could have gotten that rifle into the building and hidden it with such care without being detected?

Who could have planted the so-called magic bullet at the hospital?

Who could have placed those three empty shells to be found in the Texas School Book Depository Building? Or the pieces of bullet in the limousine? Who could have made that paper bag in which he allegedly carried that rifle into the building and left it there undetected, or placed it there after the search began? It was neither detected nor photographed when the police first photographed the area. The bag must have been made out of "magic paper" to have held the well-oiled rifle which Oswald supposedly carried through the streets of Irving, Texas, with the rifle sliding around in it, without having a trace of oil on it. The paper was capable of retaining fingerprints, yet had none despite Oswald having carried it through those streets by the top, then laying it in the back seat of the car of his fellow worker Buell Wesley Frazier, and finally carrying it by its bottom from that car into the building.

Who could have made that bag from a roll of heavy Kraft paper and left no fingerprints. And who would have done this—undetected and *inside* that building—a requirement with the bag taped together with a paper tape that was automatically wet by the dispensing machine and thus had to be used on the spot? While leaving no fingerprints on that tape, either?

Who could have pulled off all of this and more, as the official evidence requires, and have expected to get away with it, and then gotten away with it?

Very, very few.

The actual evidence, as I go into in great detail in my earlier books, is that Oswald did not and could not have fired that rifle that day. This is lied about officially, but it is that official evidence itself that establishes the truth. It also proves that he could not have been in that window at the time of the shooting.

This raises questions about the so-called investigation and whether those who saw to it that the crime itself would not be investigated were part of the conspiracy to kill.

My belief, based on what I know about the evidence and the investigation and when and by whom the decision not to investigate the crime itself was made, is that although FBI Director J. Edgar Hoover was one of those who did conspire to see to it that Oswald was held to be the lone assassin and that the crime itself would not be investigated, neither he nor the agency was part of the conspiracy to kill.

There is an adequate explanation for Hoover seeing to it that the crime was "solved" immediately by pinning it on Oswald. He had created the public image of being on top of and able to solve any crime. He and the FBI had not the slightest idea who did the job but were not about to admit it. Moreover, the FBI had failed to protect the president. So, they were under great pressure to solve the crime and solve it quickly. Oswald's arrest gave them their "solution."

The official conspiracy not to investigate the crime itself, according to the official records I got from the FBI and the Justice Department, was the idea of Deputy Attorney General Nicholas Katzenbach. He got it right after Oswald was killed and he knew there would be no trial. He conferred with Hoover on this and an FBI record I have states that Hoover agreed with him that very afternoon. (see Appendix 7) It is with this documentation that I begin *Never Again!*

However, in an LBJ phone conversation released in 1994, the extremely hawkish Walt Rostow had the same idea, perhaps a little earlier. These records, for so many years kept secret, make it possible that the idea originated with Rostow and Katzenbach liked it and adopted it as his own.

For the conspiracy to succeed, it was not essential that Oswald be convicted. What was necessary was for the actual shooters not to get caught. This meant they needed enough time to get away. Planting evidence that pointed to Oswald did give them the time to get away. If on real examination the evidence pointing to Oswald did not stack up, as it does not, by the time that could have been established the real assassins were long gone.

The framing of Oswald as the basis for the official solution may have been no more than a convenient accident. That it would hold up in court could not have been expected or depended upon. Had there been a trial based on the actual rather than the misrepresented evidence, Oswald would have been acquitted unless the case was rigged. But by then that would have made no real difference to the successful conspirators.

Jack Ruby eliminated the trial. But that does not mean that Ruby was part of the conspiracy to kill the president. His killing of Oswald was not essential to the conspirators, but it certainly did help them. It is unlikely that anyone who knew him would have trusted Ruby with knowledge of any conspiracy.

Once the shooters got away undetected, the conspiracy was a complete success, and the conspirators were in the clear. Absent a confession, they were in the clear forever. In any event, Johnson became president as soon as Kennedy died.

With the official investigation never having sought to solve the crime, there is nothing else that can be used to reason it through but an examination of motive, means, and opportunity.

Most of those who are alleged to be guilty on the basis of theories only can be easily eliminated, the anti- and pro-Castro Cubans, the Dragon Lady's Vietnamese, or the mafia. Although it is not as easy to dismiss a conspiracy of Texas oil men, several questions raise doubts about their involvement. Would they be willing to run the risk and lose all they had in trying to stop Kennedy from ending their special tax benefits, when Kennedy alone could not do that? It required Congress passing a law to eliminate their special exemption. The only justification for their running such a risk would come only when there was a probability that their exemption would be taken away from them, which simply did not exist.

While this applies to all theorized conspirators, could the Texans alone have seen to it in advance that there would not be any real investigation? That required complete control at least over the local police, the FBI and the Secret Service, control extending to everyone in all those agencies who could have been expected to have been involved in investigating the crime. Could they have been assured in advance that of all the many individuals in these policing agencies there would not be one who would become conscience-stricken and then leak the truth or confess it, and who also would not leave any written records of it or exposing it? Or naming names?

Did they, for all their influence and connections, have the capability of framing Oswald with all that required? Planting all the evidence required first that they have those who could do it and then never say a word about it. While of all those outside the government who have been suspected, they seem to have the best possibility of conceiving it and having it done, but when the planting of all the evidence and knowing all about Oswald is considered, the probability of them having been the conspirators is greatly reduced.

And in addition, would they have been able to see to it in advance that the Navy rigged an autopsy that exculpated them and pinned it on Oswald. Nor could the Texans, the mafia, or any others have arranged for those in the government to conspire not to have any real investigation and then say that Oswald was all alone in the assassination.

For all these prerequisites to be met it appears that all other than the military-industrial-intelligence complex can be eliminated. It also had a much stronger motive than any others for changing national policy, which required getting rid of Kennedy. More than any others, they had means and opportunities others did not have. This is not to say, of course, that it is a proven fact that they conspired to have the president killed. But they more than others meet the traditional motive, means, and opportunity standard. And as we have seen, there were many Strangelovians within their ranks! They are at the least the prime suspects, by the circumstantial evidence involving motive, means, and opportunity. It strongly suggests their guilt.

CHAPTER 11

AN "IRREVERSIBLE CHAIN OF EVENTS" AND "HOOVER TO THE RESCUE"

The Fall 1994 issue of the *American Prospect* carried an article entitled, "Did the U.S. Military Plan a Nuclear First Strike for 1963?" by Heather A. Purcell and James K. Galbraith.[1] Though not directly stated by them, their scholarly and thoroughly documented study firmly establishes that the military-industrial-intelligence complex had a strong motive to assassinate President Kennedy.

They draw on twenty-one authoritative sources, including Reeves's *President Kennedy*, quoted above regarding SIOP-62. They add breadth and depth to Reeves's treatment of that frightening plan. In dealing with their subject chronologically they actually build to the assassination. They make it ever starker that the Kennedy presidency that ended with his assassination was one in which he somehow frustrated the determined military plan to implement that SIOP, which would have meant the utter ruin of the world. Although thoroughly frightened by it and lacking the control civilians believed their president had exclusively over nuclear war, Kennedy somehow managed to prevent, in the phrase of the day, "mutually assured destruction."

In the course of doing this, they recall what attracted some attention in 1970, Robert Kennedy's fear expressed to the Russian ambassador at the time of the Cuba Missile Crisis, that the military would overthrow Kennedy and take power. That did get a little attention when its source, Nikita Khrushchev's *Khrushchev Remembers*, was published. (1970) That was eight years after that crisis in which John Kennedy kept his military from using it to begin a war that would devastate the world. In 1970, very few were aware of the terror that must have been in the minds of the Kennedys during that crisis when Robert Kennedy went to see Anatoly Dobrynin at the peak of that crisis. There is little doubt that what Purcell and Galbraith quote from it accurately reflects Robert Kennedy's meeting with Dobrynin:

> Even though the president himself is very much against starting a war over Cuba, an irreversible chain of events could occur against his will. . . . If the situation continues for much longer, the president is not sure that the military will not overthrow him and seize power. The American military could get out of control.[2]

That Purcell and Galbraith do not quote this until the very end of their lengthy study rather than treating it when they deal with 1962, makes it part of the unintended case of motive in the assassination. They follow it with a list of military endeavors that could have triggered the nuclear war that Kennedy prevented "the last year of his life."

They report that when Johnson assumed the Presidency he was "uneasy over the swirling rumors connecting Lee Harvey Oswald, falsely as we know, to the KGB." Here they greatly magnify the 40 million lives that could be lost which Earl Warren told his staff about. They quote journalist David Wise "hearing Johnson tell in late 1963 of recruiting Warren" that "possibly a hundred million lives were at stake here. . . ."[3]

Before they get to this end of their study, Purcell and Galbraith do make it clear that the military did plan for a nuclear attack on the USSR in 1963 and that John Kennedy prevented it. And that is a motive for getting rid of Kennedy, if not by overthrowing him, by assassinating him.

They trace this military plan for a nuclear attack back to its 1957 beginning. There is no indication of President Eisenhower's involvement, or even knowledge of it. That was when he was recovering from a heart attack. The planning was "for a preemptive nuclear strike against the USSR . . . based on our growing lead in land-based missiles," which was the SIOP approach presented to JFK in 1961 when he was green in the Presidency and recovering from the Bay of Pigs disaster. What was presented to him was that by 1963 we would have an "outright missile superiority." This presentation took place at the July 20 meeting of the National Security Council. They reproduce for the first time a declassified "EYES ONLY" memo from the LBJ Library on that meeting. Its second sentence reads: "General Lemnitzer stated that the assumption of this year's study was a surprise attack in late 1963, preceded by a period of heightened tensions." General Lyman Lemnitzer was then the chairman of the Joint Chiefs of Staff. He was not predicting an attack by the USSR. He did not project that attack for December of 1962 "because the United States would have too few missiles" then.

This formerly "EYES ONLY" memo Purcell and Galbraith expose for the first time concluded with Kennedy ordering them all to keep their mouths clamped shut: "The president directed that no member in attendance at the meeting disclose even the subject of that meeting."

In reporting that Kennedy was "displeased," Purcell and Galbraith quote from Arthur Schlesinger Jr.'s, *Robert Kennedy and His Times*,

> that President Kennedy received this annual doomsday briefing analyzing the chances of nuclear war. An Air Force General presented it, said Roswell Gilpatric, the deputy secretary of defense, 'as though it were for a kindergarten class'. . . Finally Kennedy got up and walked out in the middle of it, and that was the end of it. We never had another one.

McGeorge Bundy, Kennedy's National Security chairman, in writing about it, also used Dean Rusk's quotation of what the president said, cited above, "And we call ourselves the human race," to reflect the impact of the military's proposal on the president.

They also refer to "numerous other accounts" saying that "All agree on Kennedy's reaction." Among those they quote is Kennedy's White House counsel and chief speech writer Theodore Sorensen. And they add this from Rusk:

> That briefing confirmed, however, the harsh facts [Kennedy] already knew: (1) that neither the Soviet Union nor the United States could 'win' in any rational sense of the word; (2) that, except to deter an all-out Soviet attack, our threat of 'massive retaliation' to every Communist move was no longer credible, now that it invited our own destruction; and (3) that a policy of 'preemptive first strike' or 'preventive war' was no longer open to either side, inasmuch as even a surprise missile attack would trigger, before those missiles reached their targets, a devastating retaliation that neither country could risk or accept.

Rusk did not spell out what the problem of a "stable deterrent" was in 1961. Purcell and Galbraith say it was not that we did not have enough missiles, rather it was "the need for the Soviets to develop sufficient effective ICBM (and submarine) forces to deter us. That is an ugly and unavoidable fact." A page later they quote Rusk's comments that appear almost anguished, and for which his own account of the meeting gives no apparent rationale:

> . . . the United States has never renounced possible first use of nuclear weapons. I personally think the United States is committed to a second strike only, after we have received nuclear weapons on our soil. Under no circumstances would I have participated in an order to launch a first strike, with the possible exception of a massive conventional attack on Western Europe.

In quoting from a paper entitled "Nuclear Strategy in the Berlin Crisis," prepared for the president by the economist Thomas C. Schelling, Purcell and Galbraith say Schelling "advocated centralization of the control of nuclear weapons in the hands of the president," where most of us believed it always had been, as a "means of preventing any use by anyone not specifically authorized. . . ." His concern was that "the diffuse character of nuclear command and control in 1961 did not assure that the president in fact enjoyed the full authority over the bomb which most Americans assumed was the case. Establishing such a control became a priority for Kennedy in the months that followed."

One of Kennedy's concerns was that "miscommunication could rain down more devastation in several hours than had been wrought in all the wars in human history."[4] The full magnitude of this evaluation of the impending devastation may be impossible to appreciate, but when it is remembered that aside from all military losses on both sides and all the civilians who were killed during World War II, the Soviets alone lost 20 million people and Hitler slaughtered 6 million Jews.

Although by then the United States was "far ahead in the arms race," which it should be noted has been a cause of our increasing national debt, "the military continued to press for a rapid build-up of strategic missiles. Curtis LeMay had asked for at least 2400 Minutemen; Thomas Power of the Strategic Air Command had asked for 10,000. All were to be unleashed," as we saw in Reeves's reporting of that SIOP, "in a single paroxysm of mass annihilation, that SIOP, or Single Integrated Operational Plan . . . a recipe for blowing up the world."[5]

They quote McGeorge Bundy, Kennedy's National Security chief, as warning him on July 7, 1961, that the plan is so rigid it "may leave you with very little choice as to how you face the moment of thermonuclear truth. . . . In essence the current plan calls for shooting off everything in one shot. . . ."

"Defense Secretary McNamara and Kennedy did impose a limit of 1,000 Minuteman missiles, thus angering the Joint Chiefs, . . ." Purcell and Galbraith wrote, adding that "Kennedy also launched efforts to gain operational control of the nuclear force. . . ." They then quote Vice President Johnson's military aide Howard Burris on "the military's drive for a vast U.S. nuclear build-up despite the fact that America was already far ahead, and the resistance from JFK and McNamara." What Kennedy had been told gave him only a "glimpse of the fact that our 'nuclear superiority was so complete' as to make a first nuclear strike successful."

But despite its incompleteness, it was enough to alert "Kennedy to a danger. American nuclear superiority might be so complete that rogue elements from the military and intelligence forces, seeking to precipitate an American first strike might not feel deterred by Soviet retaliation. . . ." And this "when the president could not be sure of his control over the nuclear button."

They then quote Khrushchev, as I did earlier, to portray the fear, the horror that dominated and terrified the Kennedy brothers, who gave no other overt indication of it. The authors characterize the period from the Cuba missile crisis to the assassination and just after it as "critical to the survival of the world."

As they conclude, they sum up Kennedy's "repeated initiatives to settle conflicts and reduce tensions." They refer to "the normalization of Berlin, the withdrawal of missiles from Turkey, the no-invasion pledge on Cuba and the effort, only partially effective, to end the covert campaign (OP/MONGOOSE) against Castro, the test-ban treaty and . . . the order in October 1963 to begin a phased withdrawal from Vietnam." Their list is far from complete; they do not include his cutting of military excesses, especially those that were unneeded and dangerous. "By November 1963 (which is to say, by the time Kennedy was assassinated) the potential for 'heightened tensions' leading to uncontrollable pressures to strike had indeed been reduced."

This in every particular is the precise opposite of what the military wanted so much and strove for so hard in its concept of the country's need and of true patriotism, as they understood it. Purcell and Galbraith repeat that: "Civilian control of nuclear forces was no sure thing in 1961, . . ." because the military had contrived for that to be the reality. Their analysis is that by the time he was assassinated, Kennedy had succeeded in getting the out-of-control Strangeloves who were mostly in the military largely under control. What then were the choices of these Strangelovian super-patriots who believed so sincerely that they best understood the nation's needs, and they alone knew how to meet them? And in their minds, their president had proven beyond question that he did not understand and that he was determined to prevent their assertion of their patriotism and their dedication to country.

They had two choices. They could accept defeat in their determined effort that began in 1957 to wipe out the USSR, and with it much of Europe and Asia, as well as their coming defeat in Southeast Asia. Or they could refuse to accept defeat and eliminate the cause. This they could not do in the next year's election. Kennedy had already achieved great personal popularity. It had begun with his acceptance of responsibility for the disaster they created at the Bay of Pigs and his refusal to let them extend it to the beginning of a war that was built into the plan they gave him when he had no choice but to accept it. And it had continued to grow. There was also the near certainty that with Barry Goldwater the likely nominee of the Republicans, Kennedy's electoral victory was assured.

They could be the true patriots they believed they were, the experts who saw and understood what the young upstart president neither saw nor understood as they did, and eliminate him. There were no other forces with this motive, none even close to it, none with their dedication, and none with their power and influence, not to mention their ability to scare the life out of those who might question them.

As I said to begin with, this is not proof that they were behind the assassination. But it does answer the primary question that arises with respect to the three elements of circumstantial evidence. They more than any others had the intensity of motive and a record of attempts to achieve the same result by other means. No others even came close to that intensity of motive.

It should not be assumed that our Dr. Strangeloves were incapable of contemplating the killing of millions of innocent people or jeopardizing the lives of millions of Americans in their Cold War insanities, insanities that included the murder of individual Americans.

Consider the case of the CIA's killing of an Army scientist which was before the House Government Operations Committee, along with experiments on millions of unwitting Americans, mostly by the Army. Frank Olson was an Army scientist who was part of a CIA cell at Fort Detrick in Frederick, Maryland. In one of their earliest experiments in mind-control and mind-bending, a major CIA Cold War project, they did kill Olson, father of three young children and a much-liked, sincere man and a fine scientist. My initial interest in this came from a CIA memo for the Warren

Commission. In it the CIA evaluated, as part of a Manchurian-candidate Cold War and irrational assessment of Oswald, that in this despicable toying with human minds we were five years ahead of the Soviets. Back in the 1950s, the CIA had killed Olson but there is no reference to that in this memo or in any other known record. It was only after many years, however, after the family got a lawyer and was going to sue the CIA, that it admitted that Olson had been killed by an overdose of LSD that the agency claimed was entirely accidental. The CIA claimed that Olson had killed himself. In an out-of-court settlement it gave his wife, Alice Wicks Olson, the entirely inadequate sum of $750,000, with which to raise and educate the three children. The CIA and the Army had even ruled that Olson's death, their murder of him in their experiments, was not service connected.

The sons had reason to believe that their father was killed because he had become disenchanted with the germ-warfare work he was doing for the CIA while an Army employee, that his disenchantment made him a "security risk" to the CIA, and that it killed him to eliminate that risk.[6]

Those who have not made detailed studies of our spookeries may find it hard to believe that the CIA actually did murder people. Naturally, it and other spookeries do not ordinarily advertise their murders. But the fact is such abuse was confirmed when the CIA called its former officer, John Clement Hart, back from retirement to study the records of its abuse of the defected KGB official, Yuri Nosenko. Nosenko told the FBI what the CIA did not want believed about Oswald, that the KGB suspected he was an American "sleeper" agent and that he also was anti-Soviet and a lousy shot. Hart then testified to the House Select Committee in 1978. He attested to finding handwritten records in which a CIA official deliberated about ways of getting rid of Nosenko, destroying his credibility, or both. Hart testified that on one extreme, consideration was given to driving Nosenko insane. The CIA's abuse of Nosenko for three years would have done that to most people. On the other extreme, the plan considered was flying Nosenko over the ocean and throwing him in.[7]

That same day the local papers quoted the testimony of the assistant comptroller general of the General Accounting Office. He testified, "it's clear that this research continues. . . ." In the partial account of the past of this experimenting with living Americans by the CIA and the Army, it is reported that: "Between 1940 and 1974, experiments were performed on at least a half-million individuals, including 210,000 exposed to radiation. . . . In addition, Army researchers sprayed zinc cadmium sulfide—a chemical now associated with cancer—over more than 200 cities . . . which included Minneapolis, St. Louis, Detroit and Springfield, Ill." It earlier disclosed that other such experiments with living Americans including the dousing with germs of San Francisco and the subways of several large cities. Moreover, "the GAO found that some 100 people received LSD at five universities through tests financed by the Air Force." A few other such so-called "tests" on our own people by the Army here and abroad did receive attention, some in the courts, some on television.[8]

Or, as John Kennedy said when he walked out on the briefing on how the military was going to wipe out a major part of the world with a nuclear attack which he then could neither prevent nor control, "And we call ourselves the human race."

Millions of Americans had their lives and health experimented with by the military and the CIA without their permission being sought or obtained. An incalculably large number of them suffered, never learning the cause. Many lives were ruined. Some lives, like that of Frank Olson, were taken, all in the name of "national security."

There is also no way of knowing how many killings the CIA's Aldrich Ames was responsible for, but from the available information it is quite a few, all of whom were CIA spies or sources. The CIA drizzled out as little as it thought it could get away with and then saw to it that all of its many officers, who were so indifferent and made it possible, got away with it. That the CIA's only releases of information understated this enormously was reported by the Senate Intelligence Committee on November 2, 1994.

As the story by Walter Pincus in the next day's *Washington Post* begins, ". . . Ames has admitted to betraying more than 100 U.S. and allied government intelligence operations." The Committee report also says," Pincus continued, "the former CIA officer knew about several hundred other operations that he may have passed to Moscow. . . ." To protect himself, Ames first turned in "several KGB agents working for the United States . . . in order to make sure they did not turn him in." Asked by the committee's Senator Dennis DeConcini, "did you identify the two KGB people in the (USSR's Washington) embassy [working for the CIA]?" Ames responded, "In the embassy? Yes." Asked "did it occur to you that they might be killed?" Ames replied, "Yes, it did."[9]

There is no way of knowing how many deaths Ames was responsible for. There were so many who disappeared and whose disappearance was known to intelligence agencies. The number was so great it scared Ames himself to the point where he complained about it to the KGB. He feared it might lead to his exposure.

As the Olson and Ames cases illustrate—and they are just illustrations, not by any means a full accounting, which there can never be—killing is not unknown to the CIA as an institution or to its people. They do go in for cold-blooded murder. We know of many examples, like trying to figure out how to kill Nosenko, who in fact was a prime intelligence coup for the CIA, even though its crazies refused to believe it. Or that Miami case of dropping people into the sea from a chopper. There were many reports of the CIA doing that in Vietnam to those it suspected were Vietcong. And then, of course, there are all those plots against Castro and other heads of state.

Is there then any reason to believe that with this as their concept of patriotism, those in the CIA would not have considered getting rid of a president who opposed what it was up to and its policies in Vietnam and elsewhere?

The CIA and its people are no less patriotic than those at the top in our military. The military, along with the CIA, were cavalier in planning a nuclear attack that would have resulted in millions of deaths here and abroad. And when they could experiment with living Americans and even kill some for the sake of "national security," is there anything of which they are not capable? Including disposing of the one man who stood in their way, the one man who frustrated their plans for a disastrous nuclear attack in their concept of what our "national security" required of them.

When this is considered along with what the military did in taking control of the autopsy and seeing to it that that autopsy was incompetent, then lying and repeatedly committing perjury about it, the possibility of their involvement in the assassination of JFK cannot be easily dismissed. No others had a motive equal to this.

Hoover to the rescue?

At the moment of the assassination and for a short time thereafter, the fate of this country and the world was in question. In the midst of all this Strangelovian lunacy, the world was spared by the lunacy of the paranoid and political FBI Director J. Edgar Hoover.

Had the Texas-based 112th Army intelligence unit not told the Dallas police immediately that Oswald had defected to the Soviets and was a Red,[10] which in a short time would have emerged anyway, the world might not have survived.

Although it escaped any public comment and is little known, the vaunted head of the FBI got hysterical as soon as he heard that JFK had been assassinated. For at least a week his hysteria was reflected in virtuoso ignorance and confusion about the facts his own FBI knew. Anxious for the new president to believe that, as usual, he was on top of everything, he kept giving Johnson misinformation, some so ignorant it seems impossible that the man who had headed the FBI for forty years from its inception could have spoken so stupidly. Virtually the only thing he had straight was spelling Oswald's name. As records not still suppressed indicate, Hoover's hysteria, paranoia, and detachment from reality were still running full-tilt a week after the assassination.

It was David Wrone who put the case of Hoover's hysteria together from its own records, which I had obtained in FOIA lawsuits. And it was Wrone who first saw that in the short period after the assassination Hoover may have saved the world without the remotest notion that he had.

As I read my way through the quarter of a million JFK assassination records, which I'd gotten through a series of FOIA lawsuits that extended for more than a decade, while keeping those records exactly as I got them for history's record, I had extra copies made of some for special filing in what I called my "subject" file. In going over this subject file and making copies for his own work and teaching, Wrone noticed how wild Hoover appeared to be. This led him to set up a separate file of FBI records he called "Hoover's Hysteria."

According to recorded phone conversations disclosed in 1994, on November 29, 1963, a week after the assassination and the day Johnson appointed the Warren Commission, Hoover gave LBJ an account of the new and greater magic he attributed to the bullet which came to be known as the magic bullet, and not without cause! In the commission's evidence it is Exhibit 399. Hoover told Johnson it had hit President Kennedy's head and then fell out and was recovered. In the official story there was but one shot to the president's head and it exploded and blew out a major part of the right side of the president's head, hitting bone as it entered and as it left.

Well before that Hoover phone conversation with Johnson, the FBI lab had completed its examination of that bullet. It examined the bullet microscopically and did a spectrographic analysis of it. It did not test the bullet to determine whether it held any traces of human tissue or blood.[11] Without question, and in all the many test firings, bullets bear the marks of any bones they hit. This bullet is said to have demolished bones. Yet the FBI testified that it was virtually unmutilated, having no marks, none from hitting any bone.

Although the FBI and the commission do not agree on the career each imputed to this bullet, both agree that it did not hit the president's head and did cause a non-fatal injury to his body. So, a week after the assassination, Hoover told President Johnson that it had hit President Kennedy in his head and after exploding in his head fell out of it intact and in virtually pristine condition with not a single bone mark on it! So not only did Hoover have the history of that super-magical bullet all twisted and entirely wrong, what he told Johnson about it was absolutely impossible. Yet Hoover had the results of his own lab's testing of that bullet the day after the assassination and on that day signed a report on his lab's work he sent to the Dallas police.

Here was Hoover, who had spent forty years heading the FBI, convincing the media and the people that his was the best of such agencies and he the best of all possible heads of any of them; but when the president was killed, for all the FBI's intelligence operations and reputation of being on top of everything, he was caught by surprise. They knew almost immediately that they did not really know what had happened, except that the president had been assassinated. Hoover knew he could not possibly admit that and retain his reputation and that of the FBI.

It was when he learned very shortly after Oswald was arrested by the Dallas police that they had also identified him as a "Red," that Hoover at once faced a serious problem and a solution to that serious problem. He joined the Dallas police in labeling Oswald a Red, but he added—no doubt an instant vision if not instant realization of what his reputation and that of his FBI required—that Oswald had acted entirely alone. No conspiracy. No KGB. No Soviet involvement. Yet, ironically, at the same time the FBI captioned its records on this in terms of a conspiracy involving the USSR, Cuba, or both.

Hoover let it be known the day of the assassination that Lee Harvey Oswald was a "commie" who acted alone. So, from the very day of the assassination, government officials knew that Hoover had decided that there had been no conspiracy. Had he admitted that there had been a conspiracy, he would have had to acknowledge what would have reflected badly on him and the FBI. But the FBI could not be blamed for not penetrating a single man, so it could not be faulted for not knowing about the assassination in advance because it allegedly was the act of a lone nut.

In fact, Hoover later boasted about his instant vision the very day of the assassination when he was interviewed by William Manchester for his book, *The Death of a President.*[12] His then number four man, Cartha DeLoach, was his notetaker. DeLoach set this forth in his lengthy typed account of that interview. (see Appendix 8)

With all those Strangelovians so anxious to nuclear bomb the hell out of the USSR and other countries for no legitimate reason and with Oswald labeled as a Red, they had their excuse. But before they could do anything, Hoover let it be known that the USSR was not behind the assassination because Oswald had acted alone. That eliminated any possible justification for launching all those thousands of nuclear bombs and starting World War III, which, as we have seen, was the military's most ardent desire.

It is by his declaration that there had been no conspiracy before he knew anything really factual about the assassination at all, that the USSR was not behind it, that Hoover may well have saved the world from its worst disaster. Hoover was in such haste to protect himself and his FBI from criticism, he nullified the military's excuse for "SIOP-sing" much of the world into oblivion before the military could get together and decide to seize the opportunity the assassination provided them.

There is no way of knowing whether the military did see the assassination as a means of implementing the devastation it had planned for that very time or whether any at the top in the military deliberated using it as an excuse, as justification for their loosing all that destruction laid out in their SIOP-62. All that can be said is that the assassination did provide what they could have used to justify it, to make it appear to be necessary.

Whether or not the military did see this possibility, the fact remains that of all those who can be believed to have wanted the president eliminated, and with that eliminate his policies with which the military had such a violent disagreement, the military had by far the strongest motive, not to mention of course the means and opportunity, in the assassination.

We may never know because, as previously mentioned, there was a well-documented government conspiracy not to investigate the crime itself that was agreed to as soon as Oswald was killed and it was known there would be no trial. It also was another official decision that there was no "Red" conspiracy.

It must not be forgotten that it was at that very moment—when it knew there would be no trial because Oswald had been killed—that the Navy destroyed the autopsy report prepared in the expectation it would have to survive examination at trial. The Navy then prepared and substituted for the destroyed original autopsy report the misbegotten travesty of an autopsy report it knew would not be examined and cross-examined at any public trial. This substitute Navy autopsy report, supported by Navy perjury, was the basis for the knowingly false official "solution" that Oswald was the lone assassin, that there had not been any conspiracy to kill the president, when in fact all of the official evidence shows that he was killed by a conspiracy, a conspiracy for which the military had the strongest and most compelling of motives.

CHAPTER 12

"THE POLITICS OF LYING" AND "THE PRESS BOX MENTALITY"

The government lied to us when our president was killed. It intentionally lied and continues to lie about the assassination and its own non-investigation of it. At the same time, it improperly interferes with those who criticize it. This is not new. It is well known and established by publicly available evidence. But, for whatever reason, the news media does not deem it news worth reporting.

That the assassination was a great subversion, one in which the course of history was radically altered, is never mentioned by the media, thus leaving the people unaware of its true significance. That it was a coup d'état—not just a murder—is also apparently not news to the media; in more than thirty years it has not yet so informed the people, the people who in our system of freedom through self-government are supposed to be the controlling force.

When the president was assassinated and his assassination was supposedly investigated by the government that replaced his, the media did not meet its obligations. Instead of a critical examination of the official evidence, it accepted the lies officials told about it. This is well documented in all books, all of which rely on a critical examination of that evidence.

How can our system of government work absent an electorate adequately informed by the media?

Whether or not the media helped the assassins get away with their coup, the media did see to it that the government got away with a "white-wash" and "cover up" of the coup. That, too, is a great subversion. It is one that endangered and still endangers us and our democratic system. It is another step toward an authoritarian society, a step in addition to the one that resulted from the assassination and from the de facto government conspiracy not to investigate the crime itself, as I prove in my *Never Again!* with long secret records I obtained through lawsuits I filed under the Freedom of Information Act.

All of this and more was made possible by the official secrecy that is the curse of freedom and a democratic society. The official secrecy, however, does not exonerate the media of its responsibility. Nothing in this book is based on secrets; it is all public information, more readily available to the media than to me, an aged and infirm octogenarian. Yet for all its wealth, power, and resources, for all its highly educated and experienced reporters, editors, and pundits, none of this readily available information has been mentioned by the media. It has not troubled the people with the knowledge that their freedom, their democratic system, was and is endangered by this assassination that was a coup, that the coup was protected by the government, and that this made the government itself part of the threat to freedom and to democracy.

Lyndon Johnson became president as a consequence of the assassination. When he appointed a commission of inquiry, he gave it a political composition that is without precedent in American history. That it was unprecedented in this way was patently obvious, but the media did not question or even mention it. So, again, ordinary citizens had little opportunity to understand that or its meaning.

Under our political system the party in power, put there by the people, has the responsibility that goes with that power. This means it typically constitutes the majority on all appointive bodies, unless otherwise specified by law. But in appointing his commission to investigate the assassination that made him president, Johnson gave the other party, the Republicans, the majority on the commission and thus responsibility for what that commission decided and reported. We do not know why Johnson did this; he apparently left behind no record of his motive.

Of the seven members Johnson appointed to the commission, five were Republicans. This alone is without precedent in our history. Johnson appointed two from the Democratic Party who were not friends of the assassinated president and in fact strongly opposed many of his policies.

Because most of these seven were conservative or very conservative in their views and records and most were Republican, conservatives and Republicans would be unlikely to object to what the commission reported. On the other hand, Johnson effectively immobilized the liberals, especially of the East Coast intellectual community, by selecting liberal Republican Chief Justice Earl Warren as Commission Chairman.

In short, by his departure from precedent, Johnson saw to it that whatever the commission would conclude and report would likely be accepted.

What is almost entirely unknown, but what I prove at the very beginning of *Never Again!* and will discuss below, is that there is little question that Johnson appears to have approved the de facto government conspiracy not to investigate the crime and did so five days before he appointed his commission, only two days after the assassination.

I do not mean, nor do I believe, that Johnson himself was involved in the assassination. He was its beneficiary and that alone created suspicions; but that he was the beneficiary does not mean that he was party to it. I know of no official evidence justifying this suspicion and I know of no evidence of any kind made public by anyone at all—and I mean evidence, not conjecture—that justifies this suspicion.

Why he departed from the practice dating from our nation's founding is a legitimate question. The most obvious answer, apart from Johnson having been party to the conspiracy, is that he wanted the country to be satisfied and wanted to preserve tranquility.

Before he appointed his commission, he knew what the FBI would conclude in response to his charge to it—within a few hours of the assassination—to investigate and report on the crime. J. Edgar Hoover kept him fully informed on what the FBI had concluded and what it would say in its report. Even though Hoover never got his "facts" straight, Johnson knew the FBI believed that Oswald was the lone assassin. Transcripts of their telephone conversations and records the FBI disclosed to me prove this beyond question. Hoover had decided immediately that Oswald was the lone assassin. As we have seen, he reached this determination the afternoon of the crime, as soon as he got the first report that Oswald was allegedly some kind of "Red." That this was false made no difference to Hoover. Johnson knew that nobody in political life could expect to survive contradicting Hoover. So Johnson knew that his commission would have no option but to accept the conclusion Hoover had arrived at even before the commission had been appointed.

The commission itself confirmed this in one of its first executive sessions, an emergency session called after the end of the working day on January 22, 1964. That was before the commission was fully organized and before it held its first hearing.

The failure of the media to report or comment on the unprecedented composition of this Presidential Commission meant that the people had no way of knowing that the official investigation of the assassination from the very outset was rigged. The media thus served not as an objective source of information in this profound crisis, but instead served as an adjunct of government, reporting on its actions, no matter how wrong, as the best of possible practices in the best of possible worlds.

When the commission decided to proceed in complete secrecy, there was not a peep of protest from the media. Had the media protested, the commission might have been forced to hold its hearings in the traditional American way, in public, and would not have been able to foist its fraudulent conclusions off on the trusting public.

Had Oswald lived, there would have been a trial which would have been entirely public, and the media would have fought vigorously for a seat in the crowded courtroom. The media's acceptance of total secrecy in the hearings of the investigation of the assassination of the president, the most terrible and subversive of crimes in a country like ours, was highly unusual. One need only look at media behavior in the O. J. Simpson case when it went to court to prevent even the slightest bit of secrecy in a trial that had not yet begun. The 1994 case involved the prominent personality, TV telecaster, and hall-of-fame football hero, O. J. Simpson, who was accused by the Los Angeles police of killing his estranged wife and her friend. Any effort by the judge in this case to curb media access or curtail broadcast of the trial to ensure the possibility of a fair trial was met with media outrage. Yet it remained silent in face of the assassination of the president. It did not even ask why there was a need for secrecy. There was, of course, no such need; that secrecy could only have been for dishonest purposes. Thus, the commission was able to perpetrate the fraud it intended to perpetrate, as its own records which I obtained and published prove. The media ignored those records, too. Had the media acted as it traditionally had, all subsequent history might have been very different.

Not only did this commission proceed entirely in secret, it classified even the verbatim stenographic transcripts of all the testimony taken in its hearings—what it intended to publish and did publish! This meant that the media had no access to any of the testimony before the commission published all of it at one time a year after the assassination. Again, there was no media complaint about that, either.

The commission had no classification authority, as is clear in the documents that created it. This also was never mentioned nor protested by the media. This classification of testimony prevented the media, which had not been allowed to cover the hearings, from studying and reporting on the testimony that had been taken in secret and kept secret from it and from the people.

What the media did not know but could have learned if it had regarded the assassination of the president and its official investigations as at least as important as a sensational celebrity murder trial is that the commission held its executive sessions in such secrecy it barred its own staff from them! And then, without any authority to do so, it classified all those transcripts, TOP SECRET.

So, protected by improper and entirely unnecessary and unjustified secrecy, the commission prepared and issued its report. That report is one that cannot survive any critical examination. Given three days to read and prepare to report on it, instead of subjecting it to critical examination, the media went into ecstasies over it. There was no criticism at all; it was hailed as the best of possible reports with certain answers to all questions. So much did the media constitute itself an arm of government, the propaganda arm, the Associated Press, which serves most of the nation's media and much of that of the rest of the world, actually used as its major story on the release of that report its first chapter titled "Summary and Conclusions."

The media had previously reported on evidence that refuted the entire report, but apparently did not recall that report or ask questions about it. For example, the commission concluded that Oswald, the lone assassin, fired all the shots and fired them from above and behind the president. But at the press conference minutes after the president was pronounced dead, the Dallas doctors, who had sought to treat and who had examined the president in the Parkland Hospital emergency room, stated three times that the president had been shot from the front. The surgeon who made these statements was backed up by the hospital's chief of neurological surgery. Virtually every paper in the country printed this. It was part of the Associated Press's story. The White House disclosed the official transcript of that press conference promptly. The doctors who reported that the president's wound in the front of his neck was an entrance wound were the only doctors who saw that wound before it was altered by their emergency procedures.

The media knew that the FBI had filed its supposedly definitive report on its investigation of the assassination that had been ordered by Johnson prior to the creation of the Warren Commission. Had the media asked to see that FBI report, something that would be normal in reporting, it would have learned that the report had been classified and was withheld from the media and the public. Withholding the official FBI report on the murder of the president would normally be considered newsworthy, yet the media did not report it. Had the media pressed the issue and had been able to see that report, it would have discovered that the FBI and the Warren Commission disagreed radically on their accounts of the assassination. Both could not have been right. (In fact, neither was.) Both the FBI and the commission agreed that only three shots were fired.[1] The FBI report claimed that "Two bullets struck President Kennedy, and one wounded Governor Connally."[2] The FBI report makes no mention of the shot that had missed and struck a curbstone, wounding a bystander. However, by the time the commission was putting together its version, that missed shot had become public knowledge, requiring that it account for all wounds with two bullets in order to stick to its "lone assassin" theory. This gave rise to the so-called "single-bullet theory." That single, nearly pristine bullet, supposedly found on a stretcher at Parkland Hospital, caused all the non-fatal wounds in Kennedy and Connally according to the Warren Commission. In the FBI's account, that bullet, CE 399, wounded only the president before finding its way to that hospital stretcher.

Furthermore, if the media had asked to see that FBI report that is the commission's first record in its numbered files, it would have found in it an FBI picture of the front of the president's shirt collar that proves beyond question that no bullet went through it, as is claimed by the commission in its single-bullet theory, essential to maintaining that there was no conspiracy.

Why should the media have demanded to see the FBI report? Because the commission's report attributes still another magical property to that bullet, that it left no bullet traces on the front of the president's shirt or his tie while depositing them on the back of his shirt and his jacket. And this the media also did not report.

I have written many books on what the official evidence shows and means. But what was obvious to one man was not obvious to the many, many thousands of reporters, editors, and columnists of our media, not because they also sought the truth and disagreed with me, but because they did not seek the truth that is in those records, but rather accepted and praised the report, "the official mythology," in Orwell's words.

Thus, because the media failed itself and the public, the "official mythology" became the official fact that remains unquestioned by the media after more than thirty-one years as I write this. How was all of this possible? How could the "official mythology" become and remain official fact? How could the media continue with this fiction?

It is not because it was completely controlled by the government that the media fell into lockstep with the government and thus failed itself and the country in not meeting and serving its essential and traditional role. It was, instead, because of official secrecy and the media's uncomplaining acceptance of that official secrecy at the time of the assassination and throughout the life of the commission. It was not until two months after the report was released that the commission released the officially estimated ten million words of its appendix of testimony and exhibits, the supposed back stopping of its report. Before release to the general public, the media had only five days in which to understand and report on ten million words in twenty-six large volumes. It did not complain.

If the media had done what it should have done, it would have learned—and could not have avoided learning—that the assassination was the product of a conspiracy. When I say that the assassination was the product of a conspiracy, I am not engaging in any kind of theorizing. The official facts that I brought to light, beginning in my first book, completed in mid-February 1965, leave no question that the crime was beyond the capability of any one person and was thus a conspiracy. As previously noted, this has never been contradicted by the government or by anyone else. There is no refutation of it in any of the hundreds of thousands of pages of government records I obtained through those FOIA lawsuits. That the assassination of the president was by a conspiracy is beyond question in the misrepresented official evidence itself.

Everything I have used, beginning with those twenty-six volumes of testimony and exhibits which are supposed to prove the validity of the report, additional files that the commission did not publish, records I rescued through FOIA lawsuits, is evidence that the media could have had and did not want—official evidence, all available in my previous books.

In this book, in addressing circumstantial evidence as lawyers do, I have used in addition what those in official positions learned in the exercise of their official responsibilities to bring together some of this circumstantial evidence. These are official sources too. All of this and more was more readily accessible to the media than to me. Here, I bring together for the first time, I re-emphasize, with nothing secret, nothing private at all, only what was always readily accessible to the media. It should also be noted that the media is better equipped to do this than I am in that it can draw on official and other sources that are not available to me.

That they failed by promoting only the official mythology represents a greater danger to us than the media in authoritarian societies of both extremes. At least people in those societies know their media is the voice of the government and are, consequently, skeptical of what it reports. But we believe that from the first days of our nation, the press has been independent of and beyond interference by the government. We have then no reason to believe that the media is for all practical purposes an arm of an errant government on such momentous questions as those stemming from the assassinations and their investigations.

Popular mistrust of both government and media has been widespread since John Kennedy was assassinated. In the late 1960s, I spoke to many audiences, in person and on the radio and TV, from one end of the country to the other. I have received more than twenty thousand letters and innumerable phone calls from strangers. What stands out in these calls and letters is that the assassinations and how the government and the media treated them is the greatest single cause of popular mistrust. I believe that the JFK assassination is the second greatest cause of this permeating mistrust over those years, the first being Vietnam.

The child who wrote to me that John Kennedy "left us something," spoke for many who have written and phoned me. Despite the revisionist rewriting of our history, love, respect, and appreciation of John F. Kennedy as president is clear in those expressions to me, especially from those who tell me they were not yet born or were very young when he was assassinated. Most older Americans never did believe the official mythology.

These people long for the answer denied them by officialdom at the time of the assassination and ever since then. I read and hear it every day. The people are disillusioned with their media because of its failure to do as we have always expected it to do: Report truthfully and honestly to us. They long for an answer that cannot be given, an answer made impossible by that official conspiracy hatched as soon as it was known that Oswald had been killed and thus there would be no trial.

This is what makes it necessary, in any effort to seek an answer, to employ the traditional lawyer's approach when there is only circumstantial evidence, an answer based on motive, means, and opportunity. It is that or nothing.

David Wise's *The Politics of Lying* offers insight that can help us understand both the official secrecy and official lying as well as the media's acceptance of it that made this all possible. Official secrecy means "national security" secrecy, the government secrecy that has its roots in the Cold War and its mentality. It is not secrecy necessary to keep the nation secure, but secrecy necessary to keep essential knowledge from the people to whom the government is supposed to be accountable. To the extent that official secrecy comes to dominate, to that extent government becomes more authoritarian and less democratic. It is the secrecy that kept from the American public the military's policies that might have resulted in nuclear holocaust had Kennedy not stopped them, policies that were the responsibility of the president not the military. It is the secrecy used to prosecute Daniel Ellsberg for leaking The Pentagon Papers and the newspapers that published excerpts from them. Their publication resulted in no harm to our national security. It is the secrecy that the CIA attempted to codify in US law to criminalize those who tell government secrets, as Wise brings to light in his chapter "Secrecy, National Security and the Press."[3]

Writing of the Pentagon Papers case, Wise quotes from an earlier secret CIA study that proposed changing our laws in ways that would have had the effect of changing our democratic society to an authoritarian one. Because of the Constitution and democratic laws, the government has great difficulty in jailing those who make public use of what is rubber-stamped with a "security" classification. Referring to that formerly secret study, Wise notes that the CIA was concerned about the lack of deterrence provided by existing espionage laws since they allowed individuals to disclose classified data which they believed the American people had a right to know, as long as the government was unable to prove intent to aid a foreign government. He goes on to note that the CIA was, in effect, proposing an Official Secrets Act for intelligence information in which anything stamped secret would automatically be accepted by the courts as secret. It would increase the power of the Director of Central Intelligence "to seek court injunctions to prevent the release or publication of intelligence information."

Here some of the more preposterous CIA claims to urgent "national security" that I pointed out above should be recalled, their claims that revealing these secrets could lead to the rupture of foreign relations or even to war when such secrets involved the names of newspapers and of hotels that it had already disclosed. Based on my own not inconsiderable experiences with outrageous CIA claims and its regular lying about them under oath and in courts, there is nothing that is too ridiculous or shameful for it.

And how about our Constitution, also the CIA's Constitution, that the CIA was proposing to nullify? Basically, the CIA was endorsing the idea of "crown privilege," the basis of the British Official Secrets Act. This would be tantamount to relieving the government of the burden to prove someone guilty, putting the onus on the defendant to verify the legality of his action in disseminating the intelligence information.

What the CIA was proposing here is a return to one of the principles our Revolutionary War was fought to end, the presumption of guilt. This is an authoritarian not a democratic concept. It is the law of the police state. This had a certain appeal to those of an authoritarian turn of mind such as Senator John L. McClellan of Arkansas who sought to make the disclosure of "classified information" a felony in the wake of the publication of the Pentagon Papers in 1972. Dean Acheson also spoke out in favor of a "severe Official Secrets Act."[4]

This is the highly respected Acheson who as author of the Truman Doctrine formulated the Cold War and who was frustrated when we did not go to war with Cuba and the USSR when that dispute could be and was settled peacefully.

At the very time the CIA was cooking up its plan to bypass our legal system, violate the Constitution, and eliminate the jury, it was getting away with just such a scheme in federal district court in Baltimore.

In 1965, Eerik Heine[5] filed a slander suit against another Estonian emigre, Juri Raus, Civil Action 15952. Heine claimed, in the words of the *Washington Post* story of June 7, 1969, that "the CIA, acting through Raus, was attempting to ruin his career as an *anti*-Communist lecturer by spreading stories about him among Estonian emigres that he was a Soviet agent." (emphasis added)

Raus, meaning the CIA, was represented by the high priced lawyers, including Paul R. Connolly, a partner of the famed Edward Bennett Williams, the same Williams who spent years on the president's intelligence advisory board, ostensibly in oversight of the CIA. Hanrahan's article reported a remand from the fourth circuit court of appeals "for another hearing on specific points dealing with whether the CIA had actually given instructions to Raus concerning Heine."

Federal district court "Chief Judge Roszel C. Thomsen made it clear," Hanrahan wrote, "that [CIA Director Richard] Helms could not be compelled to answer any question if the CIA director feels that to do so would jeopardize national security."[6]

In his lectures Heine showed anti-Communist films. He says that he had been a guerrilla fighter before the Russians took over Estonia, was an anti-Nazi fighter, and then served time in a Russian prison camp. The available records give no indication that the CIA questioned any of this in court. I have five of its affidavits, four by Helms filed between December 30, 1965, and October 7, 1966, and one by the CIA's general counsel Lawrence Houston. My recollection is that they were secret affidavits, the CIA having claimed that secrecy was required by "national security."

In Helms's April 1, 1966, affidavit he refers to Raus's "employment by the Agency." Raus was not a CIA employee in the normal sense, but was an informer. In the affidavit Helms refers to Raus as "a source" for the CIA about the Soviet Union in Estonia and on "Estonian emigre activities in foreign countries as well as in the United States." (see Appendix 9)

While claiming that Raus was its informer, the CIA also admitted that not only was he a propagandist for it but that he had slandered Heine on behalf of the agency: "the defendant (Raus) was furnished information concerning the plaintiff (Heine) by the Central Intelligence Agency and was instructed to disseminate such information to members of the Legion (of Estonian Liberation) so as to protect the integrity of the Agency's foreign intelligence sources." How slandering Heine could "protect foreign intelligence sources" Helms did not state, but the court accepted that without question. (see Appendix 9)

So certain was Helms that he and it could get away with almost anything in the federal courts, his first affidavit was of but three short paragraphs of ten lines of typing!

Neither Helms nor his general counsel even suggested that Heine was not slandered. The CIA intended to damage Heine with the emigres from that part of Europe who were divided along political lines, some of whom were anti-Soviet having been pro-Nazi. The CIA preferred Raus's faction of the anti-Communist Estonians, so it set out to defame and ruin Heine's effectiveness by telling Raus to call him "a Soviet agent." The only wonder is that it did not get him killed.

This is a fair sample of what could be expected of the CIA's plan to bypass our legal system and have the courts compelled to take any CIA director's unquestioned word about anything he said, without even allowing a jury to consider it. This is the same Helms who when found guilty of perjury was defended as a true patriot by Connolly's senior partner, Edward Bennett Williams. To the CIA, felony perjury is a hallmark of patriotism. Had the CIA gotten away with what it planned, the courts without question would have to accept the word of perjurers.

The Supreme Court upheld Helms's affidavits and the decision of Judge Thomsen that Helms could not be questioned about them on the ground that "there are certain public interests that are paramount." Our Constitution apparently ceased being one of those paramount "public interests."

This is how the CIA was able to frustrate our system of justice without the 1966 plan it cooked up to make that a matter of law. As Wise said of this CIA plan of 1966, "the CIA would like to convict without proof." It "would also substitute the judgement of the director for that of a jury." It succeeded in doing so to Eerik Heine whose character it assassinated and whose anti-Communist effectiveness it eliminated.

King George and his generals would have been proud, but not so Washington, Madison, Jefferson, or Sam Adams and those others who intended to make plans like the CIA's proposal impossible in the nation they established in freedom without such authoritarian practices and "laws." Acceptance of the CIA's proposal would have been a return to what our forefathers fought against and defeated. This CIA plan would have been the beginning of the end of the right to trial by jury by rendering the jury meaningless.

Earlier in this chapter, Wise has an excellent but limited commentary on the indispensability of a free press in a democratic society. What he does not point out is that this free press enables it to inform the people so that they can make their wishes and beliefs known. He also does not point out that it is only when there is full and free discussion can most mistakes be corrected before they do great harm and government can be prevented from doing wrong:

> At the core of all this is the continuing clash between the values of a free press and those of national security. Many constitutional scholars, political leaders, jurists, and others believe those values must be "balanced" and compromised. But a democratic system requires a public informed about the decisions and actions of its political leaders. If democracy is to work, the freedom of the press to report about *the activities of government* cannot be qualified by prior restraint or subsequent punishment. The press must be free to publish no matter what the potential harm to an officially defined "national security." The risks of repression are greater. Any legal restrictions imposed upon the press in advance, or by later punishment, that limit what it can report about the government would diminish the First Amendment and change the nature of American democracy. It is always possible to rationalize the case for curbing the press in particular circumstances. But who can say, once it begins, where it will end? Freedom to publish about government is either absolute, or it does not exist. Once qualified, it may be described as something else, but not as freedom of the press.[7]

And if there is no freedom to publish there is no democracy. It means the people do not have the right to know what their government does or plans to do. As we have seen, there are extraordinary examples such as the military's plans to start a "preventive war" in secret when that is prohibited absolutely by our Constitution; or that SIOP-62, which also was the most basic violation of our Constitution and would have wiped out a major part of the world and poisoned all the rest of it in a nuclear holocaust; or, the nuclear war that would have resulted had Kennedy not blocked the military's secret intent to invade Cuba during that 1962 missile crisis. But as we have seen, the military believes that the people do not have this right to know in this militarized conception of a free and democratic society.

Wise begins the part of his book entitled "Secrecy" with a quotation from General Maxwell D. Taylor, the general in whom Kennedy placed his trust as he struggled with the Vietnam problem he had inherited. Taylor was interviewed on the CBS morning news on June 17, 1971.

He was asked, "Well, what do you make, General, of the principle of the people's right to know?" Taylor's forthright response was: "I don't believe in that as a general principle."[8] There can be no more forthright military statement that it does not believe in our Constitution, in our most basic principles.

At the very beginning of his important book, Wise states a painful but obvious truth that has become more painfully obvious since then:

> . . . large numbers of people no longer believe the government or the president. They no longer believe the government because they have come to understand that the government does not always tell the truth.
>
> This erosion of confidence between people and government is perhaps the single most significant political development in America in the past decade. Because of it, an American president today operates within a new political framework. He can no longer assume that a majority of the people will believe him.[9]

In the context of this book that "most important political development in America in the past decade" is in fact "the most important political development" since President Kennedy was assassinated.

The government's lies about the Pentagon Papers and the Vietnam war and the secrecy that made all of that possible is what Wise uses to carry this idea forward:

> The disclosures of the Pentagon Papers did demonstrate, however, how easy it is for government officials to use the security classification system to keep from public view policies, decisions, and actions that are precisely the opposite of what the public is told. In other words, through official secrecy, we now have a system of institutionalized lying.
>
> Policy makers who consider it desirable to mask their decisions or their objectives, or who wish to mislead the public or withhold information, can do so as easily as reaching for the nearest rubber stamp. In short, lying and secrecy are two sides of the same coin.

> The government can lie, withhold information, or classify it. But equally important is what the government *does* choose to communicate. And the Executive Branch has at its disposal today a large and powerful government public relations and information machine. It uses this machine to sell those policies and distribute those official truths that it wishes the public to receive.[10]

"Official truths" is a polite way of saying official lies.

As we have seen, the grim reality is that it was more than "the people" who were lied to. Those who are supposed to be responsible for making policy were also lied to by the military. Its way of making policy—by making decisions that cannot be changed—was utterly disastrous in Vietnam.

Wise concludes his first chapter by stating the importance of a free press if there is to be a free and democratic society. He then says correctly that it is "the politics of lying" that has brought these basic changes about. The American press is often called the "fourth branch of government," not because it is literally part of the government but because its role of vigorously questioning and criticizing government actions is vital. When the press fails to do this and merely accepts official "handouts" as fact, it is indulging in what Tom Wicker has called "the press box mentality," which makes it easier for government to mislead the public. This undermines public trust in government, which can be crippling to a democracy, as Wise notes: "If the governed are misled, if they are not told the truth, or if through official secrecy and deception they lack information on which to base intelligent decisions, the system may go on—but not as a democracy."[11]

This is well put. It is a basic truth. The "Politics of Lying," the phrase Wise coined and uses as his title, is as apt a description as could be of the way in which governments have come to govern and make policy. But what Wise, a member of the media, does not say of the "Fourth Branch of government," is that it also lies, and the effects of its lies are as detrimental as the lying of the other three branches.

As noted by Wise, Tom Wicker, who had been The *New York Times*'s Washington bureau chief before becoming an associate editor and one of its columnists, thereafter, retiring to a Vermont farm, has an apt description of the press that blindly accepts government handouts and reports them without questioning. He calls it the "press box mentality." Tragically, both Wise and Wicker participated in the "politics of lying" and the "press box mentality" when it came to government lies about the assassination of the president.

CBS-TV and the retired president Johnson had contracted to do three prime time specials which were filmed in September and October of 1969. CBS legendary newsman, Walter Cronkite, conducted the interviews.

When the third Johnson interview was shown on May 2, 1970, it included this message about thirty seconds into the program: "Certain material has been deleted from this broadcast at President Johnson's request, made on the ground of national security." During the filming Johnson had freely used classified documents. Following each interview, he "reserved the right to edit the CBS interviews for 'national security' reasons.'" During the third interview, he expressed "some misgivings about the Warren Commission's central finding that Lee Harvey Oswald, acting alone, had killed President Kennedy. Johnson indicated to Cronkite that he still retained some doubts and that, possibly, a conspiracy had been involved." Several weeks later, Johnson asked that these remarks be deleted.

> Cronkite, a newsman of great integrity and high professional standards, had been unhappy from the start with Johnson's right to edit the tapes. In this case he felt that Johnson was misusing his right to make deletions, since it was difficult to see how, six years after the assassination, any "national security" was involved.
>
> As the CBS interviews suggested, presidents or former presidents can freely ignore the secrecy label when it suits their purposes or invoke it to suppress embarrassing information. The system exists not so much to protect national security as to provide a flexible tool of power for political leaders.[12]

Cronkite found it only "difficult to see how" the former president's beliefs about the assassination that made him president involved any "national security." That is not only "difficult to see," it is impossible. But CBS

President-Elect John F. Kennedy and President Dwight D. Eisenhower meet at the White House, January 19, 1961. *Abbie Rowe. White House Photographs. John F. Kennedy Presidential Library and Museum, Boston.*

Meeting with Attorney General Robert F. Kennedy and J. Edgar Hoover, director of the Federal Bureau of Investigation, February 23, 1961. *Abbie Rowe. White House Photographs. John F. Kennedy Presidential Library and Museum, Boston.*

President John F. Kennedy meets with Minister of Foreign Affairs of the Soviet Union Andrei Gromyko in the Oval Office, White House, Washington, DC, March 27, 1961. *Robert Knudsen. White House Photographs. John F. Kennedy Presidential Library and Museum, Boston.*

President John F. Kennedy gestures during a press conference in the State Department Auditorium, April 21, 1961. *Abbie Rowe. White House Photographs. John F. Kennedy Presidential Library and Museum, Boston.*

President John F. Kennedy meets with the Joint Chiefs of Staff. L-R: Vice Chief of Staff of the United States Air Force, General Curtis E. LeMay; Chairman of the Joint Chiefs of Staff, General Lyman L. Lemnitzer; President Kennedy; Chief of Staff of the United States Army, General George H. Decker; Chief of Staff of the United States Navy, Admiral Arleigh A. Burke; Commandant of the United States Marine Corps, General David M. Shoup. Cabinet Room, White House, Washington, DC, May 27, 1961. *Robert Knudsen. White House Photographs. John F. Kennedy Presidential Library and Museum, Boston.*

President John F. Kennedy with Soviet Union Premier Nikita Khrushchev and others outside the Soviet Union Embassy in Vienna, Austria, June 4, 1961. *United States Information Service. Kennedy Family Collection. KFC5415P. John F. Kennedy Presidential Library and Museum, Boston.*

President John F. Kennedy meets with General Douglas MacArthur. Oval Office, White House, Washington, DC, July 20, 1961. *Robert Knudsen. White House Photographs. John F. Kennedy Presidential Library and Museum, Boston.*

President John F. Kennedy delivers a radio and television address to the nation regarding the Soviet Union's military presence in Cuba. Oval Office, White House, Washington, DC, October 22, 1961. *Robert Knudsen. White House Photographs. John F. Kennedy Presidential Library and Museum, Boston.*

President John F. Kennedy signs the Interdiction of the Delivery of Offensive Weapons to Cuba. Photographer at left is unidentified. Oval Office, White House, Washington, DC, October 23, 1962. *Cecil Stoughton. White House Photographs. John F. Kennedy Presidential Library and Museum, Boston.*

President John F. Kennedy meets with members of the Executive Committee of the National Security Council regarding the crisis in Cuba. October 29, 1962. *Cecil Stoughton. White House Photographs. John F. Kennedy Presidential Library and Museum, Boston.*

President John F. Kennedy meets with United States Air Force officers who took part in aerial photo-reconnaissance missions over Cuba. Seated on sofa (left to right): Colonel Ralph D. "Doug" Steakley, photo evaluator with the Office of the Joint Chiefs of Staff; Lieutenant Colonel Joe M. O'Grady, U-2 pilot; Major Richard S. "Steve" Heyser, U-2 pilot; Chief of Staff of the United States Air Force, General Curtis E. LeMay. Air Force Aide to the President, Brigadier General Godfrey T. McHugh (center right), stands in the background. Oval Office, White House, Washington, DC, October 30, 1962. *Robert Knudsen. White House Photographs. John F. Kennedy Presidential Library and Museum, Boston.*

President John F. Kennedy delivers a radio and television address to the nation regarding the dismantling of Soviet missile bases in Cuba. Fish Room, White House, Washington, DC, November 2, 1962. *Robert Knudsen. White House Photographs. John F. Kennedy Presidential Library and Museum, Boston.*

President John F. Kennedy meets with Assistant Secretary of State for Far Eastern Affairs, W. Averell Harriman. United Press International photographer, Frank Cancellare (with camera), stands in background; two unidentified men stand at right. Oval Office, White House, Washington, DC, November 26, 1962. *Robert Knudsen. White House Photographs. John F. Kennedy Presidential Library and Museum, Boston.*

Special counsel to the president Theodore C. Sorensen. White House, Washington, DC, January 25, 1961. *Abbie Rowe. White House Photographs. John F. Kennedy Presidential Library and Museum, Boston.*

Special assistant to the President Kenneth P. O'Donnell. White House, Washington, DC, January 25, 1961. *Abbie Rowe. White House Photographs. John F. Kennedy Presidential Library and Museum, Boston.*

President John F. Kennedy meets with special assistant to the president, Arthur M. Schlesinger Jr. Oval Office, White House, Washington, DC, July 26, 1962. *Cecil Stoughton. White House Photographs. John F. Kennedy Presidential Library and Museum, Boston.*

Fidel Castro and French journalist Jean Daniel at the Riviera Hotel on November 22, 1963, the day President John F. Kennedy was assassinated. *Marc Riboud/L'Obs/Magnum Photos.*

accepted this impossible justification for an improper demand that really involved the non-functioning, malfunctioning and misfunctioning of Johnson's administration and the legitimacy of his succession to the presidency.

When none of this was classified or even classifiable, there could not have been any legitimate "national security" element in what the people had every right to know and CBS agreed to keep them from knowing and for all of his great integrity and high professional standards, Cronkite accepted it, as he accepted his paycheck for it, in public silence.

Although Wise does not here point it out to his readers, later in his book[13] as we have seen, he reports that the CIA prepared a plan under which others of lesser importance would be jailed with the Constitutional protection of the jury eliminated for them, for ever so much less than the former president was doing.

Johnson followed the example set by Eisenhower for Donovan's biography of him[14] by having loads of classified papers trucked to him for his use, aided by the prime hawk of his administration, Walt Rostow. When Eisenhower and Johnson and others used "intelligence information" freely for their personal reasons, for publicity to improve their images and for personal profit, a reporter, even one who innocently picked up a piece of paper and gave it to a someone else who made any use of it, would face jail.

The real question is hardly one of any legitimate or rational concept of "national security," and it rarely is. But even without all the meaning it has attributed to it, this kind of information is almost never accessible to most Americans. The major media does not report it, as CBS News did not report Johnson's open and wholesale use of classified "national security" information on its show. "Unhappy" as Cronkite was and as great as his "integrity" and "high professional standards" were, he did not give this information about Johnson's public use of classified records to his audience. A staffer on those TV specials leaked a copy of what was excised to a friend of mine, and he gave it to *The Washington Post*.

But neither the *Post* nor Wise, who diminished what Johnson said and believed into "some misgivings," explained that what Johnson was actually saying is that he did not believe the conclusions of the commission, the commission he had selected with such care to reach the conclusions it did not "reach" but began its work with them already "reached."

Putting this another way, Johnson did not believe the report of the official investigation of the crime that made him president, the assassination of President Kennedy. While Johnson did not advertise it, he made his refusal to believe his own commission's report clear to his White House staff and to others before it was printed. He actually asked the FBI for more information confirming his refusal to believe that report and his belief that there had been a conspiracy. This has been in the public domain since the FBI disclosed it under FOIA pressures in December 1977 or January 1978. I have given copies of the FBI memo I quote to many reporters of all media, but I do not recall any of them ever using it.

On April 4, 1967, immediately after columnist Jack Anderson saw the FBI's chief of leaking, lobbying, and propaganda, Assistant Director Cartha DeLoach, who headed the division whose official title was "Crime Records," DeLoach wrote a memo to J. Edgar Hoover. But because nobody inside the FBI ever addressed Hoover either directly or by name, his memo was to Hoover's next in command and closest friend, Clyde Tolson. In it he recalled a phone call to him late the night before from Marvin Watson, President Johnson's longtime top assistant. In that conversation, in DeLoach's words, Watson "stated that the president had told him, in an off moment, that he now was convinced that there was a plot in connection with the assassination. Watson stated the president felt that the CIA had something to do with this plot. Watson requested any further information we could furnish in this connection would be much appreciated by him and by the president." (see Appendix 6)

Johnson was not alone in his disbelief in the conclusions of the Warren Commission. In *Whitewash IV*, I broke the news that Warren Commission member Senator Richard Russell also dissented from the commission's conclusions. As I discuss in greater detail in my unpublished manuscript, "Senator Russell Dissents,"[15] Russell, along with commission member Senator John Sherman Cooper, had refused to believe the basis of the report, the single-bullet theory. Russell had forced an executive session to record his disagreement only for the commission's general counsel, J. Lee Rankin, to see to it that the Russell record of disagreement did not exist in any commission records. When I put the proof of how he had been tricked in Russell's hands, he broke his long relationship with Johnson and encouraged my work until his dying day.

That executive session was on Friday, September 18, 1964. After it ended, without the stenographic transcript the commission had agreed would be made of all of them, Russell reported it to Johnson in a telephone call. When in response to the 1992 law requiring fullest possible disclosure of all JFK assassination records on April 15, 1994, some of Lyndon Johnson's tapings of his conversations were disclosed. When Russell told Johnson of his disagreement with this most basic of the commission's conclusions, it was because he believed that his disagreement would be noted in the report. In the Associated Press story on these tapes, Johnson is quoted as telling Russell, "I don't either" believe that theory.

The meaning of this is not in that AP story, nor to my knowledge was it given to the people by any of the media. The meaning, of course, is that the president himself did not believe the official assassination mythology he had personally endorsed when it was released. He believed it was impossible. If two commission members and the president of the United States did not believe the Warren Report, who should?

But the major media continued to support the lies the government told the people about how and by whom their president had been assassinated. Even though the president of the United States himself believed that terrible crime to be a conspiracy that remained unsolved.

Although Wise gave an understated account of Johnson's belief that the crime was unsolved, he failed to see the significance of the single-bullet theory, which is undoubtedly the biggest political lie about the assassination of President Kennedy. Wise does not include it in his otherwise excellent study of the "politics of lying." Random House does not include it in the index it had prepared for his book. That index includes not only names, but also subjects. But Wise's account of Johnson's disbelief is not indexed under Johnson or Kennedy and there is no "assassination" item in that index.

So there is this "press box mentality" of which Wicker spoke in reporting on the assassination, as there is on the editorial and op-ed pages and in book publishing. Wicker himself has come to embody that mentality he condemned. Wicker who had written a foreword for a commercial publication on the report of the House Select Committee on Assassinations which concluded that there had been a conspiracy, was approached by Random House for a blurb on Posner's *Case Closed*. Posner's book is the most deliberately, extensively, and inclusively dishonest book in support of the official assassination mythology. Yet Wicker of that "press box mentality" wrote the following which Random House used on the back cover.

> *Case Closed* is a deliberate, detailed, thoroughly documented, sometimes brutal, always conclusive destruction of one Kennedy assassination conspiracy theory after another. Posner shows them to be in some cases impossible, in others mistaken, in many dishonest, in all wishful. Yet the book's most important contribution may be Posner's thorough, dispassionate, yet rather sympathetic account of the warped and miserable life of Lee Harvey Oswald. After his book, the case of JFK is indeed closed. *Case Closed* is important.

There is no way Wicker could know of any evidence that could justify these statements. There is not a single qualification in any of his praises for Posner's work. Wicker quite obviously did not check and really could not do so on his Vermont farm. It is, in Wise's words reflecting Walter Cronkite's strong disapproval of LBJ's censorship to which he agreed, "difficult to see how" Wicker could endorse the House Committee's conclusion that there had been an assassination conspiracy and write as he did for Random House and Posner the exact opposite.

Earlier he had plugged another angled and dishonest book. That book, *Oswald's Game* by Jean Davison, was based on the commission's published work which it misused and distorted. It is not easy to be as dishonest as she was in her omissions and misuses of that material, as I told her when we were both on a radio talk show together. Yet, Wicker and Daniel Schorr provided blurbs praising that book.

Before my *Case Open* appeared and asking nothing of him, I wrote Wicker because I was and am concerned about precisely what Wise reports and exposes in his *The Politics of Lying* and that so many, including reporters who should know better, made themselves part of it. He sent me this postcard on February 3, 1994:

> Dear Mr. Weisberg:
>
> I said what I said about Case Closed because I thought it was true, and I still do. I gave the comment when asked for it by the publisher, who sent me the ms. I tell you that because I have nothing to hide, though I don't think you have any right to ask. In general, I'm sorry you feel as you do but I stand by what I said about Case Closed.
>
> Sincerely . . . . Tom Wicker
> P.S. I don't care what you may say about me in some future work. I long ago got use to criticism, and worse.

I can only wonder what Wicker's reaction would have been in his reporting days if someone had responded to him and his questioning about a very public and controversial matter, "I don't think you have a right to ask."

For the politics of lying there are different ways in which the lies are told. What we are told can be entirely false. It can be partly false. It can be false by misleading incompleteness in which some of what we are told is technically accurate but becomes false when what is omitted is known. Among the other ways in which lies can be told is by not giving the correct meaning to what is told, as with Wise's recounting of Johnson's not believing his own official solution to the assassination of President Kennedy without telling his reader that it has this meaning. Yet this non-solution to that "crime of the century" is the biggest government lie of Wise's life and that of all of us. That it is palmed off on all of us as the solution is not within his catalogue of official lies. Nor does he have any mention of the military's involvement in it and its extensive lying which was public knowledge.

I regret it for both of them and for all of us that Wise in his otherwise excellent book practices "the politics of lying" as Wicker does his "press box mentality."

CHAPTER 13

KILLING THE TRUTH

All the institutions of our society failed,[1] each and every one of them, beginning with all branches of the government, especially the executive, but also the legislative and judiciary. With the failure of these institutions, all the protections of our society, of our system of government, were made to fail and our freedom was jeopardized. Of the non-governmental institutions, the media failed miserably, disgracefully, sycophantically. All elements of the media, including book publishers. Our professors, scholars, those who teach and inform the rest of us, failed. Potentially by far the most dangerous of those who failed themselves, the people, and our democratic system is the military and its complex partners. Whether it was more than failure is the question this book raises for the first time. Even those of us known collectively as "critics" failed, as I document in my lengthy unpublished manuscript, *Inside the JFK Assassination Industry*. In it, I include myself as having failed.

The thrust of all my work, while not spelled out in my earlier books, is that in the time of great crisis, the time of the JFK assassination, all of our institutions failed then and ever since then. Our institutions ignored the criticism and persisted in their failure, refusing to meet their responsibilities to themselves and the public.

The Congress failed in allowing itself to be conned by Johnson out of investigating the crime. One of the reasons for his haste in appointing his commission was to co-opt the Congress. After the Warren Report was out,

Congress insisted on continuing to fail. As an example of this, I took a copy of *Whitewash* to the office of one of the Senators who had earned the reputation of being one of the toughest minds, Wayne Morse of Oregon. His legislative assistant was impressed by the book and what it mustered of the official evidence only and how it was put together. But when she tried to get the busy Morse to read it, he told her, in approximately these words, "If Bobby (Kennedy) accepts it, I have to accept it." Morse assumed that Bobby had accepted it. He had not. Until long after that Bobby had said not a word about it and in fact, as I show with official documents in *Post Mortem*, the chapter, "Hades not Camelot," he had refused to endorse the report when pressured to do so.

When the House of Representatives established a committee to investigate the JFK and Martin Luther King Jr. assassinations in 1976, it began with the determination to fail. It began with assumptions that guaranteed failure. They assumed that the official mythologies in both crimes were essentially correct. Instead of investigating the crimes, the Committee instead focused on refuting criticisms of the official mythologies, and, further, accepted assassination mythology spoon-fed to it by the FBI.

Each JFK hearing began with a narration of what it would deal with, and in each narration, it explicitly quoted critics that it would then address. This was the design not of the committee members but of their general counsel and staff director, G. Robert Blakey. Blakey then devoted each hearing to refuting what he said these named critics said, but there was one critic whose name he never mentioned and whose writing he raised no questions about—me. Obvious as this was, and as gross a violation of the committee's mandate as it was, it escaped political or journalistic criticism. The media was not disappointed by that approach.

Blakey, formerly a lawyer in the Department of Justice organized-crime task force, began with the hang-up that the mafia had assassinated the president. He was not able to create even a rational suspicion of that. So, after his big-league failure, he co-authored a book making that claim. His committee editor, Richard Billings, was his co-author.[2]

Blakey wound up his King work with a preposterous and entirely unproven irrational assumption that John and Jerry Ray, the brothers of the accused assassin, James Earl Ray, were involved in a conspiracy with a safely dead, wealthy Missouri racist. Blakey's source, a criminal who sought, and through his helpfulness received, special consideration for another crime for which he faced trial, fabricated the cock-and-bull nonsense that James Earl Ray got $50,000 to kill King. In fact, Ray had so little money he had to risk robbing a house of prostitution to be able to pay for a plane ticket out of Canada; and if he had had $100 more when he got to Portugal, he would have had enough for boat fare to Zimbabwe, then known as Rhodesia, which did not have an extradition treaty with the United States. Ray could not have been extradited, nor would the Rhodesian government have wanted to extradite Ray anyway.

I was James Earl Ray's investigator for the habeas corpus proceeding that was to determine whether he would get the trial he never had. With the success of that proceeding, I conducted the investigations for the two weeks of evidentiary hearings which proved unsuccessful. They ended with a something less than Solomonic decision, that guilt or innocence were immaterial to whether Ray would get that trial.

Thereafter, I spent a decade suing the Department of Justice for its records relevant to that case. All those records were readily available to Blakey. I'd already forced them into the public domain. In addition, he had the power of subpoena and could have gotten any records he wanted that way. But that legal eagle (who later became a professor of law at University of Notre Dame) was like the critics he criticized, without interest in any real investigation or with the facts developed by other investigations. Knowing full well just how exceptional a genius he is, Blakey did not speak to me or ask me what records I had which he could use or if I had any leads for him to follow. He did not even ask for the transcripts of those two weeks of evidentiary hearings in which the evidence I developed was produced in court and the witnesses I located testified. That evidence was tested in the American way, under oath and subject to cross-examination. But it proved Ray innocent, the reason for that quoted language from the judge's decision. Therefore, Blakey had no interest in it.

Can there be higher qualifications for teaching the law than a manifest contempt for evidence and preference for preconception and indulging prejudice?

There was no other Congressional investigation of either crime. Earlier, the Church committee established a JFK assassination subcommittee. Pennsylvania Republican Senator Richard Schweiker was its chairman. Colorado Democratic Senator Gary Hart was the subcommittee's only other member. He had nothing to do with what Schweiker did or reported. He did nothing at all on that subcommittee. Schweiker began like Blakey later did, but from the other side. He was hung up on the nuttier conspiracy theories and his utterly worthless report dealt with nothing else. So the Senate failed, too. Schweiker, who acted in the name of the Senate, saw to that, as Blakey did for the House.

These failures of Congress contribute to the fact that the JFK assassination is an unsolved crime, to all that this has cost the country, and to the widespread disenchantment over it.

By their failures, the courts in the early days of the Freedom of Information Act and thereafter became, and within my experience remained, an adjunct of the de facto government conspiracy to withhold—which means to keep secret—official records that contradict, and in many instances, disprove the official "solution" to the assassinations.

While what lawyers do is not usually referred to as a conspiracy, it was that and it had that effect in those many lawsuits I filed. A criminal conspiracy is an agreement between two or more people to commit an unlawful act. The agreement itself is a crime, but an overt step toward committing the unlawful act is typically required to secure a conviction. This is what they did, over and over again, each and every one of them who defended the government in those lawsuits I filed and in all the many cases of which I have knowledge and court records. Those government lawyers combined with those who swore falsely to what is material and thus, in effect, conspired with them to violate the law. They also suborned perjury, which is a felony. This was their means of keeping secret what the law said could not be kept secret. That is largely how they denied information to those of us who write to inform the people of what they need to know.

The media compounded its failure by never once reporting any of this. Government agents were accused of felonies in open court, and the accusations were proven and not once in the many times I did just that was it ever reported. Those agents were thus immune in their felonies, and they repeated them, some being promoted for it!

Once I proved in court that the agent the FBI used to offer false testimony in that case was an unindicted co-conspirator in a major case of that day. It was an unprecedented case in which the acting director of the FBI and his top assistants were to be tried for serious offenses.[3] The agent swore falsely to enable the government to illegally keep records secret, records that under the law had to be made public. And they got away with it. He sat mute in that court when I presented this information to the judge. She was offended that the government used an unindicted co-conspirator in a criminal case as an affiant before her. This was because he was in a compromised position and it compromised her. Because he was an unindicted co-conspirator, he had to do what the government wanted him to do, otherwise he could be added to the indictment as an indicted conspirator. He also would have lost his pension when he was just two years away from retirement. That agent, having done his duty as the FBI saw it, was reassigned to a field office near his home and worked for the FBI there until he retired.

But that judge said not a word about his perjury; she was, however, the only judge before whom I appeared in those many cases who ever did a thing about all the government misconduct. She banished that agent from her court but did not even expunge his proven false swearing from the court record. In any case, his false swearing, his part in that de facto conspiracy, succeeded in keeping assassination information secret.

And although that agent was an unindicted co-conspirator in that sensational case, not a word about any of this appeared in the papers or was even mentioned by the electronic media or in any magazine.

While I did not do it to get personal attention and did nothing to attract media interest in it, what I did try to do to prevent these felonies was unusual, the man-bites-dog kind of thing that the media usually loves. Instead of having my lawyer merely make allegations in pleadings, I proved those official perjuries in documented sworn affidavits. I was also always in court willing to testify and be cross-examined about what I attested to. With the prosecutor also the government's lawyer in these cases, I was in effect putting my head on the block and challenging the government to charge me with perjury. Except for being threatened by a surprised judge one time, the threat against my lawyer and me that did not work, nothing ever happened and there was never any mention of any of this outside of those court rooms.

That the government was capable of such serious misconduct before the federal courts and that the timid courts tolerated it, in particular with regard to withholding assassination information, was not news to the media. This is but one of its many and unending failures. From the very beginning, they behaved like the media in authoritarian societies. All the media not only praised the report when it was issued, while not checking it out, it also then went out of its way to ignore the serious published criticism of the report and to demean those critical books and those who wrote them.

Whitewash: The Report on the Warren Report was the first book on that subject.[4] The assassination of any president is, without question, at the very least, one of the major events in any lifetime. Yet, that first book on it, a book that has stood the test of time and is still used in colleges and universities, was not reviewed by a single newspaper or review service.

But those books that uncritically accepted the "official truth" were praised to the heavens by these same papers and all elements of the media. The most shameful example of this is the glorification of the most deliberately dishonest of those books, Gerald Posner's knowingly mistitled *Case Closed*.[5] No book on the subject was ever given the exalting and extensive attention he and his book got from the media, here and abroad, without ever being checked out by any reporter, reviewer, op ed writer, radio or TV producer, talk show staff or producer—not by a single one of those innumerable sycophants who protected errant officialdom. It is so brazenly dishonest, so vulnerable to the simplest checking of any part of it, that Posner and his publisher, Random House, must have assumed that there would be no questioning of it by the media. Random House shunned the traditional peer review of non-fiction books. It had to know that Posner's commercialization and exploitation of that great tragedy could not survive any competent peer review.

When my *Case Open*, my rebuttal of Posner's book, appeared, not a single paper reported or reviewed it.[6] No reporter or reviewer phoned to ask me a single question about it or about Posner's shameless dishonesty. Nor did anyone from any of the electronic media. It is not an everyday affair when in a field of serious writing one author refers to another one who boasts of being a "Wall Street lawyer" as a shyster, a literary thief, a literary whore, and as a writer who cannot tell the truth even by accident. If only one of these characterizations is false, there is indefensible libel. No one asked me if I had heard a word of complaint or protest from Posner or Random House, or from any lawyer representing them. I have not. Particularly not those in the business of reviewing books, those who make their living from book reviewing.

The accusations in *Case Open* are, by normal standards, major news in that field. It is also major news if they are undenied accusations, particularly after the unprecedented glorification of the book and Posner.

Then, too, how would those who treated Posner's outrageous dishonesty as virtually holy script look if they said a word about a book that showed them to be uncritical propagandists, rather than serious book critics? This is also true of all the reporters who raved about Posner and his book, without a single one checking it out as reporters are supposed to do. Not one asked anything of me when it appeared, or later when my exposure of it appeared. Nor did any of those TV producers who fought to get Posner on the tube. Of course, if they acknowledged and reported on or reviewed *Case Open*, they would be condemning themselves—all of the media, all elements of it.

This abdication and worse extended into even the most minor of the media, the JFK assassination newsletters that seem to exist only to excite their few readers with fanciful fictions. One example is Dr. Jerry Rose's *The Fourth Decade Journal*, which delayed any review of *Case Open* until the end of the usual shelf-life of most books in the chains that sell the most books in this country. In his September 1994 issue, he had an impartial review by Ohio history teacher David Keck and what is called "A Critical Review" by an aficionado of nutty conspiracy theories, Tom DeVries. The latter is twice as long as the former. Aside from DeVries's constitutional inability to understand what he does not want to understand, his life in the field in which he pretends serious scholarship and writes as an unquestioned authority based on his myriad fantasies, he spends part of his self-promotion guised as a review in defending other conspiracy-theorists from my earlier criticisms of them. DeVries endorses many by name. He pretends to deal with fact but seems unable to distinguish fact from fiction. For example, he condemns me for not including the names of those so-called "Dealey Plaza Tramps" which neither DeVries nor any other of the misguided assassination conspiracy theorists have ever shown to have any relevance to the assassination. They are in fact totally irrelevant, their identities long ago disclosed by the Dallas police, whose records as well as those of the FBI, leave it without any question that those men had no connection of any kind to the assassination.

I use this as just one illustration of how those who call themselves critics deceive and mislead the people and create diversions that never end, which seem to proliferate even more irrelevant speculation. There are many others.

Another—and this is so irrational it can hardly be believed, but it is true and unretracted or apologized for—happened when *The Fourth Decade* sponsored a conference in Providence, Rhode Island in 1993. One of its co-chairmen, George Michael Evica, a college professor, solicited a paper on me as a government agent! Had he attained even a rudimentary knowledge of the subject matter, he would have known that I filed more than a dozen FOIA lawsuits *against* the government in which I pried loose from secrecy and made available to others about a third of a million pages that had been withheld by the government. For this, Evica can regard me as some kind of government agent?

So, on all sides, from the major to the most minor of those who take supposed information to the people, the people are deceived, misled, misinformed, lied to, encouraged to credit fantasies and to have faith in those who range from insane to gross exploiters of the assassination. The people have no ready source of dependable information about the assassinations and their investigations. Save for their overwhelming disbelief in the official mythology, a belief that is a credit to the good common sense of most Americans, they would be even more confused than they are.

I have given this mixture of indulgent self-importance, stupidity, fantasy, and gross ignorance of the established assassination fact this attention because the people, including those who read and trust those so-called newsletters, are not aware of being deceived and misled by them. They are, however, insignificant in their corrupting effect and influence when compared with the major media offenders. From both extremes, people almost never have access to truth and fact of the assassinations and their investigations. As previously noted, popular awareness of this is one of the major causes of widespread distrust in the media, deserved mistrust.

I refer above to the failure of virtually all in academe, perhaps especially the eminences of the academic world. This has two major parts, each of which is indispensable to the major media and its determined failure.

One part is by ignoring the subject, great as its significance is and will continue to be in our lives and that of this country and its democratic system. When the professors do not ignore the subject, as with few conspicuous exceptions they do, they endorse the corruption of the truth and fact about it disseminated by our government. They also write texts that, true to Orwell, are used in teaching that the mythology is actuality, the truth about the assassination.

Even many children have written to me protesting what they read in their textbooks and are told by their teachers. These kids have enough sense to see through the propaganda they are required to believe is our history. These children also want the truth, something they can believe in.

This is the field of the history professors, and what have they done, at least those who do not keep their tails between their legs and their minds tightly closed? It is confirmed spectacularly by Dr. Michael Kurtz in his *Crime of the Century: The Kennedy Assassination from a Historian's Perspective.*[7] Even Kurtz's subtitle exemplifies his lack of authentic scholarship for all his PhD credentials: there were *two* Kennedy assassinations, contrary to his subtitle.

Because Kurtz is a history professor, the media greeted his book as the ultimate in scholarship and dependability, but as usual, there were no checks on his "scholarship" or even his grasp of the subject matter of his book. It was reviewed for the September 1983 *Journal of American History* by Jim Lesar, a lawyer who was educated as an historian before turning to the law. After pointing out that Kurtz draws on the uncredited work of others he then deprecates, Lesar concludes his review in these words:

> This book lacks scholarship. The author makes blatant factual mistakes and important errors of omission: Mark Lane's *Rush to Judgment* (1966) is *not* the first book on the subject; the wounding of James Tague is totally ignored. There are falsehoods: the Warren Commission was *not* "[un]aware of the FBI's real attitude toward it;" to the contrary, its members stated in their secret sessions that the FBI "would like to have us fold up and quit," and they also asserted that the FBI had concluded that Oswald was the lone assassin without having "run out all kinds of leads." Kurtz relies on the commission testimony by an FBI agent contradicted by FBI records and on the results of tests performed for the House committee on evidentiary items inexplicably different in size and shape, and weight from the original FBI specimens without evincing any awareness of the discrepancies. The book's footnotes retard rather than advance scholarship: they generally do not support the assertions made in the text, nor do they identify with requisite specificity the materials cited.
>
> In his last chapter Kurtz forgoes his vow against speculation—already broken—and reconstructs the assassination. He hypothesizes that a shot that hit Kennedy in the back—he asserts at an upward angle—was fired from the second floor of the Texas School Book Depository Building. Here he whooshes across the line separating speculation from fantasy. His assertion that 'the first two floors of the Depository were lower than the limousine at the time of the shots' requires a feat of levitation that is neither recorded on any film of the assassination nor testified to by any eyewitness.
>
> Kurtz rightly calls attention to the need for professional historians to appraise the assassination of President Kennedy and the official investigations into the crime. Unfortunately, this book does not measure up to the demands of that gargantuan task.[8]

Where Lesar refers to Kurtz "whooshing," in the official account, with which it is safely assumed Kurtz has at least a nodding acquaintance, all the shots were fired from stories higher, from the sixth floor.

In 1994 a New York university professor assigned several of the nuttier assassination books for critical analysis along with that most completely dishonest of them, Gerald Posner's *Case Closed.* Two of his students—and I am elliptical in this to protect them from retaliation—report that he announced in advance that all those who disagreed with Posner would get failing grades.

Random House asked noted historian Stephen Ambrose for a pre-publication comment on *Case Closed*, and here is what Ambrose wrote that appears on the book's back dust-jacket cover:

> Posner has done a great service, in the process of proving that a single researcher, working alone, is always preferable to a committee. This is a model of historical research. It should be required reading for anyone reviewing any book on the Kennedy assassination. Beyond the outstanding research, Posner is a dramatic storyteller. The recreation of Oswald's, and Jack Ruby's, personalities is wonderfully well done. The case has indeed been closed by Mr. Posner's work.

Asked for additional praise by *Newsday*'s Jack Sirica, who wrote a lengthy, entirely uncritical puff piece on the book, Ambrose was even more effusive. Likewise, Ambrose told Rob Zaleski for the Wisconsin *Capital Times* of October 11, 1993, that Posner's is an "absolutely flawless" and "a wonderful, fabulous book," that is both "meticulous" and "thorough."

David Wrone, a professional historian and the co-author of the only professional bibliography in the field, wrote Ambrose in detail about the flaws and errors in his comment on *Case Closed.* He concludes his letter asking Ambrose, "how it is you were tripped up on Posner's effort to depict the reality of the murder of a president?" In a somewhat snooty non-response, Ambrose told Wrone, "You write a book on the subject." He also said, "I'm always open to new evidence. . . . Even when I have to eat crow."

I gave Ambrose an invitation to such a feast and gave him "new evidence" in a letter on December 29, 1993. I began by asking Ambrose for "the basis of those comments" used by Random House and "whether you did any checking of what Posner says at all." When Ambrose did not respond after five months, I wrote him again, in greater length, including some ignorant comments he had made in his *Foreign Affairs* review of the previously quoted Reeves book. I did not expect any response, so I made it a point to say that: "In failing to respond you have made the record that will exist for history" of himself, "that can be taken as your own reflection of your regard for your reputation." Ambrose remained mute.

On the other side of the country, the eminent chairman of Stanford University's history department was "outraged" that Posner's closest approximation of total dishonesty and inaccuracy in the field, which was no easy achievement, did not get the Pulitzer Prize for history, the honor for which his three-man committee of the Pulitzer history panel had recommended it. Professor David M. Kennedy also was silent when on June 9, 1994, I asked him, "Did any of you prestigious eminences (in history) ask yourselves if you were in a position to evaluate that book by other than taking his word?"

I sent copies to several reporters, who published nothing at all about how the Pulitzer was nearly besmirched by ignorant professors who obviously did no checking at all. It turns out, they were overruled and there was no history Pulitzer in 1993.

I also expressed this concern to Roger Rosenblatt, editor-in-chief of the *Columbia Journalism Review* (CJR) for the Pulitzer committee, lacking any address for it. I also referred him to *Case Open*, as I had Professor Kennedy. I heard nothing from Rosenblatt, any Pulitzer committee member, anyone on the CJR staff, including a contributing editor I know, to whom I sent a copy of my letter along with the *San Francisco Chronicle* story reporting Kennedy's complaint. Again, with no responses from anyone.

So, it appears that neither the CJR nor the Pulitzer eminences of journalism care much about the reputation of their awards or the manner in which they are determined and by whom. I doubt very much that as an editor Rosenblatt would accept a story from a reporter who could not assure him that he had checked the facts that needed checking, especially on so controversial a subject. I also doubt very much that Ambrose or Kennedy would give other than a flunking grade to any student who could give not a single source for any paper he or she turned in. So, as I cautioned Ambrose, they were making their own records of their professional reputations for history.

With this the record of the media and their professional sources, errant government is well aware of its immunities and exploits them to perpetuate the official assassination mythology. In this, whether or not intended, it also shelters those who can, if only by circumstantial evidence, be suspected of involvement in the JFK assassination, chief among them the military and its associates in the military-industrial-intelligence complex. It is here assembled as such a case for the first time. But as with a case in court, there is no established guilt until that is decided by a jury, and in this case, there can be no jury. None, that is, but public opinion.

But that public opinion can be created only by the media, the media that failed itself and the nation from the first and continues to do so. The media that did not report about the anti-American military, although that information was much more accessible to it than to me, the media that suppressed the solidly proven facts about the JFK assassination. Most Americans have no idea what proven information is available to them, proven, truthful, accurate information.

When the media devotes any attention to books about the assassination it goes hog wild with disinformation and misinformation that it never checks out. The media elevates books like Posner's in support of the official mythology at one extreme and those like David Lifton's *Best Evidence*,[9] which is neither, at the other. As Random House avoided any peer review before publishing Posner, so also did *U.S. News and World Report* which devoted much of an issue, including the cover, to it. Likewise, *Time* magazine avoided any peer review of Lifton's concoction when it bought the rights to it from Macmillan in 1980. If *Time* had asked Macmillan if it had any peer review it would have known that Macmillan avoided that norm of nonfiction.

It is simply not possible that when mature people at Macmillan first read Lifton's book two things were not obvious. One is that what is new in the book is an absolute impossibility. The other is that it would be very profitable. So, from reliable reports, Macmillan decided to have Lifton schooled in frustrating questioning so the extensive appearances it would arrange for him to sell the book would contribute to its sale, while frustrating exposure of what is so impossible, so completely irrational, in his book.

In this, Macmillan's judgment was correct. The book enjoyed simply enormous sales and interest. It developed a cult following, the support of which Lifton still enjoys after almost a decade and a half. It was reprinted three times by different publishers. I have a copy of the 15th edition of one of those reprints published by Richard Gallen/Carroll & Graf.

Lifton's fantasy was immediately shown to be false as soon as *Time* used part of it. Two refutations came from President Kennedy's Air Force aide, General Godfrey McHugh. But by the time these refutations were published, millions of people had been deceived and their trust imposed upon by *Time*, as well as by Lifton and Macmillan.

It appears that Lifton's sole contribution to assassination mythology, in return for which he got so much money, was that the president's body was stolen from Air Force One on the trip back to Washington. It was then spirited away to the Army's Walter Reed Hospital, where the medical evidence it bore was altered, and then snuck into the Navy hospital by a back gate which had been locked securely three hours earlier as a means of crowd control. And McHugh was only one of the assassinated president's staff who never left the casket, even for a minute. For most of the trip—all but for the short period of time she stood with President Johnson when he took the oath of office—the widow sat next to the casket. So, unless they were all idiots at Macmillan and all the reprinters, they knew that what Lifton claimed was a spectacular fraud. But like Hitler's statement about making a lie credible—make it a very big one—they all recognized that this fraud had the profit potential it reached.

Between the extremes of Posner and Lifton, each of whom knew what he was doing, is a strange man with the strangest books, and like Lifton, has a claque that adores him, regards him as a national treasure. Harrison Livingstone's first two books were *High Treason* and *High Treason 2.*[10] Of those books on the lunatic fringe of disagreement with the official mythology, only Lifton's has had more sales and reached and misled more people than Livingstone's second book. His third, *Killing the Truth*, is admirably self-descriptive.[11] These and other books of that genre in disagreeing with the official mythology are the major force in the creation of their own mythologies, which are extended and enhanced by the so-called newsletters such as *The Fourth Decade*.

Livingstone's major contribution to these mythologies is not of his own invention. He adopted it and presented it as his own. It is based on the palpably false claim that in the assassination the back of the president's head was blown out. To make this seem credible an entire additional series of mythologies was necessary, but they did not tax Livingstone's facility in creating them. His capacity for invention was inexhaustible.

Illustrative of how the established fact means nothing to those like Livingstone is that he wrote and published two books supposedly on the assassination without ever studying the best of the films of it, that taken by Abraham Zapruder. It has been available for examination at the National Archives from the time the first of the commission's records were accessible. Bootleg copies have been readily available since not later than 1967. And his co-author in his second book has excellent prints, the best in private hands, that as a film technician he made from the original or from a copy made from the original.

When Livingstone phoned to tell me he was working on a documentary for television and was for the first time going to examine that film, he asked what he should look for in it. "Harry," I told him, "you will not want to see that. It will make you very unhappy." In response, he insisted in approximately these words: "I want to know the truth, regardless of what it is." So I explained to him where in that film, after the fatal head shot that did blow out the right side of the president's head, he would see several clear frames that show the back of the head intact, with not a speck of blood on it, on the shirt collar or on the jacket. Three weeks later he called to thank me, to say, "I was wrong and I'm glad to know it."

Faced with the fact that he had made a small fortune from a book that claims the back of the head was blown out, and firm in the conviction that whatever enters his mind is true because he is always right, he convinced himself that the Zapruder film was doctored. That invention is essential in his personal "killing the truth."

The frames of that film are but eight millimeters wide. Alteration of them would require micro forgery not only of the original but of all the copies made from it, not all of which were in government hands. Without forging the original and every print, the forgery would have been easily exposed and that of the frames most often and carefully examined. Aside from all the many problems in creating such a forgery on what is magnified greatly in being printed and ever so much more when projected, can it be imagined how conspicuous the most miniscule marking on the tiny frames would be when projected? Including the sprocket holes on the side by means of which the film is moved through the camera, the film is but a half-inch wide. When enlarged and projected onto a screen, magnification is enormous. The screen on which I projected that film for study is *five feet wide*! But the film itself is a trifle more than a quarter of an inch in width.

The incredible irrationality of this and more like it was no barrier to being published. If rationality had ever been a factor in his publication, he wouldn't have been able to publish anything.

Absolutely convinced that this complete impossibility was the reality as soon as it emerged from his mind, he then convinced himself that I was a co-conspirator in the assassination. Even before that, he had insisted to me that others he named also were co-conspirators, and there was no fact that dented the firmness of his conviction about this childish fabrication.

But what choice did he have? Could he admit, especially to himself, that all the work which he was so proud of was nonsense? Of course not, so he conjured this enormous conspiracy against him by those who really wanted only to have nothing to do with him. When others found out that he was firmly convinced of the validity of all this and so much more craziness, they used him to get vengeance they wanted on others. They fed him more nonsense; the wilder it was, the more impressed he was with it.

He even expected and demanded that those who had nothing to do with the assassination confess to him their involvement in it. He demanded of me, in writing, that I pressure them to confess, which I could not do in any event. When they did not confess, his abuses of and threats to them were indecent and irrational beyond belief, as was the childish trick he used to try to get confirmation from them of what they were not in any way involved in.

And so emerged his third book, the central doctrine of which was the assassination conspiracy he adopted from a fake book, *Farewell America*, by the SDECE, the French intelligence service. When I told him this, and that I had proven it to be a fraud, he asked, "But it tells the truth, doesn't it?" When I replied with an emphatic "no!" that merely added to his conviction that I was a co-conspirator with one of his and the French SDECE's more prominent men in the vast Texas-wide conspiracy Livingstone took from this fake book.

Crazy as it so obviously is, his book, like Lifton's and Posner's, had no peer review. Based on the sale of his second book, the publisher, Carroll & Graf, anticipated great profits, so why jeopardize all that money with any peer review?

There is one point of rationality in Livingstone's personal "killing the truth," where he writes, "maybe I am crazy." But in private conversation with Livingstone, records of which I have, he detailed how he would steal a fine print of the Zapruder film. And he followed up with another letter, boasting how he had pulled that off.

These are the writers loved by the publishers, the authors of the most terrible books that make money by deceiving people and rewriting our history. I give much more detailed attention to these works of disinformation in my lengthy unpublished book manuscript, *Inside the JFK Assassination Industry*.

By their invalid criticism of the military, about which valid criticism could and should easily have been made, Lifton and Livingstone both contributed much to the unwillingness of the media and the public to credit any legitimate criticisms of the military or even to consider them. With the media in particular, the endless repetition of such disgraceful fabrications as Lifton's—that it snatched the body from a military plane; took it in secret to one military hospital where military doctors altered it and the evidence it held; then, in a military ambulance, secretly took it to another military hospital so that the military doctors there could prepare and issue a phony autopsy report—is enough to persuade most of the media that all criticism of the military must be ignored entirely or must meet a far higher level of substantiation than is the usual media standard. Lifton's kind of preposterous fabrication built sympathy for the military and distracted from its record that required careful examination and understanding. It also destroyed willingness to consider whether there had been an assassination conspiracy because it required a simply enormous number of military people to know about it, to have been involved in it, and to have maintained perpetual secrecy about it.

Aside from this practice of Hitler's dictum about the big lie, the lie was made even bigger because to begin with the snatching of the body required knowledge of and participation in it by the president's own staff and even his *widow*!

The more attention Lifton got as he barnstormed this country and Canada, the more exposure Macmillan arranged for him, especially on radio and TV. Having prepared him to deflect answers to any embarrassing questions, the more any criticism of government of any kind was discredited, at least in the minds of rational people. It also had the same effect on the willingness of reasonable people to consider that the government lied in its claimed assassination solution or that the assassination was by a conspiracy.

As book publishers, Random House and Macmillan are major media. Each of them commercialized and exploited the assassination from opposite extremes; each of them misled and confused their trusting readers and most of the American public, and thus each contributed significantly to the across-the-board failures of the major media. For money and nothing else.

When CBS gave Posner major attention in its 1993 television special on the assassination, it had a poll taken. After that major propaganda effort that reached a large percentage of the American people, a larger majority than ever ironically refused to believe it and the official mythology—*nine out of ten Americans*!

Although *Case Open* was published on the cheap, without a single ad for it and not a single review in any newspaper or magazine, I received innumerable phone calls and several hundred letters from strangers within a few weeks. Not one failed to praise it and to thank me for writing it.

The major media confused the people more, but it did not persuade them to believe the official mythology, a rare tribute to the common sense of the people on this question. In all, I reached only an insignificantly tiny percentage of the people compared with these fraudulent books, but the reaction to *Case Open* was 100 percent disagreement with Posner and the official mythology, with the exception of a single letter from one of Posner's fans, defending himself, not Posner.

So, despite the fact that virtually no one has access to factual writing about the assassination, an overwhelming majority refuse to believe either the official mythology or the private defenses of it. This represents quite a large potential market for honest, factual books, but I know of no publisher who has sought or commissioned such a book on the assassination.

The policy of publishers from the moment of the assassination and the attitude it represents is one of the reasons the conspiracy to assassinate President Kennedy has continued to avoid exposure. It is the counterpart of the government conspiracy not to investigate that I expose in *Never Again!*

There is no way any private person or persons can now solve the crime. And all the years of misleading and lying to the people from both extremes has served to protect those conspirators who carried out their coup that set the world on its now disastrous course.

CONCLUSION

WAKETH THE WATCHMAN?

This book, this approach, this reasoning and mustering of facts which address motive, means, and opportunity, is made necessary by the de facto government conspiracy not to investigate the assassination of President Kennedy itself, by its foisting off on the sorrowing and trusting people of an "official truth" that I contend stands as the official mythology, by the palpably false and dishonest "solution" to what was correctly called "the crime of the century," and by the failures of the media to do as it should have done. This leaves nothing but circumstantial evidence—motive, means, and opportunity—to arrive at what might be the most dependable of possible explanations of the crime.

In this approach, no other force or combination of forces can equal in motive that of the military-industrial-intelligence complex, particularly given the military's determined opposition to President Kennedy's policies and his refusal to accept the policies they pressed upon him endlessly and which they, when they could, imposed upon him. They did this despite their knowledge that it was the opposite of what he wanted, that it was not the national policy that only the president and Congress possess the Constitutional authority to set. They severely limited what he as president could do.

Article 1, Section 1 of the Constitution reads, "All legislative Powers herein granted shall be vested in a Congress of the United States, which shall consist of a Senate and a House of Representatives." This Article deals with the powers and responsibilities of the Congress. In Section 8 of Article 1, the declaring of war and what relates to it is reserved to the Congress *exclusively*. (emphasis added) Section 8 begins, "The Congress shall have the Power To," followed by the enumeration of those powers exclusively of Congress. In it we find:

> To define and punish Piracies and Felonies committed on the high Seas, and Offenses against the Law of Nations;
>
> To declare War, grant letters of Marque and Reprisal, and make Rules concerning Captives on Land and Water;
>
> To raise and support Armies, but no Appropriation of Money to that Use shall be for a longer Term than two Years;
>
> To provide and maintain a Navy;
>
> To make Rules for the Government and Regulation of the land and Naval Forces;
>
> To provide for calling forth the Militia to execute the Laws of the Union, suppress insurrections and repel Invasions;
>
> To provide for organizing, arming, and disciplining the Militia, and for governing such Part of them as may be employed in the Service of the United States, reserving to the States respectively, the Appointment of the Offices, and the Authority of training the Militia according to the discipline prescribed by Congress; . . .

Article II, Section 1 begins, "The executive Power shall be vested in the president of the United States of America." It goes on to define his term, how he shall be elected, removed, paid, and the oath he must take. His role as commander in chief is stated at the beginning of Section 2:

> The President shall be Commander in Chief of the Army and Navy of the United States, and of the Militia of the several States when called into the actual Service of the United States; he may require the Opinion in writing of the principal Officer in each of the executive Departments, upon any Subject relating to the Duties of their respective Offices, and he shall have the power to grant Reprieves and Pardons for Offenses against the United States, except in cases of impeachment.

Under our Constitution the power to declare war is vested exclusively in the Congress. The president may not declare or start a war under the Constitution. His sole duty, as conceived and assigned to him relating to war, is as commander in chief of the armed forces.

Over the years, presidents have usurped powers not given them. And there was nothing Congress could do about that other than impeach the president or withhold money from his office and/or the armed forces, neither of which is a reasonable means of controlling any president without causing the greatest of difficulties. That in our entire history only one president has been impeached,[1] illustrates how under most circumstances that is not a reasonable means of controlling any out-of-control president. So, over the years, many of them have usurped the war-making powers they are denied under the Constitution. Truman took us into an extremely costly and hurtful war in Korea, where we are still bogged down. Johnson did the same in Vietnam. His successor, Nixon, kept us there. Nixon could have ended that war much sooner than he did, but did not because doing so would likely have threatened his prospect of re-election. Billions of dollars and countless lives were lost and ruined in that undeclared war he could have settled years earlier on better terms than the total, ignominious defeat suffered because he did not.

By calling war a "police action," war has been redefined to allow for the president to violate the clear language of the Constitution. No president has the authority to start a war, whether it be called a "police action" or a "preventive war" which the Eisenhower administration considered launching against the Soviet Union. *Any* kind of war, under the Constitution, can only be started with a declaration of it, which is a right and power vested exclusively in the Congress.

This was true of the Bay of Pigs. It was true at the time of the Cuba Missile Crisis. It was true of the war in Vietnam begun in the Eisenhower administration under pressure from Vice President Nixon and Secretary of State John Foster Dulles. It was true of any implementation of the subhuman SIOP military scheme for devastating much of the world and poisoning the rest. It is true of all the wrongful things our military did to increase our involvement in Vietnam by violating the wishes and orders of its commander in chief.

All those presidents who involved us in undeclared wars, no matter how they redefined "war" and rewrote the Constitution, were lawless presidents, and in each and every one of those undeclared wars the country suffered greatly for it. The framers of the Constitution were wiser than those presidents who waged those many undeclared wars.

Each of these instances where the military usurped the power of Congress to declare war or the powers of the president as commander in chief resulted in costly disasters.

But so many presidents, so many generals and admirals, believed that they knew and understood better than those who created this nation and stated its principles, setting forth in clear language who has what powers and who does not. None ever learned from the disasters this caused the entire nation, save for the great profits of a tiny minority. All believed they were wiser than the Founding Fathers, and none learned from the past.

As the people are never told and only a very few understand, each and every violation of the Constitution has had disastrous consequences and costs that have brought the country to its present wretched and dangerous condition, financially, economically, politically and socially. The life of the nation has been controlled for years by violations of the Constitution, all given fine-sounding rationales to make them acceptable, like "preventive war." There is no such thing. Preventive war entails surreptitiously starting a war which only the Congress can legally do. And it cannot, under the Constitution, escape that responsibility by giving it a different name or by paying no attention when a president wages war without a Congressional declaration.

All these unconstitutional military activities, wars by different names, have had significant economic and social costs, which have crippled our nation, ballooned the national debt, and prevented us from addressing our pressing problems.

All of this traces back to the military, past and present, that has been in virtually constant violation of the Constitution. The military of tunnel vision that conceives of itself as patriotic, not recognizing or even caring that this kind of "patriotism" requires genuine subversion of our Constitution. The military regards itself as omniscient, and its critics as obstacles or worse.

Consider the military leadership during the Eisenhower administration. It drew up plans for a sneak attack, war by stealth, against the Soviet Union when it was on its knees after the unimaginable devastation it suffered in World War II, the military of the so-called "preventive war."

The military that agreed to the Bay of Pigs invasion plan concocted by its partner, the Central Intelligence Agency, was well aware that plan had disastrous failure built into it. That plan had as its real purpose starting a war with tiny Cuba to salvage the purposely flawed operation and save face for the president. They had deliberately and thoroughly deceived the president in order to create the conditions for beginning another undeclared war, still another violation of the Constitution. Fortunately, President Kennedy refused to be suckered into that evil, that certain disaster, even if Cuba would inevitably have been defeated.

The military that wanted war instead of peace at the time of the Cuba Missile Crisis; the military and its complex partner the CIA that then violated orders in flying prohibited U-2 flights over the USSR at the height of that crisis; the military that opposed the peace with which that crisis ended; the military that wanted to attack Cuba even after the crisis was resolved peacefully. Despite its determined effort, peace was achieved.

The military that had arranged for it and not the president, to control the use of nuclear weapons, and for it to be able to just wipe out much of the world and poisoning the rest of it with its SIOP-62 contrary to the expressed desires of the president as commander in chief.

The military that insists there is an urgent need for more and more advanced equipment and means of waging war, including more nuclear weapons when our stockpile is ever so much greater than is required to destroy the world. This, at the same time we are supposed to be reducing and then eliminating them, as we demand that others reduce and eliminate theirs. Yet we increase and update ours, adding to the national debt to do that, which greatly hampers our ability to address genuine national needs. For example, because of extravagant military spending, millions of Americans are without medical care. Those who clamor for still more military expenditures are the same ones who saw to it that health-care reform could not be enacted by Congress in 1994.

Referring to the military, Hamilton wrote in *The Federalist Papers* that "For it is a truth, which the experience of ages has attested, that the people are always most in danger when the means of injuring their rights are in the possession of those of whom they entertain the least suspicion."

President Eisenhower, after a long professional lifetime in the military, having led it in war and with the foresight that came from looking back on his own mistakes, warned in his farewell address on leaving office on January 17, 1961:

> . . . we must guard against the acquisition of unwarranted influence, whether sought or unsought, by the military-industrial complex. The potential for the disastrous rise of misplaced power exists and will persist. We must never let the weight of this combination endanger our liberties or our democratic processes.

As we have seen, this was more than a warning. It was a prediction, and it came to pass almost immediately. That was the year of the SIOP. It was the year before the prescient and popular novel, *Seven Days in May*, by Fletcher Knebel and Charles W. Bailey II, two experienced Washington correspondents, laid Eisenhower's warning out so terrifyingly.

In modern times, it is this kind of dedicated military "patriotism" that inflicted military dictatorships on the world, or the tyrants selected by the military and kept in power by it.

With this only part of the public record we have seen, and that only part of the full record; with this concept of patriotism that dominates those who control the military, how much of an added step is it to eliminate the man who stood in the way of all those military plans, hopes, aspirations, when that was the only way they could be achieved? How, with their beliefs, could they regard the president as other than unpatriotic? Strong and fixed was their belief that they were the true patriots, that they understood the country's need better than anyone. This is the *public* record of the military which has never been assembled and made comprehensible for the people, as to a degree, I try to do here. And this is only the *public* record.

This is the military that goes off and wages war on its own during the undeclared war in Vietnam. David Wise, who in *The Politics of Lying* makes a strong case that lying, and the secrecy that makes it possible, is national policy, tells how one general in Vietnam involved forty thousand American men and four hundred fighter-bombers in unauthorized attacks in North Vietnam. In so doing, he jeopardized lives and those costly planes for almost half a year.[2] Consider also how such a policy resulted in the My Lai massacre being briefed "as one of our successful operations."[3]

For almost half a year one general allegedly waged his private war, undetected and uncontrolled? Can that be believed? Not if he told Congress the truth in testifying that this was approved and encouraged all the way up to the Joint Chiefs of Staff!

Wise had no secret sources on this, yet none of the media ever put it all together so the people could know and understand it, the people whose sons' and daughters' lives were endangered and wasted by the general encouraged to wage that unauthorized war by all above him, other than the president. It was all public, published. Wise merely put it together to give it meaning. Here is his source note:

> The Max Frankel quote is from his reply to Daniel P. Moynihan in *Commentary*, July 1971, p. 16. The data on the number of planes and men under the command of General John D. Lavelle are from *Newsweek*, June 26, 1972, p.17. Lavelle's testimony is from the *New York Times*, June 13, 1972, pp. 1, 6. His claim that his superiors tacitly encouraged his actions is from the *New York Times*, October 7, 1972, p. 6. General John D. Ryan's testimony that he was prevented from telling the truth by Melvin Laird is from the *Washington Post*, September 26, 1972, p. 1.[4]

This was not important enough for any of the well-staffed components of the major media to have put it together and let the people know about it, when knowing about it could have had some meaning and might have saved lives and millions, if not billions, of dollars. But none did.

Aside from the unending failure to either investigate or report impartially on the assassination and its investigations, this gets us to the major media's failure to report the truth about that undeclared, unconstitutional war in Vietnam and the evaluation of our military. Nonetheless, Wise defends the media, which is not unexpected for a man who was for so long a Washington correspondent for a major newspaper:

> Granted that the government can use backgrounders to shape the truth, there are other factors that may lead to news distortion. Misinformation may result not only from government manipulation but from the shortcomings and failures of the press itself.
>
> No institution is without flaws, or exempt from criticism. Much of the recent criticism of the press, however, has arisen from suspect motives and had tended to focus on false issues.[5]

That might have been true of the media at the time he writes about in his chapter, "The Government and the Press." There, he is talking about the beleaguered Nixon administration. But it is not true of the military. As I note above, reporters in Vietnam knew our military was lying, and they reported that in *foreign* papers, not for Americans to read and understand.

Without realizing that it relates to himself, too, in what he omits about the press and the assassination, and his avoidance of that in his cataloging of official lying, here is how Wise concludes this chapter:

> There is, of course, only one side that a constitutionally free press can be on, and that is the side of truth. But to fulfill that role requires a singular tough-mindedness. The press, despite criticism from political leaders, needs to question, probe, analyze, and interpret more, not less. It should resist government pressures and self-generated pressures. It must not succumb to the seduction of power, nor automatically accept government handouts and leaks as fact. If the press acts as a mere transmission belt for government pronouncements, then it contributes to the credibility gap, and to the erosion of trust that has already divided the people from their government.[6]

Who in the media did not fail "to fulfill that role" of the "constitutionally free press," did not "succumb to power" and did not "succumb" to "government handouts and leaks" when the president was assassinated? Did *any* component of any of the media ever "question, probe, analyze, and interpret" the report on the assassination and its investigations? Was there a greater issue? One more important to the nation, to the political system, to its integrity, its future, to the trust of the people in their government and their media? One that bore more on the integrity of the administration brought into power by that assassination? One that was more a challenge to the media and to its integrity?

Can there be a matter of greater importance than a coup d'état in our country? Is it not also true that what I here put together for the first time about the military is a matter of quintessential importance to the nation?

Wise's last words in his very important book are an excellent statement of the role of the media in a democratic society, and what it must do to fulfill its constitutional role, the role it did not fulfill. He writes about media acceptance and publishing what is given to it for use without attribution in backgrounders. He says what is obvious, that the media as a whole should insist on being able to identify its quoted sources:

> More important than this, however, is that the press—particularly at a time when it has been under government pressure and attack—continue to question, probe, analyze, and interpret the statements and actions of the government. The press, of all our institutions, must surely have learned over the past two decades that what the government says may not be true. If there is any one major shortcoming of the American press over recent years, it has been the tendency to accept the word of the government despite repeated evidence that—particularly in the national security area—the government may be lying.[7]

When the president was assassinated, this is precisely what the media *failed* to do, *abdicating* its responsibility to "question, probe, analyze, and interpret the statements and actions of the government." It similarly failed when faced with what the military was doing. Wise continues by quoting from Supreme Court Justice Hugo Black, who wrote a memorable opinion in the Pentagon Papers case. "In the First Amendment," he wrote, "the Founding Fathers gave the free press the protection it must have to fulfill its essential role in our democracy. The press was to serve the governed, not the governors. . . . The press was protected so that it could bare the secrets of government and inform the people. Only a free and unrestrained press can effectively expose deception in government. . . . How can you give your consent to be governed," he asked, "when you are misled and lied to?"[8]

Under our Constitution, the media is "free and unrestrained" by the government. But the Constitution does not protect the people from the restraints the media imposes on itself.

While it may be possible, as Wise writes, "to debate the meaning of 'the consent of the governed' and the role of public opinion in a democracy," what it is *not* possible to debate is that by every measure, by every poll, there was and is no "consent of the governed" on the record of all governments since the assassination of President Kennedy. Not when at the end of 1993, *nine out of every ten Americans were entirely dissatisfied with it.* And save for those that reported this statistic, the entire media was silent.

Does not this and its failure to report fully and truthfully about the military justify the above observation that: "All the talk about democracy is nonsense!"? Does this not also lend credence to Wise's trenchant observation, "If they (the people) are misled, if the truth is concealed from them . . . then the American experiment is doomed to end in repression and failure"?

The media that knows the government lies to it and to the people nonetheless reported all its lies about the assassination of President Kennedy as the truth. There is nothing more subversive of our democracy than a real or de facto coup d'état, which is the inevitable result of an assassination. There is thus nothing in this country as vital to our democracy or as urgently needed as having "the secrets of government" exposed, as Justice Black noted. And, as he further noted, that for the media be able to do this, as it must for a democratic society to be viable, the "Founding Fathers gave the free press the protection it must have to fulfill its essential role in our democracy."[9]

With regard to that assassination, its investigation and the official lying about it, including the lying by the military about the wretchedly poor and misleading autopsy it controlled and reported on, the media has failed to "fulfill its essential role."

In considering this one part of the circumstantial-evidence case against the military, its deliberately false and dishonest autopsy report about which it did commit repeated perjury, the autopsy report that is basic in any criminal investigation, I am reminded that none of the media reported what I brought to light in *Post Mortem*. The first thing the military did when the autopsy examination was about to be started was to expel all civilians from the autopsy room and place a military guard around it to prevent any civilians from entering. And as I also report there, also not to be reported by the media, all the military personnel at the autopsy were given the written threat that if anyone there ever uttered a word about that autopsy, they would be subject to court martial.

By the way, the military alone had both the "means" and the "opportunity" to control that autopsy examination and what it reported. As I also brought to light in *Post Mortem*, it used that means to alter basic facts of the crime such as the wounds and their location in what the autopsy pathologist—this military pathologist—has in his second autopsy report. This without any comment from the media or denial from this military pathologist. And, again, without any media attention, I reported that he actually burned the autopsy report he had drafted, a report which would have been subjected to examination and cross-examination at Oswald's trial, as soon as the military knew that Oswald had been killed and there would be no trial.

This should be clearly understood as without precedent in our nation's history. What also must be clearly understood is the fact that this sordid story of how the autopsy of the president was handled by the military was unreported by the media on its own and even after I published it.

The second autopsy report, the one written after the military knew Oswald was dead, *was substantively altered by the military.* As noted above, those alterations were of the most basic facts of the crime—the location and description of the president's bullet wounds. *Three* military pathologists testified falsely about their autopsy examination and their report on it, the second and third by swearing falsely their agreement with the first!

There were official, *non-military* examinations by the most eminent experts the government could get, and their report proves that the *military* autopsy report did lie about the most basic of the medical evidence in its second autopsy report, the one the military knew would not be subject to rigorous, public examination.

All of this I published in 1975; all of it based on official records that had been hidden, suppressed, or both. All of it and ever so much more *official* proof that related to it, without a word of protest from anyone in the military. And the media ignored this incredible military performance, its ghastly record when the president, its commander in chief, was assassinated.

Was there ever in our history any greater need to "bare the secrets of government and inform the people?"

The media did not "fulfill its essential role in our democracy" by reporting this on their own, when it could have easily obtained the official proof. It then failed itself and the rest of us and our democratic system by not reporting it when I published it and made it freely available to all.

This *official, military* record alone requires that the military be suspected. That there is a clear and substantial case of "motive" I have demonstrated in this book.

When I was a child more than six decades ago, we were taught American history in a way that it is not taught today. We were taught, for example, that the writer Tom Paine was among the greatest of American heroes when our Founding Fathers fought against such awful, intimidating odds to establish the first really democratic society. We were taught that to a large degree Jefferson was indebted to Tom Paine for his magnificent Declaration of Independence. Despite the primitive nature of both printing and distribution in those days, Paine's revolutionary writing in support of a free and democratic society was read by a greater percentage of Americans than anything ever written by any American since then.

One of his enduring phrases with which he described the great dangers and problems confronting our forebears in establishing freedom and democracy is, "These are the times that try men's souls."[10]

We were taught to respect and admire Tom Paine and what he risked to write and speak so forthrightly to inspire those who fought against such great odds. But today our children complete high school, even college, without ever hearing his name. There have been many changes in our lives and what our youth are taught since I was a boy, but I believe failing to include any mention of Tom Paine in educating our youth is inconsistent with teaching them the great traditions and revolutionary beliefs on which our society is based.

In our modern life, has there ever been anything that "tries men's souls" more than what I set forth in this book? None of this was ever put together by the media for the people to understand. As Justice Black reminded us, "The press was protected so that it could bare the secrets of government and inform the people, its essential role in our democracy."

But the watchmen over our democracy did not fulfill "that essential role" when it needed to be done at the time of that assassination, that coup d'état, or then in that radical and disastrous change in national policy that followed that coup. It has not fulfilled its Constitutional role since its initial failure to do so. And thus, there lingers the question: Was the Kennedy assassination a military coup d'état? Will our media ever fulfill that watchman role assigned it by our Constitution?

Waketh the watchman?

The old saying of ancient times, when cities were protected at night by watchmen, is: "Lest the Lord guard the city, the watchman waketh in vain." The lord of our safety, of our independence, of the protection of our Constitution and all that it means, is the watchman of the constitutionally free media with its "essential role in our democracy."

Waketh that watchman now!

AFTERWORD

Long after I had written, retyped, and distributed copies of this book to a few of my friends, David Wrone sent me a June 19, 1995, *New Yorker* article that, while sitting and thinking after I read it, brought a bit more back to mind. This *New Yorker* article, about which more in a moment, turned my mind back to the time of the 1962 Cuba Missile Crisis. I had evolved my contemporaneous analysis of it before the Wednesday preceding the resolution of that crisis. The book on it that I had planned had the working title, *Tiger to Ride*, with the thrust of the book being that Khrushchev, in precipitating that crisis, gave John Kennedy his own "tiger to ride" to avoid World War III. If there now still be any doubt about the correctness of that analysis, I recommend to doubters this *New Yorker* article by Richard Rhodes, "The General and World War III." Below this title, in smaller type, is the headline, "Curtis LeMay believed that the only sure defense was to launch a preemptive first strike. During the Cuban missile crisis he almost did it." As a note to myself, I wrote another title: "Our Would-Be and Almost-Was Hitler."[1]

Rhodes's account is of how perilously close LeMay came to launching World War III and how devastating it would have been. Rhodes also reports, what to me was for the first time, some of the Hitlerian accomplishments for which LeMay struggled so hard to achieve and finally succeeded in doing in North Korea.

Of LeMay's killing of civilians in Japan in World War II, Rhodes quotes LeMay himself as saying of the fire-bombing of Tokyo that "probably more persons lost their lives by fire in Tokyo in a 6-hour period than at any time in the history of man." Due to his nocturnal fire-bombings "sixty-three Japanese cities had been totally or partially burned out and more than a million Japanese civilians killed."

At the beginning of the Korean war, LeMay asked to "turn SAC [Strategic Air Command] loose with incendiaries," but this blitzkrieg of civilians with fire from the air was denied him. However, later, he was able to do it "piecemeal, and carried" it out "brutally, burning out cities and breaking big agricultural dams, scouring an entire valley of peasant villages and rice paddies as far as twenty-seven miles downstream. . . . He later claimed that "we killed off—what—twenty percent of the population of [North] Korea." Civilians: women, children, and old men.[2]

When he outlined what he had in mind for Russia to a committee appointed by President Eisenhower and was told, "But, General, that's not national policy," he responded, "I don't care. It's my policy. That's what I'm going to do." In 1954, he estimated that "virtually all of Russia would be a smoking, radiating ruin at the end of two hours."[3]

Rhodes writes that "During the Cuban Missile crisis, the determination of LeMay and some of his subordinates to follow military logic, subverting presidential authority to do so, nearly led to full-scale nuclear war with the Soviet Union. The United States came closer to self-inflicted nuclear destruction at that time than most Americans realize."[4]

But Kennedy did end the prospect of such an unimaginable disaster with peace. On leaving a Joint Chiefs of Staff meeting with him after the crisis, which we won by getting those missiles out peacefully, as Rhodes writes, "LeMay came out saying, 'We lost! We ought to just go in there today and knock 'em off.'"

If there remain any who question my use of "Strangelovian," referring to some of our military, I would also refer them to this Rhodes's article.

And then Richard Rhodes's masterful book, *Dark Sun: The Making of the Hydrogen Bomb*, appeared.[5] It is a truly horrifying book that more than justifies Rhodes's earlier Pulitzer for his *The Making of the Atomic Bomb*. It turns out that Rhodes's *New Yorker* article is a more subdued and much shorter version of what he has in his new book, mostly in its last chapter, "Scorpions in a Bottle," which adds to what is known about LeMay and the Cuba missile crisis.

It is in every sense a remarkable book, a remarkable literary and historical achievement. Although it is not uncommon for publishers to exaggerate in puffing up books on their dust jackets, the blurbs on this one do not exaggerate. It sometimes understates, and it includes a rough guide to the contents. I therefore quote it at some length:

> In this brilliant, riveting, major work of history, science and politics, Richard Rhodes, . . . tells for the first time the secret story of how and why the hydrogen bomb was made; traces the path by which "the Bomb," the supreme artifact of twentieth-century science and technology, became the defining issue of the Cold War; and reveals how close the world came to nuclear destruction before the United States and the former Soviet Union learned the lesson of nuclear stalemate—a stalemate, Rhodes makes clear, that forced the superpowers to tenuous truce for more than four decades, in the end bankrupting and destroying the Communist state and foreclosing world-scale war . . . the week of the 1962 Cuban missile crisis when Curtis LeMay goaded President Kennedy to attack the USSR with everything in the U.S. arsenal, this book is full of unexpected—and sometimes hair-raising—revelations based on previously undisclosed Soviet as well as U.S. sources:. . .
>
> The Soviet Union was essentially defenseless against atomic bombing until at least 1960.
>
> Building the Strategic Air Command, Curtis LeMay made persistent attempts to acquire control of U.S. nuclear weapons independent of presidential authorization.
>
> SAC flew daily intelligence missions over the Soviet Union throughout the 1950s, including deliberately provocative overflights of Soviet cities by squadrons of aircraft in broad daylight.
>
> At the height of the Korean War, President Truman traded the U.S. Joint Chiefs of Staff nine atomic bombs for General Douglas MacArthur's head. . . .
>
> Not Robert Openheimer, as he was accused, but physicist and superhawk Edward Teller, delayed the development of the hydrogen

> bomb; but for Teller's obsession with megaton yields, the U.S could have tested a half-megaton thermonuclear by 1949.
>
> During the Cuban missile crisis, SAC put 7,000 megatons into the air, menaced the Soviet Union with an unauthorized missile launch and deliberately flew bombers toward Soviet targets. The first and only direct nuclear confrontation between the superpowers was also very nearly the last.[6]

As Rhodes writes and proves, LeMay and other generals did in fact have control over nuclear weapons independent of presidential control. Scary enough with generals like LeMay, but not him alone.

Scary that a president like Truman had to bargain with his military to be able to fire an insubordinate general who had needlessly caused thousands of American deaths through his insubordination and could have started World War III.

The last two pages of Rhodes's final chapter, "Scorpions in a Bottle," underscores the danger of a nuclear confrontation with the Soviet Union that was being pushed by the military but resisted and finally averted by President Kennedy's peaceful resolution of the Cuba Missile crisis, which did not sit well with Curtis LeMay who chewed Kennedy out and came out of Kennedy's meeting with the Chiefs saying, "We ought to just go in there today and knock 'em off." Rhodes also notes how, at the height of the crisis, "bombers deliberately flew past their turnaround points toward Soviet airspace, an unambiguous threat which Soviet radar operators would certainly have recognized and reported." What LeMay and no one in the government knew at the time was that Soviet forces in Cuba actually had twenty nuclear warheads that could have been targeted on U.S. cities as far north as Washington, D.C., not to mention some nine tactical nuclear missiles that Soviet field commanders were authorized to use. The amount of devastation on both sides would have been considerable, resulting in an estimated 100 million deaths, a figure considered extremely conservative by a 1984 World Health Organization study. While Kennedy succeeded in ending the crisis peacefully, LeMay never got over his conviction that it ended in failure. Rhodes notes, "How extraordinary that Curtis LeMay believed for the rest of his life that the United States "lost" the Cuban missile crisis and the Cold War. If John Kennedy had followed LeMay's advice, history would have forgotten the Nazis and their terrible Holocaust. Ours would have been the historic omnicide."[7]

What could have been is what would have been had it not been for John Kennedy who was president, had he not had the insight and understanding that saved the world from his generals who his brother told the Soviet ambassador he feared might overthrow him. As in the end he was overthrown by being assassinated.

Who had, or could have had, stronger motive than those of the LeMay mindset?

The books that get the most major-media attention are not those like Richard Rhodes's *Dark Sun*, which record how John Kennedy saved us and the world from the LeMays he feared would revolt and take control of the country and of the world, and do to it what Rhodes puts so starkly.

The LeMay mindset was not uncommon in the upper echelons of the military, as we have seen. Further confirmation of this can be found in Dino A. Brugioni's 1992 book, *Eyeball to Eyeball: The Inside Story of the Cuban Missile Crisis*. Brugioni was in the top ranks of the CIA's National Photographic Interpretation Center and a dedicated cold-war believer. In it he tells the following story:

> The president, on April 22, 1961, appointed General Maxwell Taylor to head an investigation of the CIA's role in the Bay of Pigs disaster and the next day asked Attorney General Bobby Kennedy to assist Taylor in the investigation. Other members of the Taylor probe panel included CIA director Allen Dulles and Admiral Arleigh A. Burke, the chief of naval operations. Information from their report was leaked to Charles J. V. Murphy, Washington bureau chief for *Fortune* magazine. Murphy wrote an account of the Bay of Pigs invasion highly critical of President Kennedy and thereby incurred the president's wrath. The president was furious. Suspecting that General Cabell had leaked the information, he asked for his resignation. Cabell tried to explain to the president that he was not the source of the leak, but to no avail. On January 31, 1962, he resigned as deputy director

> and retired from the Air Force. He was replaced by Lieutenant General Marshall "Pat" Carter. A number of years after President Kennedy's death, Murphy was doing another story related to intelligence and Lundahl [director of the CIA's National Photographic Interpretation Center] and I were directed to cooperate with him. He revealed to us that Admiral Arleigh Burke had been the source of the Bay of Pigs information. The admiral felt that the president had "chickened out" in not calling for Navy fighter aircraft to cover the Bay of Pigs invasion. Murphy said that Burke had nothing but disdain for President Kennedy and his "bagman" at the Department of Defense, McNamara.[8]

This displays insubordination and opposition to the president's policy, when the president alone is elected to decide what policy should be. Open opposition to his policy and interference with it was not at all uncommon in the high command of all branches of the military.

This gets little to no attention from the major media. What the major media loves, and sees to it gets the widest possible attention, is the revisionism, the rewriting of history to obscure the truth, the reality: the unimaginable, unprecedented virtual end of the civilized world JFK prevented. Had it not been for him, our generals' actions would have precipitated a nuclear war in which few would have survived. But they failed, thanks to Kennedy, and to him alone.

Nonetheless, those who rewrite our history, Kennedy's history in particular, are lauded with fame and fortune. Such books have no problem finding publishers who promote them and the major media willingly adds to this profitable commercial endeavor, profitable to all but the misled and misinformed people.

What we have three decades after his assassination is the corruption of all in our society, and not just by the military. It is also by those whose political careers are made possible and advanced by keeping ours a military-oriented society with a bankrupting military economy. It is, too, by all of the media which supports the military, military policy and orientation and the rewriting of our history and that of John Kennedy, as well as its unending, unquestioning support of the official mythology of his assassination and in its refusal to publish the known and established truth about that assassination.

Were this to change, the people, most of whom have doubts, would be asking questions not only about the assassination but about all that followed it.

The difference between our media and that of the authoritarian systems we abhor is a difference in degree only. The people do not begin with the understanding that their media is controlled by the government, which it isn't. So our people do not have the reason people in authoritarian systems have for not believing what the elements of their media tell them. But the result is the same, pervasive doubt and cynicism.

And so it is that our people have not had the circumstantial evidence of motive, means, and opportunity of the assassination presented to them by our media, as I have tried to do in this book. My hope is that by making this case, which may perhaps be added to in the future, we may correct our corrupted system so that it may again work as visualized by those greatest of political thinkers who established our democratic society.

BIBLIOGRAPHY

Abel, Elie. *The Missile Crisis*. Philadelphia: Lippincott, 1965.

Bell, Bill. "Cool JFK in Tapes of Crisis in 1962." *New York Daily News*, July 28, 1994, 1994, 6.

Blakey, G. Robert and Richard N. Billings. *Fatal Hour: The Assassination of President Kennedy by Organized Crime*. New York: Berkley Books, 1992.

Blight, James G., Bruce J. Allyn, and David A. Welch. *Cuba on the Brink: Castro, the Missile Crisis, and the Soviet Collapse*. New York: Pantheon Books, 1993.

Brown, Anthony Cave. *"C": The Rise and Fall of Sir Stewart Graham Menzies, Spymaster to Winston Churchill*. New York: Macmillan, 1987.

Brugioni, Dino A., and Robert F. McCort. *Eyeball to Eyeball: The Inside Story of the Cuban Missile Crisis*. New York: Random House, 1991.

Countering Criticism of the Warren Report: Dispatch to Chiefs, Certain Stations and Bases. 1967. Edited by Central Intelligence Agency.

Daly, Christopher B. "Ex-Director Faults CIA Of Carter Era; Reports 'Irrelevant,' Turner Tells Meeting." *The Washington Post*, December 3, 1994, 11.

Daniel, Jean. "When Castro Heard the News." *The New Republic*, December 7, 1963, 7–9.

Davison, Jean. *Oswald's Game*. 1st ed. New York: W.W. Norton, 1983.

DeLoach, C. D. *FBI Memorandum DeLoach to Mohn*. (62-109060-4172). Washington, D.C., 1966.

DeLoach, C. D. *FBI Memorandum: C. D. DeLoach to Tolson*, 1967.

Donovan, Robert J. *Eisenhower: The Inside Story*. New York: Harper & Collins, 1956.

Dulles, Allen. "Statement by Mr. Allen Dulles Director of the Central Intelligence Agency to the Senate Foreign Relations Committee on 31 May 1960." Edited by Central Intelligence Agency. Washington, D.C., 1960.

Eisenhower, Dwight D. "Farewell Address." 1961. https://www.eisenhowerlibrary.gov/sites/default/files/research/online-documents/farewell-address/1961-01-17-press-release.pdf.

Esterline, Jacob D. Memorandum. Edited by Central Intelligence Agency. 1960.

Evans, C. A. Memorandum, Evans to Belmont 11/25/1963. Edited by Federal Bureau of Investigation. Washington, D.C, 1963.

FBI. *Investigation of the Assassination of John F. Kennedy November 22, 1963.* Edited by U.S. Department of Justice Federal Bureau of Investigation. Washington, D.C.: U.S. Government Printing Office, 1963.

Ford, Gerald R. and John R. Stiles. *Portrait of the Assassin.* New York: Simon and Schuster, 1965.

Frankenheimer, John and Rod Serling, *Seven Days in May.* United States: Paramount Pictures, 1964.

Fulbright, J. William. "Speech in U.S. Senate." *Congressional Record.* Washington D.C.: U. S. Government Printing Office., 1960, 14734.

Hamilton, Alexander, and Clinton Rossiter. 1961. *The Federalist Papers; Alexander Hamilton, James Madison, John Jay. A Mentor book, MT328.* New York: New American Library.

Hanrahan, John. "CIA Chief Faces Quiz in Agent Slander Suit." *The Washington Post,* June 7, 1969, 7.

Helms, Richard. *Affidavit in Eerik Heine v Juri R*aus April 1, 1966.

Helms, Richard. *Affidavit in Eerik Heine v Juri Raus October 7, 1966.* (Civil Action 15952).

Hepburn, James. *Farewell America.* Vaduz: Frontiers, 1968.

House Select Committee on Assassinations. Hearings. Washington D.C.: U.S. Government Printing Office. 1978.

Hunt, E. Howard. *Undercover; Memoirs of an American Secret Agent.* New York: Berkeley Publishing, 1974.

Hunt, Linda. *Secret Agenda: The United States Government, Nazi Scientists, and Project Paperclip, 1945 to 1990.* New York: St. Martin's Press, 1991.

"Jaworski Reportedly Had Role in Setting Up C.I.A. Aid Conduit." *New York Times*, November 6, 1973, 25.

Karnow, Stanley. *Vietnam: A History*. New York: The Viking Press. 1983.

Keck, David M. "Case Open: A Review." *The Forth Decade: A Journal of Research on The John F. Kennedy Assassination,* 1994. 1 (2): 19-21.

Kennedy, Robert F. *Thirteen Days; A Memoir of the Cuban Missile Crisis.* New York: W. W. Norton, 1969

Khrushchev, Nikita Sergeevich, and Edward Crankshaw. *Khrushchev Remembers*. Boston: Little, Brown, 1970.

Knebel, Fletcher, and Charles W. Bailey. *Seven Days in May*. New York: Harper & Row, 1962.

Kurtz, Michael L. *Crime of the Century: The Kennedy Assassination from a Historian's Perspective*. Knoxville: University of Tennessee Press, 1982.

Lechuga, Carlos. *In the Eye of the Storm: Castro, Khrushchev, Kennedy and the Missile Crisis*. Translated by Mary Todd. Melbourne, Australia: Ocean Press, 1995.

Lesar, James H. "Crime of the Century: The Kennedy Assassination from a Historian's Perspective." *Journal of American History* 1983, 70 (2), 469.

Lifton, David S. *Best Evidence: Disguise and Deception in the Assassination of John F. Kennedy*. New York: Macmillan, 1980.

Livingstone, Harrison Edward. *Killing the Truth: Deceit and Deception in the JFK Case*. New York: Carroll & Graf Publishers, 1993.

Livingstone, Harrison Edward, and Robert J. Groden. *High Treason 2: The Great Cover-Up: The Assassination of President John F. Kennedy*. New York: Carroll & Graf, 1992.

———. *High Treason: The Assassination of JFK & The Case for Conspiracy*. New York: Carroll & Graf, 1998.

Manchester, William. *The Death of a President: November 20-November 25, 1963*. New York: Harper & Row, 1967.

Marcus, Jon. "New Cuba Tapes Show Congressional Leadership Wanted an Invasion." *Associated Press*, December 21, 1994.

McGrory, Mary. "Rebel Without a Trace." *The Washington Post,* November 6, 1994, C1.

McKnight, Gerald D. *Breach of Trust: How the Warren Commission Failed the Nation and Why*. Lawrence, KS.: University of Kansas Press, 2005.

Meagher, Sylvia. *Accessories After the Fact: The Warren Commission, the Authorities, and the Report*. New York: Vintage Press, 1976.

Newman, John M. *JFK and Vietnam: Deception, Intrigue, and the Struggle for Power*. New York, NY: Warner Books, 1992.

O'Donnell, Kenneth P., and David F. Powers. *"Johnny, We Hardly Knew Ye"; Memories of John Fitzgerald Kennedy*. 1st ed. Boston: Little, Brown, 1972.

Paine, Thomas. *Common Sense*. London: J. Watson, 1850.

Pincus, Walter. "According to panel, CIA Should Lock Its Internal Watchdog in the Doghouse." *The Washington Post*, Nov 03, 1994, 23.

———. "Panel Head Presses Clinton, CIA to Close Gap." *The Washington Post*, December 3, 1994, 11.

———. "Senior CIA Official Criticizes Past Estimates, Urges Change in Emphasis." *The Washington Post*, September 24, 1994, 23.

Posner, Gerald L. *Case Closed: Lee Harvey Oswald and the Assassination of JFK*. New York: Random House, 1993.

Purcell, Heather A., and James K. Galbraith. "Did The U.S. Military Plan a Nuclear First Strike for 1963?" *The American Prospect* (19): 88. 1994.

Reeves, Richard. *President Kennedy: Profile of Power*. New York: Simon & Schuster, 1993.

Rhodes, Richard. *The Making of the Atomic Bomb*. New York: Simon & Schuster, 1986.

———. *Dark Sun: The Making of the Hydrogen Bomb*. New York: Simon & Schuster, 1995.

———. "The General and World War III". *The New Yorker* 1995, 71 (17): 47.

Roffman, Howard. *Presumed Guilty: Lee Harvey Oswald in the Assassination of President Kennedy.* Rutherford, NJ: Farleigh Dickinson University Press. 1975.

Rossiter, Clinton Lawrence, and Charles R. Kesler. *The Federalist Papers: Alexander Hamilton, James Madison, John Jay*. New York: Signet Classic, 2003.

Rusk, Dean, Richard Rusk, and Daniel S. Papp. *As I Saw It.* 1st ed. New York: W.W. Norton, 1990.

Schlesinger, Arthur M. *A Thousand Days; John F. Kennedy in the White House.* Boston: Houghton Mifflin, 1965

Senate Foreign Relations Committee. "Events Incident to the Summit Conference." Edited by United States Senate. Washington, D.C.: U.S. Government Printing Office, 1960.

Shapiro, Margaret. "Russian Missile Center Has Electricity Cut Off." *The Washington Post,* September 22, 1994, a26.

"Shuttle Crew Plucks Satellite from Its Orbit." 1994. *The Washington Post,* September 16, 1994, 3.

Smith, R. Jeffrey. "Clinton Decides to Retain Bush Nuclear Arms Policy." *The Washington Post,* September 22, 1994, 1.

Sorensen, Theodore C. *Kennedy.* New York, Harper & Row,1965.

Sparrow, John. "After the Assassination." *Times Literary Supplement,* December 14, 1967, 1217–1222.

———. *After the Assassination: A Positive Appraisal of the Warren Report.* New York: Chilmark Press, 1967.

Warren, Commission. *Report of the President's Commission on the Assassination of President John F. Kennedy.* Vol. Book, Whole. Washington, D.C.: U.S. Government Printing Office, 1964.

Warren Commission. *Investigation of the Assassination of President John F. Kennedy: Hearings Before the President's Commission on the Assassination of President John F. Kennedy.* Washington, D.C.: U.S. Government Printing Office, 1964.

Weiner, Tim. 1994. "Director Of C.I.A. To Leave, Ending Troubled Tenure." *New York Times,* December 29, 1994, 1994, 1.

Weisberg, Harold. 1966a. *Whitewash II: the FBI-Secret Service Cover-up.* Hyattstown, MD.

———. *Whitewash: The Report on the Warren Report.* Hyattstown, MD: Weisberg, 1966.

———. *Oswald in New Orleans.* New York: Canyon Books, 1967.

———. *Case Open: The Unanswered JFK Assassination Questions.* New York: Carroll & Graf, 1994.

———. *Photographic Whitewash; Suppressed Kennedy Assassination Pictures.* Hyattstown, MD: Weisberg, [1967] 1976.

———. *Post-Mortem: JFK Assassination Cover-up Smashed!.* Frederick, MD: Weisberg) 1969.

———. *Never Again! The Government Conspiracy in the JFK Assassination.* New York: Carroll & Graf, 1995.

Weisberg, Harold, and Jim Lesar. *Whitewash IV: Top Secret JFK Assassination Transcript.* Frederick, MD.: Weisberg, 1974.

Wise, David. *The Politics of Lying: Government Deception, Secrecy, and Power.* New York: Random House, 1973.

———. "Patrician for the C.I.A." *New York Times*, December 11, 1994, BR9.

Wrone, David R. *The Freedom of Information Act and Political Assassinations.* Stevens Point, Wi.: Foundation Press, 1978.

———. *The Zapruder Film: Reframing JFK's Assassination.* Lawrence, KS: University Press of Kansas, 2003.

APPENDIX 1

EXCULPATING OSWALD

There is much evidence that the Warren Commission and FBI gathered, but suppressed, misrepresented, or simply ignored which unquestionably exonerates Lee Harvey Oswald as the so-called "lone-nut" assassin. Harold Weisberg, Sylvia Meagher, Howard Roffman, Gerald McKnight, David Wrone, among a few others, have laid out and discussed in great detail this evidence in their published works, evidence which Harold Weisberg on occasion draws on in this manuscript. In this appendix we present a few examples of the significant pieces of that evidence, although clearly not all, which exonerate Oswald and should help explain why Weisberg so often refers to the "solution" or conclusion of the *Warren Report* as "mythology."

1. Did Oswald bring the alleged assassination weapon, the Mannlicher Carcano rifle, to the Texas School Book Depository (TSBD) on the morning of the assassination, as the Warren Commission (WC) claimed?

TSBD employee, Jack Dougherty, whose job was to check employees coming into work, in testimony before the WC, positively swore twice that Oswald had nothing in his hands when he entered the building on the morning of Nov. 22, 1963.[1]

In addition, the paper bag that allegedly was constructed to carry the disassembled weapon and found on the 6th floor of the TSBD had no evidence of oil stains from the well-oiled Mannlicher Carcano. FBI expert James Cadigan was unable to find any marks, scratches, abrasions or other indications that would tie the bag to the rifle.[2]

2. Did Oswald fire the Mannlicher Carcano rifle that day?

There is no evidence that the Mannlicher Carcano was even fired that day (by Oswald or anyone else). Neither the Dallas Police nor the FBI swabbed the barrel to see if the weapon had been fired since it was last cleaned, a basic test in any murder investigation involving a firearm.

Even more conclusive, paraffin casts of Oswald's cheeks showed no residue, indicating he had not fired the rifle. Most revealing is an internal FBI memorandum from Assistant Director Alan Belmont to Clyde Tolson, Hoover's deputy. Belmont writes, ". . . our Laboratory experts testified to the WC that the paraffin tests were essentially negative. In addition, highly technical examinations made by the Atomic Energy Commission and our Laboratory on the paraffin casts could not connect Oswald with the rifle."[3]

3. Oswald's whereabouts just prior to the assassination.

TSBD employee Carolyn Arnold, who was interviewed by the FBI but never called as a witness by the WC, stated that she had seen Oswald on the first floor at 12:25 p.m., just five minutes prior to the assassination. The FBI, however, had recorded 12:15 p.m. as the time she saw Oswald. But the proof that Arnold actually saw Oswald on the first floor at 12:25 p.m. can be found in an internal FBI document, a radiogram dated 3/31/1964.[4] She also confirmed this time in a November 27, 1978, *Dallas Morning News* article.[5] Several other witnesses placed Oswald on the first floor of the TSDB just prior to the assassination.

4. Problems with the testimony of Howard Brennan, the one eyewitness who claimed to have seen Oswald in that 6th floor window with a rifle.

Brennan said that the gunman he saw in that 6th floor window was standing, which would have meant he had to have shot his rifle through a double window pane.

He testified that the person he saw in that window was wearing a different color shirt than the one Oswald wore that day.

He never testified to seeing that gunman actually fire his weapon.

He never positively identified Oswald during two police lineups, even though he admitted to seeing Oswald on television prior to the lineups.

The Zapruder film actually shows Brennan not looking up at the TSBD at the time of the assassination, but looking over his right shoulder.[6]

5. Two films taken just before and at the time of the assassination show no one in that 6th floor window, from which the WC concluded Oswald had shot and killed President Kennedy.

A film taken by Charles Bronson which captured the TSBD minutes before the assassination and also showed the exact moment that the fatal shot struck Kennedy was reviewed by the Dallas FBI but never sent to Washington, nor was it seen by the Warren Commission. It was not until 1978 that the public became aware of the film due to the efforts of Harold Weisberg, who forced the release of the Dallas field office's assassination files. *The Dallas Morning News* ran a story on Bronson and reproduced stills and frames from his film. The *News* reported, "Bronson's still photographs of the motorcade were crisp and clear." Gerald McKnight added, "Bronson's film showed President Kennedy enough to reveal that there had been nobody at the sixth-floor window seconds before the assassination. There were ninety-two frames of that window—the alleged "sniper's nest"—alone."[7]

Another film taken by Robert J. E. Hughes also shows that there was no one in that 6th floor window, the alleged "sniper's nest." Both the FBI lab and the Navy Photographic Interpretation Center examined this film taken just prior to the assassination and found that: "No images that could be interpreted as an individual or individuals were found in any of the exposures."[8]

6. Rifle tests that actually undermine the claim that Oswald had the capability to carry out the assassination.

It should first be noted that the rifle that was used for these tests after significant repairs and alterations, was no longer the same rifle Oswald allegedly used. Most significantly, shims had to be inserted to elevate the scope and move it to the left.[9]

Sylvia Meagher presented a useful summary of these rifle tests in her *Accessories After the Fact*, pp. 107–108, in which she began by pointing out: "It must be emphasized at once that these tests have not the slightest claim to being comparable with the performance credited to Oswald by the Warren Commission. The tests used three master riflemen whose skill was as superior to Oswald's as a chief surgeon's to an intern. In 1959 Oswald qualified as a marksman, the minimum classification used in the Marine Corps, scoring 191 on a scale of 190–250, after which he had had no target practice of significance and no proven practice with the Carcano rifle. This alone is sufficient to invalidate the tests as in any sense comparable with or indicative of the skill allegedly demonstrated by Oswald. In addition, the tests utilized stationary rather than moving targets. Each participant was told to take as much time as he wished for the first shot; it will occasion no surprise that they all hit the first target, but it should be borne in mind that the alleged assassin did not enjoy such an advantage."[10]

Yet, despite all these advantages, none of these master riflemen was able to duplicate Oswald's feat of firing the Mannlicher Carcano three times in 5.6 seconds, hitting the president twice and killing him, as well as severely wounding Governor Connally. As Ms. Meagher concludes: "The conditions under which the rifle tests were conducted , the introduction of shims to correct the telescopic sight, and the unresolved questions related to the mounting of the scope—all these only reinforce the impression that the Commission indulged in self-deception in finding that Oswald had the capability to carry out the feat no less remote than his actual skill than a flight to the moon."[11]

The exculpatory evidence discussed above is largely drawn from the Warren Commission's own investigation. There is perhaps no greater example of this basic point than the Commission's endorsement of the so-called "single-bullet theory:" that one bullet, specifically CE 399, caused all the non-fatal wounds to President Kennedy and Governor Connally. This theory is not only central to their case that Oswald was the lone assassin, but it is also contradicted by the testimony they took and ballistics tests performed. All this is indicative of the kind of painstaking work responsible critics have been doing for decades, which unfortunately has been largely ignored by the media. In addition to Mr. Weisberg's considerable contributions, we list below some of the most important works of other responsible critics.

McKnight, Gerald D. *Breach of Trust: How the Warren Commission Failed the Nation and Why.*

Meagher, Sylvia. *Accessories After the Fact: The Warren Commission, the Authorities, and the Report.*

Roffman, Howard. *Presumed Guilty: Lee Harvey Oswald in the Assassination of President Kennedy.*

Wrone, David R. (ed.) *The Legal Proceedings of Harold Weisberg v. General Services Administration.*

Wrone, David R. *The Zapruder Film: Reframing JFK's Assassination.*

APPENDIX 2

OPERATION NORTHWOODS

THE JOINT CHIEFS OF STAFF
WASHINGTON 25, D.C.

UNCLASSIFIED

13 March 1962

MEMORANDUM FOR THE SECRETARY OF DEFENSE

Subject: Justification for US Military Intervention in Cuba (TS)

1. The Joint Chiefs of Staff have considered the attached Memorandum for the Chief of Operations, Cuba Project, which responds to a request of that office for brief but precise description of pretexts which would provide justification for US military intervention in Cuba.

2. The Joint Chiefs of Staff recommend that the proposed memorandum be forwarded as a preliminary submission suitable for planning purposes. It is assumed that there will be similar submissions from other agencies and that these inputs will be used as a basis for developing a time-phased plan. Individual projects can then be considered on a case-by-case basis.

3. Further, it is assumed that a single agency will be given the primary responsibility for developing military and para-military aspects of the basic plan. It is recommended that this responsibility for both overt and covert military operations be assigned the Joint Chiefs of Staff.

For the Joint Chiefs of Staff:

SYSTEMATICALLY REVIEWED
BY JCS ON 21 May 84
CLASSIFICATION CONTINUED

L. L. Lemnitzer

L. L. LEMNITZER
Chairman
Joint Chiefs of Staff

1 Enclosure
Memo for Chief of Operations, Cuba Project

EXCLUDED FROM GDS

EXCLUDED FROM AUTOMATIC
REGRADING; DOD DIR 5200.10
DOES NOT APPLY

TOP SECRET SPECIAL HANDLING NOFORN

TOP SECRET
JCS 1969/321
12 March 1962
Page 2165

UNCLASSIFIED

COPY NO. 1
SPECIAL DISTRIBUTION

NOTE BY THE SECRETARIES
to the
JOINT CHIEFS OF STAFF
on
NORTHWOODS (S)

A report* on the above subject is submitted for consideration by the Joint Chiefs of Staff.

F. J. BLOUIN
M. J. INGELIDO
Joint Secretariat

* Not reproduced herewith; on file in Joint Secretariat

EXCLUDED FROM GDS
EXCLUDED FROM AUTOMATIC
REGRADING; DOD DIRECTIVE
5200.10 DOES NOT APPLY

TOP SECRET
JCS 1969/321

2165

NOFORN

9 March 1962

COPY ___ OF ___ COPIES
SPECIAL DISTRIBUTION

UNCLASSIFIED

REPORT BY THE DEPARTMENT OF DEFENSE AND
JOINT CHIEFS OF STAFF REPRESENTATIVE ON THE
CARIBBEAN SURVEY GROUP

to the

JOINT CHIEFS OF STAFF

on

CUBA PROJECT (TS)

The Chief of Operations, Cuba Project, has requested that he be furnished the views of the Joint Chiefs of Staff on this matter by 13 March 1962.

EXCLUDED FROM GDS

UNCLASSIFIED

~~TOP SECRET SPECIAL HANDLING NOFORN~~

JUSTIFICATION FOR US MILITARY INTERVENTION IN CUBA (TS)

THE PROBLEM

1. As requested* by Chief of Operations, Cuba Project, the Joint Chiefs of Staff are to indicate brief but precise description of pretexts which they consider would provide justification for US military intervention in Cuba.

FACTS BEARING ON THE PROBLEM

2. It is recognized that any action which becomes pretext for US military intervention in Cuba will lead to a political decision which then would lead to military action.

3. Cognizance has been taken of a suggested course of action proposed** by the US Navy relating to generated instances in the Guantanamo area.

4. For additional facts see Enclosure B.

DISCUSSION

5. The suggested courses of action appended to Enclosure A are based on the premise that US military intervention will result from a period of heightened US-Cuban tensions which place the United States in the position of suffering justifiable grievances. World opinion, and the United Nations forum should be favorably affected by developing the international image of the Cuban government as rash and irresponsible, and as an alarming and unpredictable threat to the peace of the Western Hemisphere.

6. While the foregoing premise can be utilized at the present time it will continue to hold good only as long as there can be reasonable certainty that US military intervention in Cuba would not directly involve the Soviet Union. There is

* Memorandum for General Craig from Chief of Operations, Cuba Project, subject: "Operation MONGOOSE", dated 5 March 1962, on file in General Craig's office.

** Memorandum for the Chairman, Joint Chiefs of Staff, from Chief of Naval Operations, subject: "Instances to Provoke Military Actions in Cuba (TS)", dated 8 March 1962, on file in General Craig's office.

UNCLASSIFIED

as yet no bilateral mutual support agreement binding the USSR to the defense of Cuba, Cuba has not yet become a member of the Warsaw Pact, nor have the Soviets established Soviet bases in Cuba in the pattern of US bases in Western Europe. Therefore, since time appears to be an important factor in resolution of the Cuba problem, all projects are suggested within the time frame of the next few months.

CONCLUSION

7. The suggested courses of action appended to Enclosure A satisfactorily respond to the statement of the problem. However, these suggestions should be forwarded as a preliminary submission suitable for planning purposes, and together with similar inputs from other agencies, provide a basis for development of a single, integrated, time-phased plan to focus all efforts on the objective of justification for US military intervention in Cuba.

RECOMMENDATIONS

8. It is recommended that:

a. Enclosure A together with its attachments should be forwarded to the Secretary of Defense for approval and transmittal to the Chief of Operations, Cuba Project.

b. This paper NOT be forwarded to commanders of unified or specified commands.

c. This paper NOT be forwarded to US officers assigned to NATO activities.

d. This paper NOT be forwarded to the Chairman, US Delegation, United Nations Military Staff Committee.

UNCLASSIFIED

~~TOP SECRET SPECIAL HANDLING NOFORN~~

UNCLASSIFIED

MEMORANDUM FOR THE SECRETARY OF DEFENSE

Subject: Justification for US Military Intervention in Cuba (TS)

1. The Joint Chiefs of Staff have considered the attached Memorandum for the Chief of Operations, Cuba Project, which responds to a request* of that office for brief but precise description of pretexts which would provide justification for US military intervention in Cuba.

2. The Joint Chiefs of Staff recommend that the proposed memorandum be forwarded as a preliminary submission suitable for planning purposes. It is assumed that there will be similar submissions from other agencies and that these inputs will be used as a basis for developing a time-phased plan. Individual projects can then be considered on a case-by-case basis.

3. Further, it is assumed that a single agency will be given the primary responsibility for developing military and para-military aspects of the basic plan. It is recommended that this responsibility for both overt and covert military operations be assigned the Joint Chiefs of Staff.

* Memorandum for Gen Craig from Chief of Operations, Cuba Project, subject, "Operation MONGOOSE", dated 5 March 1962, on file in Gen Craig's office

UNCLASSIFIED

~~TOP SECRET SPECIAL HANDLING NOFORN~~

TOP SECRET - SPECIAL HANDLING NOFORN

APPENDIX TO ENCLOSURE A

DRAFT

MEMORANDUM FOR CHIEF OF OPERATIONS, CUBA PROJECT

Subject: Justification for US Military Intervention in Cuba (TS)

1. Reference is made to memorandum from Chief of Operations, Cuba Project, for General Craig, subject: "Operation MONGOOSE", dated 5 March 1962, which requested brief but precise description of pretexts which the Joint Chiefs of Staff consider would provide justification for US military intervention in Cuba.

2. The projects listed in the enclosure hereto are forwarded as a preliminary submission suitable for planning purposes. It is assumed that there will be similar submissions from other agencies and that these inputs will be used as a basis for developing a time-phased plan. The individual projects can then be considered on a case-by-case basis.

3. This plan, incorporating projects selected from the attached suggestions, or from other sources, should be developed to focus all efforts on a specific ultimate objective which would provide adequate justification for US military intervention. Such a plan would enable a logical build-up of incidents to be combined with other seemingly unrelated events to camouflage the ultimate objective and create the necessary impression of Cuban rashness and irresponsibility on a large scale, directed at other countries as well as the United States. The plan would also properly integrate and time phase the courses of action to be pursued. The desired resultant from the execution of this plan would be to place the United States in the apparent position of suffering defensible grievances from a rash and irresponsible government of Cuba and to develop an international image of a Cuban threat to peace in the Western Hemisphere.

UNCLASSIFIED

5

Appendix to Enclosure A

TOP SECRET - SPECIAL HANDLING NOFORN

4. Time is an important factor in resolution of the Cuban problem. Therefore, the plan should be so time-phased that projects would be operable within the next few months.

5. Inasmuch as the ultimate objective is overt military intervention, it is recommended that primary responsibility for developing military and para-military aspects of the plan for both overt and covert military operations be assigned the Joint Chiefs of Staff.

SECRET - SPECIAL HANDLING NOFORN

ANNEX TO APPENDIX TO ENCLOSURE A UNCLASSIFIED

PRETEXTS TO JUSTIFY US MILITARY INTERVENTION IN CUBA

(Note: The courses of action which follow are a preliminary submission suitable only for planning purposes. They are arranged neither chronologically nor in ascending order. Together with similar inputs from other agencies, they are intended to provide a point of departure for the development of a single, integrated, time-phased plan. Such a plan would permit the evaluation of individual projects within the context of cumulative, correlated actions designed to lead inexorably to the objective of adequate justification for US military intervention in Cuba).

1. Since it would seem desirable to use legitimate provocation as the basis for US military intervention in Cuba a cover and deception plan, to include requisite preliminary actions such as has been developed in response to Task 33 c, could be executed as an initial effort to provoke Cuban reactions. Harassment plus deceptive actions to convince the Cubans of imminent invasion would be emphasized. Our military posture throughout execution of the plan will allow a rapid change from exercise to intervention if Cuban response justifies.

2. A series of well coordinated incidents will be planned to take place in and around Guantanamo to give genuine appearance of being done by hostile Cuban forces.

a. Incidents to establish a credible attack (not in chronological order):

(1) Start rumors (many). Use clandestine radio.

(2) Land friendly Cubans in uniform "over-the-fence" to stage attack on base.

(3) Capture Cuban (friendly) saboteurs inside the base.

(4) Start riots near the base main gate (friendly Cubans).

7

Annex to Appendix to Enclosure A

~~TOP SECRET - SPECIAL HANDLING - NOFORN~~

(5) Blow up ammunition inside the base; start fires.

(6) Burn aircraft on air base (sabotage).

(7) Lob mortar shells from outside of base into base. Some damage to installations.

(8) Capture assault teams approaching from the sea or vicinity of Guantanamo City.

(9) Capture militia group which storms the base.

(10) Sabotage ship in harbor; large fires -- napthalene.

(11) Sink ship near harbor entrance. Conduct funerals for mock-victims (may be lieu of (10)).

b. United States would respond by executing offensive operations to secure water and power supplies, destroying artillery and mortar emplacements which threaten the base.

c. Commence large scale United States military operations.

3. A "Remember the Maine" incident could be arranged in several forms:

a. We could blow up a US ship in Guantanamo Bay and blame Cuba.

b. We could blow up a drone (unmanned) vessel anywhere in the Cuban waters. We could arrange to cause such incident in the vicinity of Havana or Santiago as a spectacular result of Cuban attack from the air or sea, or both. The presence of Cuban planes or ships merely investigating the intent of the vessel could be fairly compelling evidence that the ship was taken under attack. The nearness to Havana or Santiago would add credibility especially to those people that might have heard the blast or have seen the fire. The US could follow up with an air/sea rescue operation covered by US fighters to "evacuate" remaining members of the non-existent crew. Casualty lists in US newspapers would cause a helpful wave of national indignation.

4. We could develop a Communist Cuban terror campaign in the Miami area, in other Florida cities and even in Washington.

The terror campaign could be pointed at Cuban refugees seeking haven in the United States. We could sink a boatload of Cubans enroute to Florida (real or simulated). We could foster attempts on lives of Cuban refugees in the United States even to the extent of wounding in instances to be widely publicized. Exploding a few plastic bombs in carefully chosen spots, the arrest of Cuban agents and the release of prepared documents substantiating Cuban involvement also would be helpful in projecting the idea of an irresponsible government.

5. A "Cuban-based, Castro-supported" filibuster could be simulated against a neighboring Caribbean nation (in the vein of the 14th of June invasion of the Dominican Republic). We know that Castro is backing subversive efforts clandestinely against Haiti, Dominican Republic, Guatemala, and Nicaragua at present and possible others. These efforts can be magnified and additional ones contrived for exposure. For example, advantage can be taken of the sensitivity of the Dominican Air Force to intrusions within their national air space. "Cuban" B-26 or C-46 type aircraft could make cane-burning raids at night. Soviet Bloc incendiaries could be found. This could be coupled with "Cuban" messages to the Communist underground in the Dominican Republic and "Cuban" shipments of arms which would be found, or intercepted, on the beach.

6. Use of MIG type aircraft by US pilots could provide additional provocation. Harassment of civil air, attacks on surface shipping and destruction of US military drone aircraft by MIG type planes would be useful as complementary actions. An F-86 properly painted would convince air passengers that they saw a Cuban MIG, especially if the pilot of the transport were to announce such fact. The primary drawback to this suggestion appears to be the security risk inherent in obtaining or modifying an aircraft. However, reasonable copies of the MIG could be produced from US resources in about three months.

7. Hijacking attempts against civil air and surface craft should appear to continue as harassing measures condoned by the government of Cuba. Concurrently, genuine defections of Cuban civil and military air and surface craft should be encouraged.

8. It is possible to create an incident which will demonstrate convincingly that a Cuban aircraft has attacked and shot down a chartered civil airliner enroute from the United States to Jamaica, Guatemala, Panama or Venezuela. The destination would be chosen only to cause the flight plan route to cross Cuba. The passengers could be a group of college students off on a holiday or any grouping of persons with a common interest to support chartering a non-scheduled flight.

a. An aircraft at Eglin AFB would be painted and numbered as an exact duplicate for a civil registered aircraft belonging to a CIA proprietary organization in the Miami area. At a designated time the duplicate would be substituted for the actual civil aircraft and would be loaded with the selected passengers, all boarded under carefully prepared aliases. The actual registered aircraft would be converted to a drone.

b. Take off times of the drone aircraft and the actual aircraft will be scheduled to allow a rendezvous south of Florida. From the rendezvous point the passenger-carrying aircraft will descend to minimum altitude and go directly into an auxiliary field at Eglin AFB where arrangements will have been made to evacuate the passengers and return the aircraft to its original status. The drone aircraft meanwhile will continue to fly the filed flight plan. When over Cuba the drone will being transmitting on the international distress frequency a "MAY DAY" message stating he is under attack by Cuban MIG aircraft. The transmission will be interrupted by destruction of the aircraft which will be triggered by radio signal. This will allow ICAO radio

TOP SECRET SPECIAL HANDLING NOFORN

UNCLASSIFIED

stations in the Western Hemisphere to tell the US what has happened to the aircraft instead of the US trying to "sell" the incident.

9. It is possible to create an incident which will make it appear that Communist Cuban MIGs have destroyed a USAF aircraft over international waters in an unprovoked attack.

a. Approximately 4 or 5 F-101 aircraft will be dispatched in trail from Homestead AFB, Florida, to the vicinity of Cuba. Their mission will be to reverse course and simulate fakir aircraft for an air defense exercise in southern Florida. These aircraft would conduct variations of these flights at frequent intervals. Crews would be briefed to remain at least 12 miles off the Cuban coast; however, they would be required to carry live ammunition in the event that hostile actions were taken by the Cuban MIGs.

b. On one such flight, a pre-briefed pilot would fly tail-end Charley at considerable interval between aircraft. While near the Cuban Island this pilot would broadcast that he had been jumped by MIGs and was going down. No other calls would be made. The pilot would then fly directly west at extremely low altitude and land at a secure base, an Eglin auxiliary. The aircraft would be met by the proper people, quickly stored and given a new tail number. The pilot who had performed the mission under an alias, would resume his proper identity and return to his normal place of business. The pilot and aircraft would then have disappeared.

c. At precisely the same time that the aircraft was presumably shot down a submarine or small surface craft would disburse F-101 parts, parachute, etc., at approximately 15 to 20 miles off the Cuban coast and depart. The pilots returning to Homestead would have a true story as far as they knew. Search ships and aircraft could be dispatched and parts of aircraft found.

11

Annex to Appendix to Enclosure A

TOP SECRET SPECIAL HANDLING NOFORN

ENCLOSURE B

FACTS BEARING ON THE PROBLEM

1. The Joint Chiefs of Staff have previously stated* that US unilateral military intervention in Cuba can be undertaken in the event that the Cuban regime commits hostile acts against US forces or property which would serve as an incident upon which to base overt intervention.

2. The need for positive action in the event that current covert efforts to foster an internal Cuban rebellion are unsuccessful was indicated** by the Joint Chiefs of Staff on 7 March 1962, as follows:

> " - - - determination that a credible internal revolt is impossible of attainment during the next 9-10 months will require a decision by the United States to develop a Cuban "provocation" as justification for positive US military action."

3. It is understood that the Department of State also is preparing suggested courses of action to develop justification for US military intervention in Cuba.

* JCS 1969/303
** JCS 1969/313

APPENDIX 3

CIA INTERNAL MEMORANDUM NOVEMBER 18, 1960

SECRET

18 November 1960

MEMORANDUM FOR: C/WH/4/FI

SUBJECT: QDDALE Correspondence

1. Attached to this memorandum are the most recent pieces of correspondence from QDDALE. I have looked through it hurriedly and see nothing of particular moment. I would suggest, however, you screen it again before passing on to PA.

2. For PA: You should be aware of and somewhat interested in the fact that QDDALE has established a new (and according to him productive) channel to President Elect Kennedy through George Smathers. According to QDDALE Smathers conversations with the President Elect have lead QDDALE now to take the position that he should not go along with the Department of State and have the dictator step down. It appears that Mr. Kennedy may take a considerably more conservative position than many people in the Department and "the fun house."

Jacob D. Esterline
Chief, WH/4

Attachment:

QDDALE Correspondence

Document on FRD forwarded to PA on 23 Feb 1961 - Miscellaneous correspondence to WH/H/C2 - for filing see log

SECRET

D0477

APPENDIX 4

CIA MEMORANDUM FOR THE RECORD

 CONFIDENTIAL

CENTRAL INTELLIGENCE AGENCY
WASHINGTON 25, D. C.

14 May 1962

MEMORANDUM FOR THE RECORD:

SUBJECT: Arthur James Balletti et al - Unauthorized Publication or Use of Communications

1. This memorandum for the record is prepared at the request of the Attorney General of the United States following a complete oral briefing of him relative to a sensitive CIA operation conducted during the period approximately August 1960 to May 1961. In August 1960 the undersigned was approached by Mr. Richard Bissell then Deputy Director for Plans of CIA to explore the possibility of mounting this sensitive operation against Fidel Castro. It was thought that certain gambling interests which had formerly been active in Cuba might be willing and able to assist and further, might have both intelligence assets in Cuba and communications between Miami, Florida and Cuba. Accordingly, Mr. Robert Maheu, a private investigator of the firm of Maheu and King was approached by the undersigned and asked to establish contact with a member or members of the gambling syndicate to explore their capabilities. Mr. Maheu was known to have accounts with several prominent business men and organizations in the United States. Maheu was to make his approach to the syndicate as appearing to represent big business organizations which wished to protect their interests in Cuba. Mr. Maheu accordingly met and established contact with one John Rosselli of Los Angeles. Mr. Rosselli showed interest in the possibility and indicated he had some contacts in Miami that he might use. Maheu reported that John Rosselli said he was not interested in any remuneration but would seek to establish capabilities in Cuba to perform the desired project. Towards the end of September Mr. Maheu and Mr. Rosselli proceeded to Miami where, as reported, Maheu was introduced to Sam Giancana of Chicago. Sam Giancana arranged for Maheu and Rosselli to meet with a "courier" who was going back

25X1 ... 10/1/86
Copy No. 2 of 2

Page 1 of 3 pages

CONFIDENTIAL

and forth to Havana. From information received back by the courier the proposed operation appeared to be feasible and it was decided to obtain an official Agency approval in this regard. A figure of one hundred fifty thousand dollars was set by the Agency as a payment to be made on completion of the operation and to be paid only to the principal or principals who would conduct the operation in Cuba. Maheu reported that Rosselli and Giancana emphatically stated that they wished no part of any payment. The undersigned then briefed the proper senior officials of this Agency on the proposal. Knowledge of this project during its life was kept to a total of six persons and never became a part of the project current at the time for the invasion of Cuba and there were no memoranda on the project nor were there other written documents or agreements. The project was duly orally approved by the said senior officials of the Agency.

2. Rosselli and Maheu spent considerable time in Miami talking with the courier. Sam Giancana was present during parts of these meetings. Several months after this period Maheu told me that Sam Giancana had asked him to put a listening device in the room of one Phyllis McGuire, reported to be the mistress of Giancana. At that time it was reported to me that Maheu passed the matter over to one Edward Du Boise, another private investigator. It appears that Arthur James Balietti was discovered in the act of installing the listening device and was arrested by the Sheriff in Las Vegas, Nevada. Maheu reported to me that he had referred the matter to Edward Du Boise on behalf of Sam Giancana. At the time of the incident neither this Agency nor the undersigned knew of the proposed technical installation. Maheu stated that Sam Giancana thought that Phyllis McGuire might know of the proposed operation and might pass on the information to one Dan Rowan, another friend of McGuire's. At the time that Maheu reported this to the undersigned he reported he was under surveillance by agents of the Federal Bureau of Investigation, who, he thought, were exploring his association with John Rosselli and Sam Giancana incident to the project. I told Maheu that if he was formally approached by the FBI, he could refer them to me to be briefed that he was engaged in an intelligence operation directed at Cuba.

3. During the period from September on through April efforts were continued by Rosselli and Maheu to proceed with the operation. The first principal in Cuba withdrew and another principal

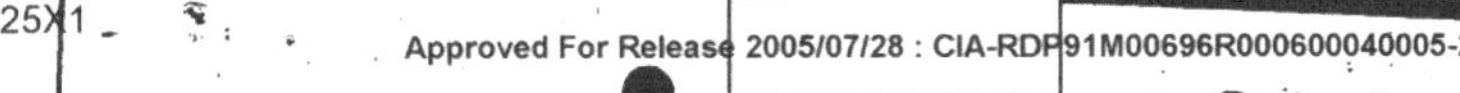

was selected as has been briefed to The Attorney General. Ten thousand dollars was passed for expenses to the second principal. He was further furnished with approximately one thousand dollars worth of communications equipment to establish communications between his headquarters in Miami and assets in Cuba. No monies were ever paid to Rosselli and Giancana. Maheu was paid part of his expense money during the periods that he was in Miami. After the failure of the invasion of Cuba word was sent through Maheu to Rosselli to call off the operation and Rosselli was told to tell his principal that the proposal to pay one hundred fifty thousand dollars for completion of the operation had been definitely withdrawn.

4. In all this period it has been definitely established from other sources that the Cuban principals involved never discovered or believed that there was other than business and syndicate interest in the project. To the knowledge of the undersigned there were no "leaks" of any information concerning the project in the Cuban community in Miami or in Cuba.

5. I have no proof but it is my conclusion that Rosselli and Giancana guessed or assumed that CIA was behind the project. I never met either of them.

6. Throughout the entire period of the project John Rosselli was the dominant figure in directing action to the Cuban principals. Reasonable monitoring of his activities indicated that he gave his best efforts to carrying out the project without requiring any commitments for himself, financial or otherwise.

7. In view of the extreme sensitivity of the information set forth above, only one additional copy of this memorandum has been made and will be retained by the Agency.

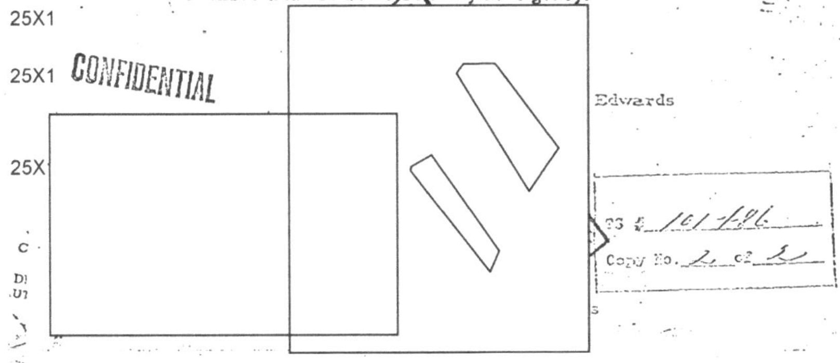
25X1

25X1 CONFIDENTIAL

Edwards

25X1

TS # 161196

Copy No. 2 of 2

APPENDIX 5

ALLEN DULLES TO SENATE FOREIGN RELATIONS COMMITTEE, MAY 3, 1960

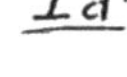

STATEMENT BY
MR. ALLEN W. DULLES
DIRECTOR OF CENTRAL INTELLIGENCE
to the
SENATE FOREIGN RELATIONS COMMITTEE
ON 31 MAY 1960

The duty of the Central Intelligence Agency under statute and under National Security Council directives pursuant to statute, is to provide the President and the National Security Council with evaluated intelligence relating to our national security.

The Agency has no policy or police functions.

In addition, however, the Agency has the duty, within policy limitations prescribed by the President and State Department, to do whatever is within its power to collect and produce the intelligence required by the policy makers in government, to deal with the dangers we face in the world today, a nuclear world.

Increasingly over the past ten years, the main target for our intelligence collection has been the U. S. S. R., its military, its economic, and its subversive potential.

The carrying out of this task has been rendered extremely difficult because the Soviet Union is a closed society.

Great areas of the U. S. S. R. are curtained off to the outside world. Their military preparations are made in secret. Their military hardware, ballistic missiles, bombers, nuclear weapons, and submarine forces, as far as physically possible, are concealed from us. They have resisted all efforts to realize mutual inspection or "open skies."

Declassified by Senate Foreign Relations Committee
date 10 March 1975

This document may be downgraded to Confidential when separated from the balance of the testimony.

TS #172676
COPY
No. 2 of 15 Copies

TOP SECRET

The ordinary tools of information gathering, under these circumstances are not wholly adequate. These ordinary tools include both the normal overt means of obtaining information, and the classical covert means generally referred to as espionage.

It is true that from these sources and from the many Soviet defectors who have come over to the Free World and from disaffected and disillusioned Soviet nationals, we obtain very valuable information.

However, these sources and other sources developed through the application of various scientific techniques, while very helpful, did not give us the full intelligence protection this country required against the danger of preparation for surprise attack against us, from bases which might remain unknown and by weapons, the strength and power of which we might not be able adequately to evaluate.

Almost equally serious had been our lack of knowledge of Soviet defense measures against our retaliatory striking power.

Shackled by traditions, we were seeing the power of attack grow while the ability to secure the intelligence necessary for defense against attack was slipping, bound down in part by tradition.

For example, while Soviet spy trawlers can lurk a few miles off our shores and observe us with impunity, the Soviets cry "aggression" when a plane, invisible to the naked eye, flies over it some fifteen miles above the ground.

Either, theoretically, could carry a nuclear weapon. The trawler could deal a much more serious nuclear blow than a light reconnaissance plane.

But, of course, as we well know, no one would think of starting a nuclear war with either an isolated plane or ship.

In this age of nuclear peril we, the Central Intelligence Agency, felt that a new approach was called for in the whole field of intelligence collection.

* * * * *

TOP SECRET

TOP SECRET

This was the situation, when in 1954, almost six years ago, consultation was initiated on new intelligence collection techniques. We consulted with a group of highly competent technicians in and out of government. From our discussions there emerged the concept of a high-flying, high performance reconnaissance plane. In the then state of the art of aeronautics, it was confidently believed that a plane could be designed to fly unintercepted over the vitally important closed areas of the Soviet Union, where ballistic, nuclear, and other military preparations against us were being made.

We also believed, as a result of these consultations, that the art of photography could be so advanced as to make the resolution of the pictures taken, even at extreme altitudes, of very great significance. On both counts the accomplishments exceeded expectations.

While the developmental work for this project, pursuant to high policy directive was in process, there came the Summit Conference of July 1955.

Here, in order to relax the growing tensions resulting from the danger of surprise attack, the President advanced the "open skies" proposal. Moscow summarily rejected anything of this nature, and Soviet security measures continued to be reinforced.

Accordingly, the U-2 project was pushed forward rapidly, and about a year after the 1955 summit meeting the first operational U-2 flight over the Soviet Union took place. For almost four years the flight program has been carried forward successfully.

Speed in getting the program underway had been a top priority. We were then faced, that is in 1955-1956, with a situation where the Soviets were continuing to develop their missiles, their heavy bomber and bomber bases, and their nuclear weapons production without adequate knowledge on our part.

This was considered tobe an intolerable situation; intolerable both from the viewpoint of adequate military preparation on our part to meet the menace; intolerable from the point of view of being able effectively to take countermeasures in the event of attack.

TOP SECRET

-3-

TOP SECRET

It was recognized at the outset that this U-2 project had its risks and had a limited span of life due to improvement of counter measures; that a relatively fragile single-engine plane of the nature of the U-2 might one day have a flame-out or other malfunction in the rarified atmosphere in which it had to travel. If that resulted in a serious and prolonged loss of altitude, there was danger of failure and discovery.

To stop any enterprise of this nature because there are risks, would be, of course, in this field, to accomplish very little.

While air reconnaissance is an old and tried method of gaining intelligence, a peacetime operation of this particular type and on this scale was unique.

But I submit that we live in an age when old concepts of the limits of "permitted" techniques for acquiring information are totally outdated. They come from the horse and buggy days.

I see no reason whatever to draw an unfavorable distinction between the collection of information by reconnaissance at a high altitude in the air and espionage carried on by individuals who illegally operate directly within the territory of another state.

In fact, the distinction, if one is to be drawn, would favor the former. The illegal espionage agents generally attempt to suborn and subvert the citizens of the countries in which they operate. High level air reconnaissance in no way disturbs the life of the people. It does not harm their property. They do not even notice it.

I believe these techniques should be universally sanctioned on a mutual basis and become an accepted and agreed part of our international arrangements.

The USSR has known a good deal about these flights for the last four years. It has studiously refrained from giving the people of the Soviet Union the knowledge they now admit they had.

* * * *

With respect to the U-2 project, I am prepared to support and document these conclusions:--

TOP SECRET

-4-

TOP SECRET

First, that this operation was one of the most valuable intelligence collection operations that any country has ever mounted at any time, and that it was vital to our national security.

Second, that the chain of command and authority for the project was clear.

Third, that every overflight was carefully planned, fully authorized, and, until May 1, 1960, effectively carried out.

Fourth, that the technical and logistic support was prompt and efficient.

Fifth, that the security which was maintained for this project over a period of more than five years has been unique.

I shall deal with these points in the inverse order in which I have presented them.

First - security. The project was run by a small, closely knit organization at headquarters and in the field. Knowledge of the operation was restricted to a minimum. Over more than five years, since the inception of the project, there has never been any damaging disclosure to interfere with the program.

The existence of the U-2 aircraft was, of course, well known, though its full capabilities, particularly the altitude and range were not disclosed. It had important weather and air sampling capabilities which were effectively used and which afforded natural cover for the project. These weather capabilities were open and publicized.

For example, as far as I know the U-2 is the first aircraft that has ever flown over the eye of a typhoon. It was used very effectively out in the Far East to learn about typhoons which cause so much damage, and we have a very extraordinary series of pictures of the U-2 looking right down at the eye of a typhoon from several miles above the top of it. Of course, the U-2 also had very valuable characteristics as a reconnaissance plane for peripheral flights.

With regard to technical and logistic support: -- from the inception of the project, CIA has called on the United States Air Force for support in the form of technical advice and assistance in those fields

TOP SECRET

-5-

where the Air Force has the most expert knowledge. These included advice on aircraft design and procurement, operational training of air crews, weather, aero-medicine and communications. I may say the Air Force liberally gave all this support to us.

The CIA also drew on the technical knowledge and advice of those members of the United States Intelligence Board with particular competence in the field of intelligence priorities, - targeting and the like. Each mission was carefully planned with respect to the highest priority requirements of the Intelligence Community.

The project has been directed by a senior civilian in CIA with high competence in this area of work. He was responsible directly to me and, of course, to General Cabell.

Since the inception of CIA - going back for ten years - personnel from the military services, including the Air Force, have been detailed to CIA for tours of duty. We have had as many as 8 or 9 hundred of them at one time. These personnel take their orders from CIA, not from their parent service, during their period of detail. The U-2 project, under its civilian director, drew upon both the military and civilian personnel in the Agency. They were assigned to duties in headquarters and in the field staffs which were responsible for carrying out the technical functions of the program. They were chosen in view of their particular qualifications for this particular project.

Third, every overflight, from the inception of the project, and every phase of it, was carefully planned and staffed.

From time to time intelligence requirements were reviewed, and programs of one or more missions were authorized by higher authority.

Within the authority thus granted, specific flights could then be carried out on the order of the Director of Central Intelligence, as availability and readiness of aircraft and of pilot and as weather conditions permitted.

TOP SECRET

On the afternoon of 30 April last, after carefully considering the field report on the weather and other determining factors affecting the flight then contemplated, and after consultation with General Cabell and other qualified advisors in the Agency, and acting within existing authority to make a flight at that time, I personally gave the order to proceed with the flight of May first.

There was no laxity or uncertainty in the chain of command in obtaining the authority to act or in giving the order to proceed. With respect to the flight authorized on April 30, the same careful procedures were followed as had been followed in the many preceding successful flights.

* * * *

Now I wish to discuss the value to the country of these flights from the intelligence viewpoint and from the viewpoint of national security considerations. I shall do this within the limitations of what I think both you and I feel are the necessary security restrictions.

Under the law setting up the Central Intelligence Agency, as Director, I am enjoined to protect "intelligence sources and methods from unauthorized disclosure." Naturally I recognize this Committee as an authorized body to whom disclosures can properly be made that should not be made publicly. In so doing I wish to keep within the bounds of what I believe you would agree to be in the national interest to disclose, even here.

I feel that you should share the facts which I confidently believe justified the obvious risks of this project. Such risks were recognized and evaluated at all stages of the project.

For many years, the United States Intelligence community has been directing its efforts to provide the information which would help to meet the threat of surprise attack. Every available means in the classifical intelligence field have been utilized, and over recent years these have been valuably supplemented by the highly technical electronic and other scientific means to which I have referred.

Our main emphasis in the U-2 program has been directed against five critical problems affecting our national security. These are: the Soviet bomber force, the Soviet missile program, the Soviet atomic energy program, the Soviet submarine program. These are the major

TOP SECRET

-7-

TOP SECRET

elements constituting the Soviet Union's capability to launch a surprise attack. In addition, a major target during this program has been the Soviet air defense system with which our retaliatory force would have to contend, in case of an attack on us and a counter-attack by us.

Today, the Soviet bomber force is still the main offensive long range striking force of the Soviet Union. However, the U-2 program has helped to confirm that only a greatly reduced long-range bomber production program is continuing in the Soviet Union. It has established, however, that the Soviet Union has recently developed a new medium range bomber with supersonic capabilities.

The U-2 program has covered many Soviet long-range bomber airfields, confirming estimates of the location of bases and the disposition of Soviet long-range bombers. It has also acquired data on the nuclear weapons storage facilities associated with them.

Our overflights have enabled us to look periodically at the actual ground facilities involved.

With respect to the Soviet missile test program -- this I shall illustrate graphically by showing you the photograph of these facilities, including both their ICBM and their IRBM test launching sites which could, of course, also become and may well be, operational sites.

Our photography has also provided us valuable insight into the problem of Soviet doctrine regarding ICBM deployment. It has taught us much about the use which the Soviets are making of these sites for the training of troops in the operational use of the short and intermediate range ballistic missiles.

The program has provided valuable information on the Soviet atomic energy program. This information has been included in the estimate which we give periodically to the Joint Committee on Atomic Energy, but without referring to the actual source of our data. This has covered the production of fissionable materials, weapons development and test activities, and the location, type, and size of many stockpile sites.

TOP SECRET

-8-

COPY

This document consists of 18 pages

No. 2 of 15 copies

~~TOP SECRET~~

The project has shown that, despite Mr. Khrushchev's boasts that the Soviets will soon be able to curtail the production of fissionable materials for weapons purposes, the Soviets are continuing to expand fissionable material capacity.

The Soviet nuclear testing grounds have been photographed more than once with extremely interesting results. The photography has also given us our first firm information on the magnitude and location of the USSR's domestic uranium ore and uranium processing activities, vital in estimating Soviet fissionable material production. We have located national and regional nuclear storage sites and forward storage facilities.

In general, the program has continued to give useful data on the size and rate of growth of Soviet industry.

The material obtained has been used for the correction of military maps and aeronautical charts.

Among the most important intelligence obtained is that affecting the tactics of the United States deterrent air strike force. We now have hard information about the nature, extent, and in many cases, the location of the Soviet ground-to-air missile development. We have learned much about the basic concept, magnitude, operational efficiency, deployment, and rate of development of the Soviet air defense system, including their early warning radar development.

We have obtained photographs of many scores of fighter air fields previously inadequately identified, and have photographed various fighter-types vainly attempting to intercept the U-2. All of this has proved invaluable to SAC in adjusting its plans to known elements of the opposition it would have to face.

As a result of the concrete evidence acquired by the U-2 program on a large number of targets in the Soviet Union, it has now been possible for U. S. commanders to make a more efficient and confident allocation of aircraft, crews and weapons.

U-2 photography has also made it possible to provide new and accurate information to strike crews which will make it easier for them to identify their targets and plan their navigation more precisely.

~~TOP SECRET~~

-9-

COPY

This document consists of 10 pages

No. 2 of 15 copies

TOP SECRET

We have obtained new and valuable information with regard to submarine deployment and the precise location of their submarine pens.

In the opinion of our military, of our scientists, and of the senior officials responsible for our national security, the results of the program have been invaluable.

The program has had other elements of value. It has made the Soviets less cocky about their ability to deal with what we might bring against them.

They have gone through four years of frustration in having the knowledge since 1956 that they could be overflown with impunity, that their vaunted fighters were useless against such flights, and that their ground-to-air missile capability was inadequate.

Khrushchev has never dared expose this to his own people. It is only after he had boasted, and we believe falsely, that he had been able to bring down the U-2 on May 1 by a ground-to-air missile while flying at altitude, that he has allowed his own people to have even an inkling of the capability which we possessed.

His frustrated military, many of whom know the facts, are far less confident today than they otherwise would have been.

At the same time, in competent military circles among our allies, the evidence of American capability demonstrated by the present disclosure of the U-2 flights has given a new and better perspective of our own relative strength as compared with that of the Soviet Union.

* * * *

At this point I propose to show you some photographs to support my presentation regarding the intelligence value of the project.

* * * *

Now I shall present the facts with regard to the dispatch of the May 1 flight and the ensuing developments insofar as the intelligence aspects are concerned and insofar as they are known to us.

As to the timing of the flight, there is, of course, no good time for a failure.

TOP SECRET

-10-

TOP SECRET

I have already presented the circumstances under which I assumed direct responsibility for dispatching this flight.

If this flight had been a success, we would have covered certain targets of particular significance and we would, in the normal course, have wished to analyze its results before scheduling a further mission. When it failed, it was obvious even before we received instructions that we would not try again before studying the cause and effects of failure. In either event, success or failure, after this flight we were not preparing to fly again for several weeks and until further policy guidance was received.

With respect to the timing of the flights, the President, in his speech of May 25, had this to say: "As to the timing, the question was really whether to halt the program and thus forego the gathering of important information that was essential and that was likely to be unavailable at a later date. The decision was that the program should not be halted."

"The plain truth is this: when a nation needs intelligence activity, there is no time when vigilance can be relaxed. Incidentally, from Pearl Harbor we learned that even negotiation itself can be used to conceal preparations for a surprise attack."

I would point out, also, that if you turn off all flights for months before international meetings and then for some time after such meetings and before trips to the Soviet Union of high American officials or trips here of Soviet officials; if you also estimate that in times of tension flights should be stopped because they might increase the tension, and in times of sweetness and light they should not be run because it would disturb any "honeymoon" in our relations with the Soviet Union; if, on top of this, you take into account that in much of the Soviet Union most days of the year are automatically eliminated because of weather and cloud cover and low Arctic sun, - then you can understand the problem of timing of flights.

If you asked me whether or not a flight would have been made after this particular flight, I cannot give you the answer because I do not know. At the time, we had no authority for any mission other than the one that was then undertaken.

TOP SECRET

-11-

COPY

This document consists of 11/20 pages

No. 2 of 15 copies

TOP SECRET

With respect to the flight itself, when the aircraft did not reach its destination within the flight time and fuel capacity given it, it was presumed to be down. But at first we did not know where. It could have been within friendly territory, in hostile desert, or in uninhabited territory, or within hostile territory where if alive the pilot would have been quickly apprehended as was the case. We did not know whether the plane was intact or destroyed, the pilot alive or dead.

I shall deal in a moment with the statements which were issued during this period of uncertainty.

The question of course arises as to what actually happened to cause this aircraft to come down deep in the heart of Russia.

Let me remind you first that the returns are not yet all in, and so our picture is not complete. However, we do have a considerable body of evidence that permits a reasonable judgment with a high degree of confidence.

Our best judgment is that it did not happen as claimed by the Soviets. That is, we believe that it was not shot down at its operating altitude of around 70,000 feet by the Russians. We believe that it was initially forced down to a much lower altitude by some as yet undetermined mechanical malfunction. At that lower altitude, it was a sitting duck for Soviet defenses, whether fighter aircraft or ground-to-air fire or missiles.

As to what happened at the lower altitude, we are not sure. The pilot may have bailed out at any time or he may have crash landed. The aircraft was equipped with a destruction device to be activated by the pilot as he leaves the aircraft. Again we do not know whether or not he attempted to do so. It should be noted, however, that no massive destruction device capable of ensuring complete destruction could be carried in this aircraft as weight limitations were critical, and every pound counted.

Thus, whether or not the destruct device was used, one might expect sizable and identifiable parts of the aircraft and its equipment to remain.

TOP SECRET

-12-

TOP SECRET

As to the nature and cause of the suspected malfunction, we are not prepared to pass judgment. But let me remind you that this aircraft and this pilot had proven their high degree of reliability in many technically similar flights, inside and outside friendly territory. When operating as in this case, about 1200 miles within unfriendly, heavily-defended territory, there can be no cushion against malfunction.

* * * *

There has been much comment and questioning with regard to the pilot and his behavior after apprehension. Of course, we only have the Soviets' report on all of this, and we should accept it with caution.

All of the pilots engaged in this enterprise were most carefully selected. They were highly trained, highly motivated, and, as seemed right, well compensated financially. But no one in his right mind would have accepted these risks for money alone.

Since the operational phase of the program started, the reliability record of the plane, for a craft of this character, was little short of phenomenal. It was a tribute to the high skill of the designer, the maintenance crews, and the pilots. Until the May first flight, over about a four-year period of operations, no plane had been lost over unfriendly territory in the course of many, many missions. Several were lost during the training period at home and in friendly territory abroad.

Francis Gary Powers, the pilot on the May 1 flight, is a fourth generation American citizen, born in Jenkins, Kentucky, about 31 years ago. He received a BA degree from Milligan College, Tennessee, in September 1956. Scholastically he was high average. He joined the Air Force in the fall of 1950, as a private and served in an enlisted status until November 1951, when he was discharged as a Corporal in order to enter the Aviation Cadet School to train as a pilot. He attended the Air Force Basic and Advance Pilot Training School at Greenville, Mississippi. Upon completion of this training in December 1952, he was commissioned as a Second Lieutenant.

TOP SECRET

-13-

TOP SECRET

His first duty assignment was as an F-84 Commando Jet Pilot with the 468th Strategic Fighter Squadron at Turner Air Force Base, Georgia. He resigned his Air Force Reserve Commission under honorable conditions in May 1956. The reason for such resignation was to join the project we are discussing.

His record with the Air Force had been uniformly good. He was given a special security screening by the Air Force and also a supplemental check by the security office of the CIA.

During his Air Force career, he received training with respect to his behavior and conduct in event of capture, and after entering the employ of the Agency, he took the Agency's escape and evasion course at our training station here in the United States in June of 1956. He had subsequent training in escape and evasion after his assignment to his overseas post in August 1956.

An Air Force Major Flight Surgeon assigned to CIA who worked with the U-2 pilots during their training in the United States and continuously during their stay overseas, had this to say in regard to Francis Powers, ". . . During the period of my assignment as Flight Surgeon at Adana, I not infrequently shared a room with Mr. Powers and participated in social, flying, and mission duties with him. In my opinion Mr. Powers was outstanding among the pilots for his calmness under pressure, his precision, and his methodical approach to problems. I have flown considerably in jets with Mr. Powers. I would consider him temperate, devoted, perhaps more than usually patriotic, and a man given to thinking before speaking or acting."

It should be remembered that Powers was a pilot, navigator, a well-rounded aviator trained to handle himself under all conditions, in the air or if grounded in hostile territory. He was not trained as an "agent" as there were no foreseeable circumstances, even the present ones, where he would act as such. Furthermore, such training would have been incompatible both temperamentally and with the strenuous technical demands of his flight missions.

The pilots of these aircrafts on operational missions, and this was true in the case of Powers, received the following instructions for use if downed in a hostile area:

TOP SECRET

-14-

~~TOP SECRET~~

First, it was their duty to ensure the destruction of the aircraft and its equipment to the greatest extent possible.

Second, on reaching the ground it was the pilot's first duty to attempt escape and evasion so as to avoid capture, or delay it as long as possible. To aid him in these purposes and for survival he was given the various items of equipment which the Soviets have publicized and which are normal and standard procedure, selected on the basis of wide experience gained in World War II and in Korea.

Third, pilots were equipped with a device for self destruction but were not given positive instructions to make use of it. In the last analysis, this ultimate decision has to be left to the individual himself.

Fourth, in the contingency of capture, pilots were instructed to delay as long as possible the revelation of damaging information.

Fifth, pilots were instructed to tell the truth if faced with a situation, as apparently faced Powers, with respect to those matters which were obviously within the knowledge of his captors as a result of what fell into their hands. In addition, if in a position where some attribution had to be given his mission, he would acknowledge that he was working for the Central Intelligence Agency. This was to make it clear that he was not working for any branch of the armed services, and that his mission was solely an intelligence mission.

These instructions were based on a careful study of our experience in the Korean war of the consequences of brain-washing and of the extent of information which could be obtained by these and other means available to the Soviets.

Whether or not in this instance the pilot complied with all of these instructions, it is hard to state today with the knowledge we have. However, a careful review of what he has said does not indicate that he has given to the Soviets any valuable information which they could not have discovered from the equipment they found upon the pilot's person or retrieved from the downed aircraft.

I would warn, of course, against putting too much belief in what Powers may say, particularly if he is later put on trial. By that time they will have had a more thorough opportunity for a complete brain-washing operation which might well produce a mixture of truth and fiction.

* * * *

~~TOP SECRET~~

-15-

~~TOP SECRET~~

I will now deal with the "cover story" statements which were issued following May 1.

When a plane is overdue and the fact of its takeoff and failure to return is known, some statement must be made, and quickly. Failure to do so, and, under normal conditions, to start a search for the lost plane, would in itself be a suspicious event.

Thus, when the U-2 disappeared on May first and did not return to its base within the requisite time period after its takeoff, action was required.

For many years, in fact since the inception of the operation, consideration has been given to the cover story which would be used in the case of the disappearance of a plane which might possibly be over unfriendly territory.

Because of its special characteristics, the U-2 plane was of great interest to the U. S. weather services and to the National Advisory Committee for Aeronautics, the predecessor of NASA. NASA was very much concerned with the scientific advances which operations of these U-2s could make towards greater knowledge of the upper atmosphere and for other scientific purposes. As already indicated, U-2s have now undertaken many weather and related missions and their functions in this respect have been publicized by NASA, and this publicity has been distributed freely to the world.

It was therefore natural that NASA's operations be used to explain the presence of U-2s at various bases throughout the world, although NASA did not participate in the development of intelligence devices, nor did they participate in the planning and conduct of any intelligence missions.

Accordingly, when the May first flight was lost, an initial statement was issued on May 2nd by the Base Commandant at Adana that a U-2 aircraft, engaged in upper air studies and operating from the base was down, and oxygen difficulties had been reported. This was identified in the press as a NASA plane. A search for the plane was initiated in the remote areas of eastern Turkey.

COPY

This document consists of 18 pages

No. 2 of 15 copies

TOP SECRET

On May 5, early in the day by our time, Khrushchev made his claim that "an American aircraft crossed our frontier and continued its flight into the interior of our country ... and ... was shot down." At that time, Khrushchev gave no further details of significance.

Apparently as an attempt at deception, Khrushchev followed up his speech the next day by distributing photographs of a pile of junk -- according to experts, pieces of an old Soviet fighter plane -- possibly for the purpose of making us think that the U-2 plane had been effectively destroyed. Since the fake wreckage was quickly identified for what it was, this particular ruse had no effect.

The NASA statement which followed the Khrushchev speech of May 5 developed somewhat further the original cover story. Also on May 5, the Department of State issued a further release which generally followed the cover story. Mr. Dillon has covered this in his testimony before this Committee on May 27.

At this time - on 5-6 May - we still did not know whether the plane or any recognizable parts of it or the pilot were in Soviet hands, or whether the pilot was dead or alive. Furthermore, then we did not know whether Khrushchev desired to blow up the incident as he later did, or put it under the rug and spare his people the knowledge that we had been overflying them.

Hence, in this situation, there seemed no reason at that time to depart from the original cover story.

These two press releases attributed to NASA were worked out in consultation between CIA and NASA and after conferring with the Department of State.

These statements did not come out of any lack of forethought or attention to their preparation or lack of coordination. The basic cover story had been developed some years ago for the exigency of a failure, and this original cover story was on May 5 modified to meet our then estimate of what was best to say in the light of what little we knew about the details of the May 1 flight failure.

Subsequently, on May 7, Khrushchev adduced evidence that he had the pilot alive, and quoted his purported statements. He also

TOP SECRET

-17-

TOP SECRET

produced certain of the contents of the plane and later various parts of the plane itself. This clearly disclosed the true nature of the mission on which the plane was engaged.

The cover story was outflanked.

The issue then was whether to admit the incident but deny high level responsibility, or to take the course that was decided upon and clearly expressed in Secretary Herter's statement of May 9 and in the President's statement of May 11, and his address of May 25.

In Mr. Herter's appearance before this Committee, he has dealt with the statements which were issued during the period after May 6, except for the two statements involving NASA which I have covered.

I would only add that in my opinion, in the light of all the factors involved, the decision taken to assume responsibility in this particular case was the correct one. Denial, in my opinion, over the long run would have been tortuous and self defeating.

Those who took this decision knew that I was ready to assume the full measure of responsibility and to cover the project as a technical intelligence operation carried out on my own responsibility as Director of CIA. This alternative, too, was rejected because of the many elements making it hardly credible over the longer run.

* * * *

This concludes my statement respecting the intelligence aspects of the U-2 project.

TOP SECRET

-18-

COPY

This document consists of 18 pages

No. 2 of 15 copies

APPENDIX 6

FBI MEMORANDUM DELOACH TO TOLSON, APRIL 4, 1967

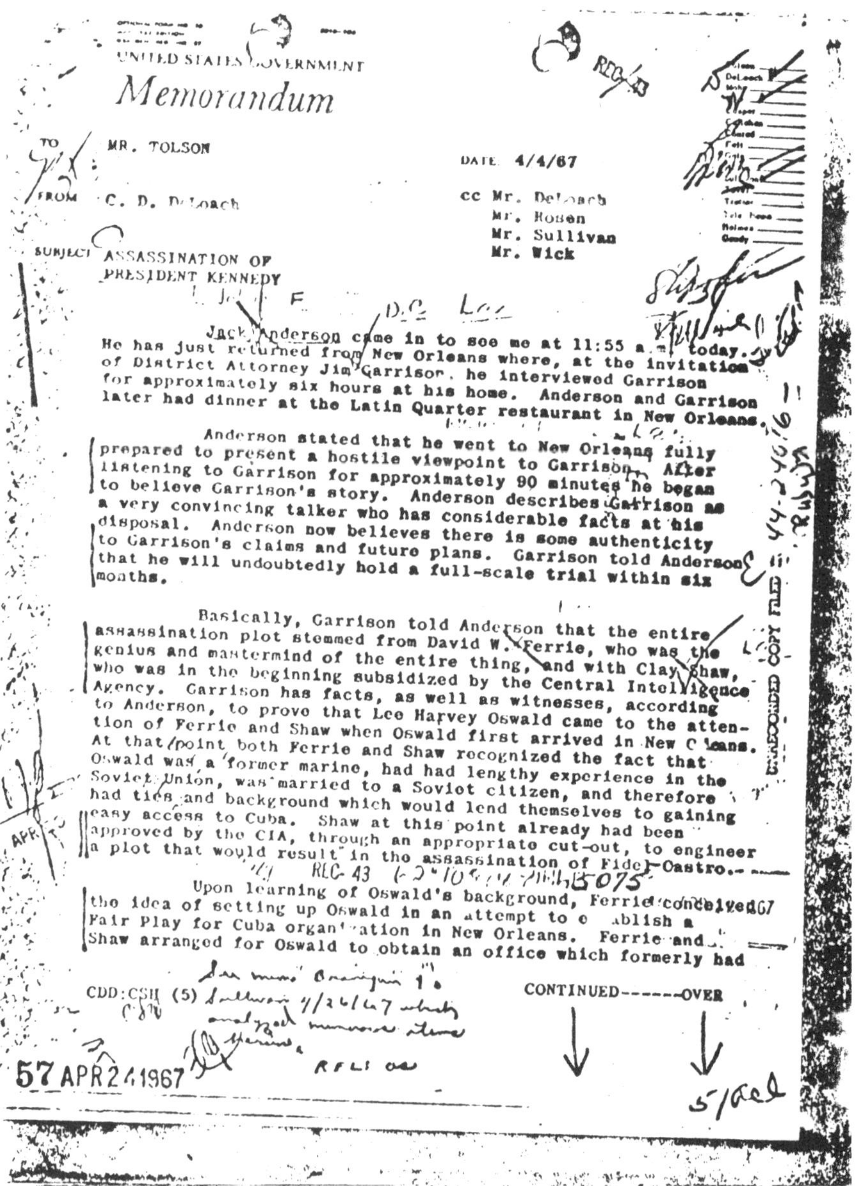

UNITED STATES GOVERNMENT

Memorandum

TO : MR. TOLSON

DATE: 4/4/67

FROM : C. D. DeLoach

cc Mr. DeLoach
Mr. Rosen
Mr. Sullivan
Mr. Wick

SUBJECT: ASSASSINATION OF PRESIDENT KENNEDY

Jack Anderson came in to see me at 11:55 a.m. today. He has just returned from New Orleans where, at the invitation of District Attorney Jim Garrison, he interviewed Garrison for approximately six hours at his home. Anderson and Garrison later had dinner at the Latin Quarter restaurant in New Orleans.

Anderson stated that he went to New Orleans fully prepared to present a hostile viewpoint to Garrison. After listening to Garrison for approximately 90 minutes he began to believe Garrison's story. Anderson describes Garrison as a very convincing talker who has considerable facts at his disposal. Anderson now believes there is some authenticity to Garrison's claims and future plans. Garrison told Anderson that he will undoubtedly hold a full-scale trial within six months.

Basically, Garrison told Anderson that the entire assassination plot stemmed from David W. Ferrie, who was the genius and mastermind of the entire thing, and with Clay Shaw, who was in the beginning subsidized by the Central Intelligence Agency. Garrison has facts, as well as witnesses, according to Anderson, to prove that Lee Harvey Oswald came to the attention of Ferrie and Shaw when Oswald first arrived in New Orleans. At that point both Ferrie and Shaw recognized the fact that Oswald was a former marine, had had lengthy experience in the Soviet Union, was married to a Soviet citizen, and therefore had ties and background which would lend themselves to gaining easy access to Cuba. Shaw at this point already had been approved by the CIA, through an appropriate cut-out, to engineer a plot that would result in the assassination of Fidel Castro.

REC-43

Upon learning of Oswald's background, Ferrie conceived the idea of setting up Oswald in an attempt to establish a Fair Play for Cuba organization in New Orleans. Ferrie and Shaw arranged for Oswald to obtain an office which formerly had

CDD:CSH (5)

CONTINUED------OVER

57 APR 24 1967

UNRECORDED COPY FILED

Mr. Tolson

been rented by an anti-Castro organization. Ferrie and Shaw also conceived the idea of sending Oswald to Mexico in a fake attempt to obtain permission to re-enter the Soviet Union. Garrison, according to Anderson, can prove that Oswald did this merely to establish a good atmosphere so that he could gain ready access to Cuba.

Garrison claims that it was at this point that Oswald became disillusioned and refused to go through with the plot to assassinate Castro. Upon returning to New Orleans from Mexico, Oswald advised both Ferrie and Shaw that he would not go through with their plans. Shaw and Ferrie, being guided by several Cubans in their midst, then conceived the idea (mostly because of the fiasco at the Bay of Pigs) of assassinating President Kennedy. Ferrie and Shaw believed that Oswald could be the "patsy" and instructed him to go to Dallas for the purpose of the assassination.

They also engineered the idea of him buying the gun under the name of A. J. Hidell, and the use of the mails in procuring this gun so that it would be an open, public record which could be traced to Oswald. They additionally told Oswald that he should keep certain papers in his possession which would trace back to the gun.

On the day of the assassination, Ferrie traveled to Houston, allegedly for the purpose of ice skating. Witnesses at the ice skating rink remember Ferrie as being at the rink and have indicated to Garrison that Ferrie, while he did not ice skate, did stand near a pay telephone at all times on the day of 11/22/63.

Garrison also has witnesses who will testify that Jack Ruby was the eyes and ears for Ferrie at all times. Ruby sent two of his people to Houston so that, upon the uccess of the assassination attempt, these two people could use a local pay phone to advise Ferrie of the success of the plot. Garrison claims that a long distance phone call from Dallas to Houston could, of course, have been traced; hence the desirability of using the local phone. Anderson stated that Ruby was defin[illegible]ly in on the plot and was later instructed by Ferrie and Shaw to take care of Oswald.

2

Mr. Tolson

Anderson next sprang the "Sixty-four dollar question." He stated that at the close of Garrison's six-hour recitation of facts, he (Anderson) was of the opinion that Garrison was not only sincere, but very convincing. Anderson stated that Garrison firmly believed his facts. Anderson then told me that he bluntly asked Garrison why Garrison had not given all these convincing facts to the FBI, whereupon Garrison replied, "I got started off on the wrong foot with the FBI." Garrison added, "I would be more than willing to give the FBI everything I have and let them finish the investigation if they so desire."

Anderson told me that he, of course, is now in a position to contact Garrison and indicate that the FBI will or will not take over this case. I told Anderson that the FBI would not under any circumstances take over the case. I stated that Garrison had made it quite plain that he did not want the cooperation of the FBI and, as a matter of fact, Garrison had threatened to put handcuffs on any of our agents who approached him for information.

I also told Anderson that, while we of course would accept any information that was voluntarily given to us, we at the same time would not take over Garrison's "dirty laundry."

Anderson told me that if the Bureau had any change of policy in the above regard he would appreciate knowing about it. I told him we would keep his offer in mind; however, there definitely would be no change of policy.

Anderson also told me that he had discussed this entire matter with George Christian, the President's Press Secretary, at the White House. He stated that Christian was also convinced that there must be some truth to Garrison's allegations. Christian told Anderson to get in touch with the FBI. Anderson stated he had already been planning to do this, but that he now especially wanted to advise us of the full facts because of Christian's request.

In this connection, Marvin Watson called me late last night and stated that the President had told him, in an off moment, that he was now convinced that there was a plot in connection with the assassination. Watson stated the President felt that CIA had had something to do with this plot. Watson requested that any further information we could furnish

3

Mr. Tolson

in this connection would be most appreciated by him and the President. I reminded Watson that the Director had sent over to the White House some weeks back all the information in our possession in connection with CIA's attempts to use former agent Robert Maheu and his private detective outfit in contacts with Sam Giancana and other hoodlums, relative to fostering a plot to assassinate Castro. Watson stated this was true and he remembered our memorandum in this regard, but that if we had anything else we should by all means forward it to the White House. I told him we had no further information in this regard.

ACTION: For record purposes. There is no need to make further contact with Anderson.

4

APPENDIX 7

FBI MEMORANDUM EVANS TO BELMONT, NOVEMBER 25, 1963, WITH KATZENBACH MEMO

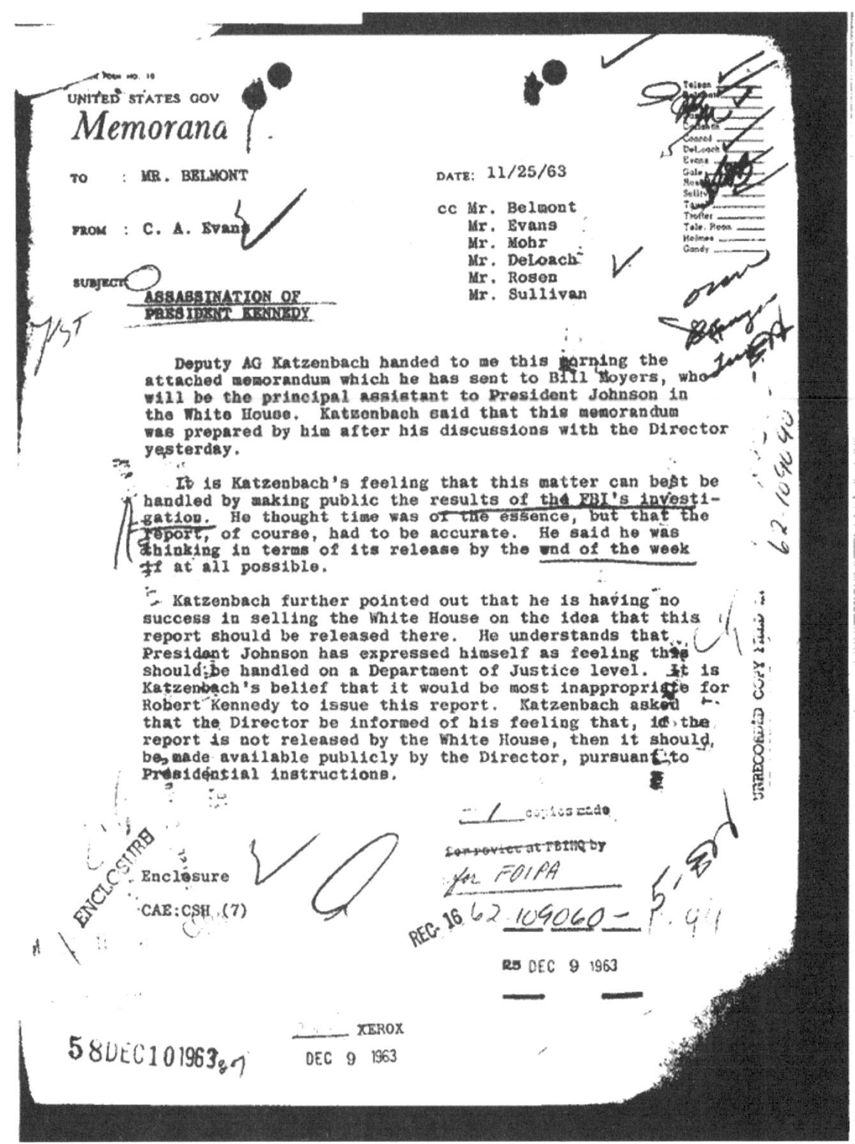

UNITED STATES GOV

Memorana

TO : MR. BELMONT

DATE: 11/25/63

FROM : C. A. Evans

cc Mr. Belmont
Mr. Evans
Mr. Mohr
Mr. DeLoach
Mr. Rosen
Mr. Sullivan

SUBJECT: ASSASSINATION OF PRESIDENT KENNEDY

Deputy AG Katzenbach handed to me this morning the attached memorandum which he has sent to Bill Moyers, who will be the principal assistant to President Johnson in the White House. Katzenbach said that this memorandum was prepared by him after his discussions with the Director yesterday.

It is Katzenbach's feeling that this matter can best be handled by making public the results of the FBI's investigation. He thought time was of the essence, but that the report, of course, had to be accurate. He said he was thinking in terms of its release by the end of the week if at all possible.

Katzenbach further pointed out that he is having no success in selling the White House on the idea that this report should be released there. He understands that President Johnson has expressed himself as feeling this should be handled on a Department of Justice level. It is Katzenbach's belief that it would be most inappropriate for Robert Kennedy to issue this report. Katzenbach asked that the Director be informed of his feeling that, if the report is not released by the White House, then it should be made available publicly by the Director, pursuant to Presidential instructions.

Enclosure
CAE:CSH (7)

ENCLOSURE

REC-16 62-109060-

25 DEC 9 1963

XEROX
DEC 9 1963

58DEC101963

UNRECORDED COPY FILED IN 62-109090

93

November 25, 1963

MEMORANDUM FOR MR. MOYERS

It is important that all of the facts surrounding President Kennedy's Assassination be made public in a way which will satisfy people in the United States and abroad that all the facts have been told and that a statement to this effect be made now.

1. The public must be satisfied that Oswald was the assassin; that he did not have confederates who are still at large; and that the evidence was such that he would have been convicted at trial.

2. Speculation about Oswald's motivation ought to be cut off, and we should have some basis for rebutting thought that this was a Communist conspiracy or (as the Iron Curtain press is saying) a right-wing conspiracy to blame it on the Communists. Unfortunately the facts on Oswald seem about too pat--too obvious (Marxist, Cuba, Russian wife, etc.). The Dallas police have put out statements on the Communist conspiracy theory, and it was they who were in charge when he was shot and thus silenced.

3. The matter has been handled thus far with neither dignity nor conviction. Facts have been mixed with rumour and speculation. We can scarcely let the world see us totally in the image of the Dallas police when our President is murdered.

I think this objective may be satisfied by making public as soon as possible a complete and thorough FBI report on Oswald and the assassination. This may run into the difficulty of pointing to inconsistencies between this report and statements by Dallas police officials. But the reputation of the Bureau is such that it may do the whole job.

62-109060 -

[R] - ITEM IS REC

The only other step would be the appointment of a Presidential Commission of unimpeachable personnel to review and examine the evidence and announce its conclusions. This has both advantages and disadvantages. It think it can await publication of the FBI report and public reaction to it here and abroad.

I think, however, that a statement that all the facts will be made public property in an orderly and responsible way should be made now. We need something to head off public speculation or Congressional hearings of the wrong sort.

Nicholas deB. Katzenbach
Deputy Attorney General

[R] - ITEM IS RESTRICTED

APPENDIX 8

DELOACH NOTES ON HOOVER INTERVIEW

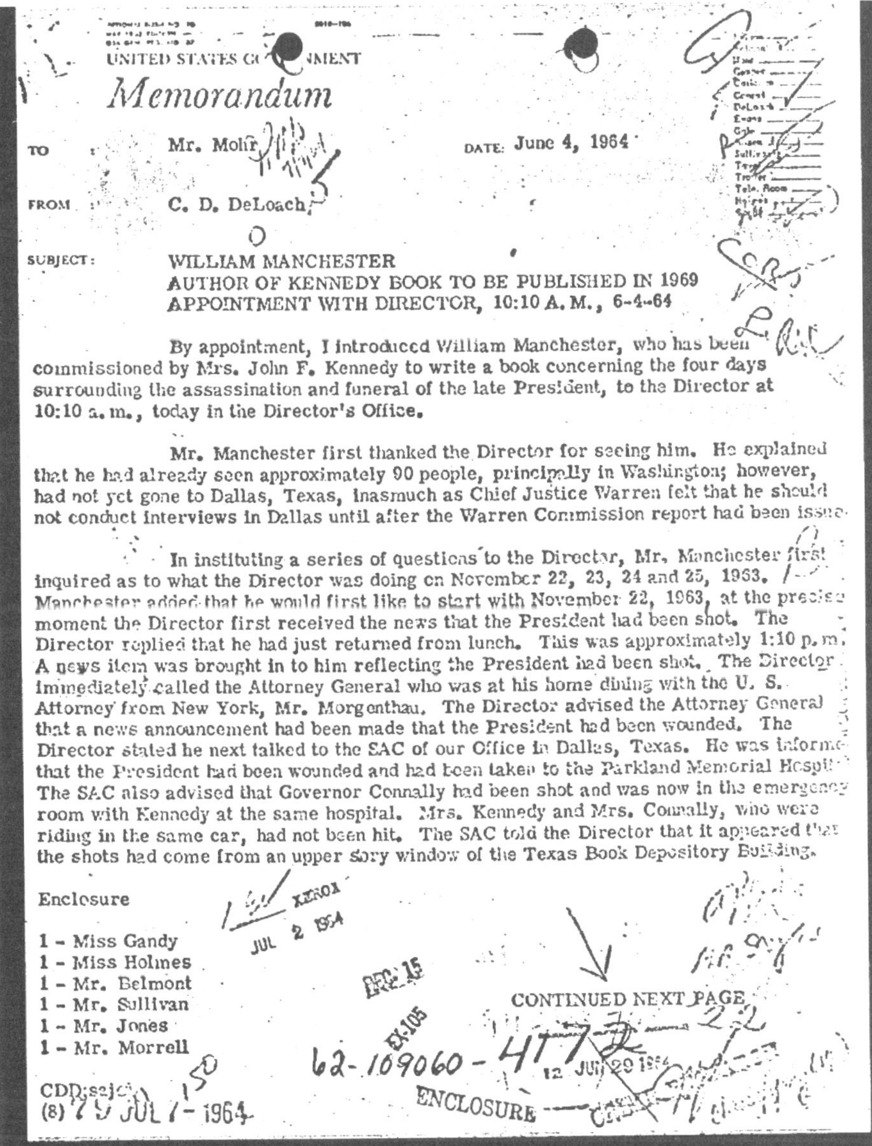

UNITED STATES GOVERNMENT

Memorandum

TO: Mr. Mohr

DATE: June 4, 1964

FROM: C. D. DeLoach

SUBJECT: WILLIAM MANCHESTER
AUTHOR OF KENNEDY BOOK TO BE PUBLISHED IN 1969
APPOINTMENT WITH DIRECTOR, 10:10 A.M., 6-4-64

By appointment, I introduced William Manchester, who has been commissioned by Mrs. John F. Kennedy to write a book concerning the four days surrounding the assassination and funeral of the late President, to the Director at 10:10 a.m., today in the Director's Office.

Mr. Manchester first thanked the Director for seeing him. He explained that he had already seen approximately 90 people, principally in Washington; however, had not yet gone to Dallas, Texas, inasmuch as Chief Justice Warren felt that he should not conduct interviews in Dallas until after the Warren Commission report had been issued.

In instituting a series of questions to the Director, Mr. Manchester first inquired as to what the Director was doing on November 22, 23, 24 and 25, 1963. Manchester added that he would first like to start with November 22, 1963, at the precise moment the Director first received the news that the President had been shot. The Director replied that he had just returned from lunch. This was approximately 1:10 p.m. A news item was brought in to him reflecting the President had been shot. The Director immediately called the Attorney General who was at his home dining with the U. S. Attorney from New York, Mr. Morgenthau. The Director advised the Attorney General that a news announcement had been made that the President had been wounded. The Director stated he next talked to the SAC of our Office in Dallas, Texas. He was informed that the President had been wounded and had been taken to the Parkland Memorial Hospital. The SAC also advised that Governor Connally had been shot and was now in the emergency room with Kennedy at the same hospital. Mrs. Kennedy and Mrs. Connally, who were riding in the same car, had not been hit. The SAC told the Director that it appeared that the shots had come from an upper story window of the Texas Book Depository Building.

Enclosure

1 - Miss Gandy
1 - Miss Holmes
1 - Mr. Belmont
1 - Mr. Sullivan
1 - Mr. Jones
1 - Mr. Morrell

XEROX JUL 2 1964

REC 15

EX-105

CONTINUED NEXT PAGE

62-109060-4772

12 JUN 29 1964

ENCLOSURE

CDD:sajc
(8) 79 JUL 1 - 1964

DeLoach to Mohr 6-4-64
Re: William Manchester, Author of Kennedy Book
To Be Published in 1969
Appointment with Director, 10:10 a.m., 6-4-64

The Dallas Office additionally advised the Director shortly after 2:00 p.m. that day that the President had died. The Director immediately called the Attorney General once again and told him of the death of his brother. At this time the Director inquired as to whether the Attorney General planned to go to Dallas. The Director stated that he had advised the Attorney General that if such plans were in the making he would facilitate his departure and arrival. The Director told Manchester that shortly thereafter our Dallas Office called once again to indicate that the President's body would be immediately flown back to Washington and that the Vice President had already been sworn in as President. The Director later called the Attorney General once again and told him that the FBI was moving into the investigation. The Director advised Manchester that the FBI took this action despite the fact that there was no law making it a Federal violation to assassinate the President.

At this point the Director gave Manchester a brief history of the assassination of SAC Shanahan in Chicago, Illinois, in the middle 1920's. There was no Federal law against assaulting or murdering an FBI Agent at that time. The Director told Manchester he initiated action to make it a Federal crime to assault or kill an FBI Agent so that proper action could be taken in Federal court rather than a local court in such matters.

The Director told Manchester that if the FBI had taken custody of Lee Harvey Oswald, Jr., Oswald would never have been killed by Jack Ruby. The Director stated that the murder of Oswald by Ruby naturally gave rise to considerable speculation and rumor. All of this could have been avoided had the Dallas police taken proper action to protect Oswald.

The Director told Manchester that the FBI immediately entered the case, despite non-jurisdiction, and that we interviewed Oswald as soon as he was made available. The Director stated that on the evening of November 22, 1963, at approximately 7:25 p.m. President Johnson called him at his home and requested that the FBI take complete charge of the case involving the assassination. The Director stated he advised the President that the FBI had already entered the case and that we would, of course, go all out in this matter. The Director also told the President that he was concerned about the great amount of publicity coming out of Dallas.

The Director then told Manchester that the Dallas police had given out considerable information received as a result of FBI findings, particularly from our Laboratory. He added that on the 4th or 5th day following the assassination he instructed our SAC in Dallas to contact Chief of Police Curry and order him to make no further statements to the press with respect to the evidence or investigation surrounding the assassination. The Director told Manchester that this Chief of Police could have told

- 2 -

DeLoach to Mohr 6-4-(

Re: William Manchester, Author of Kennedy Book
To Be Published in 1969
Appointment with Director, 10:10 a.m., 6-4-64

him to go to hell; however, he had recognized the obvious necessity and logic of such instructions and had complied. The Director explained to Manchester at some length the necessity to keep physical evidence confined prior to the prosecution of an individual.

The Director told Manchester that on Saturday evening, November 23, 1963, our Dallas Office had received an anonymous telephone call indicating that plans had been made to murder Oswald when he was removed from the Dallas City Jail. The FBI informed the Dallas Chief of Police immediately. The Director told Manchester that original plans for removal of Oswald had been made for 10:00 p.m. that Saturday night. The Chief of Police, however, changed these plans by acceding to the pressure of the press that Oswald be removed at a convenient time so that communications media could cover the event. Our Dallas Office again called the Dallas Police Department on Sunday morning, November 24, 1963, and reminded that Department of the same anonymous telephone call. At that time the Chief of Police assured our Dallas Office that all precautions were being taken to protect Oswald.

The Director informed Manchester that following the President's call at 7:25 p.m., November 22, 1963, he gave specific instructions that the FBI do everything possible to thoroughly investigate this case. The Director stated that additional personnel were immediately sent to Dallas. He told Manchester this was necessary inasmuch as our Dallas Office and FBI Headquarters, as well as other offices, received hundreds and hundreds of phone calls, telegrams and letters setting forth leads in this case.

Manchester inquired as to whether the Director placed any significance to the anonymous phone call concerning the plan to murder Oswald. The Director replied that we had no way of knowing at the time whether any importance should be attached or not; however, we did have the responsibility to immediately notify the Dallas police, which we did.

The Director characterized Jack Ruby as somewhat of a "police buff." As a result of his friendship with a number of police officers he had easy accessibility to the Dallas Police Department. The Director stated that he did not know whether Ruby's reported insanity was of the sincere or faked type inasmuch as we were not psychiatrists. He stated that Ruby had given the excuse that he had killed Oswald because of his obvious affection for the late President and the fact that he wanted to prevent any further sorrow to Mrs. Kennedy inasmuch as she would necessarily have to return to Dallas and testify against Oswald.

- 3 -

DeLoach to Mohr 6-4-64
Re: William Manchester, Author of Kennedy Book
To Be Published in 1969
Appointment with Director, 10:Da.m., 6-4-64

Manchester inquired as to the exact location of the Director at the time Oswald was killed on Sunday, November 24, 1963. The Director replied that he was at home. He stated that the Dallas Office contacted him immediately following this event. Manchester inquired as to the Director's immediate reaction. The Director replied that his first thought was how such an event could take place, particularly under a system of civilized justice. The Director added that he had ordered an immediate check on Jack Ruby and particularly to ascertain if there had been a relationship between Ruby and Oswald.

Manchester inquired as to whether the Director was watching television at the time of Oswald's murder. The Director replied in the negative. He stated he was working on official papers at the time. The Director added that he usually saved Sundays to review lengthy documents and memoranda as well as to prepare himself for interviews, hearings, etc.

Manchester inquired as to what the Director was doing on Friday morning, November 22, 1963, prior to the assassination. The Director replied that he was conducting business as usual, that he had had a number of interviews that particular morning.

Manchester inquired as to the physical location of the wire service ticker machine. He was told that it is located across the hall and that pertinent wire service items are brought in to the Director immediately.

The Director told Manchester that his first conversation on November 22, 1963, with our Dallas Office occurred at approximately 1:48 p.m. The Director was advised at that time that the President was not believed to be dead yet but that he had suffered a mortal wound. The Director mentioned that on the occasion of his second call to the Attorney General, the Attorney General had indicated that he had also been in touch with a number of the Presidential Staff and had been informed of a number of details concerning the shooting and the fact that the President had died.

Manchester inquired as to the Director's opinion of the Attorney General's reaction upon being informed that the President had been shot. The Director replied that the Attorney General had been silent for a few moments and had then requested that the Director keep him informed of any further facts received concerning this matter. The Director told Manchester that the Attorney General is usually very quiet in manner until he has all the necessary facts of a given situation. The Director stated that the Attorney General was not the explosive type unless he became angry.

- 4 -

DeLoach to Mohr 6-4-64
Re: William Manchester, Author of Kennedy Book
To Be Published in 1969
Appointment with Director, 10:10 a.m., 6-4-64

Manchester told the Director that the President's call to the Director at 7:25 p.m., November 22, 1963, appeared to be one of the first calls that the President made upon returning to Washington that evening. The Director replied that he would surmise that this was correct. The Director added that our investigation proceeded forthwith; however, it was not until Monday or Tuesday of the following week that the President decided to name a Presidential Commission to look into the assassination. The Director told Manchester that an FBI report had been sent to the Warren Commission within ten days after the President had set up this body. The Director stated that he personally had appeared before the Warren Commission and that he considered their questioning of him to be quite thorough. He stated that thoroughness was necessary on the part of the Commission inasmuch as this would serve to assist in quelling gossip and speculation in the future. The Director quickly added, however, that rumors will continue concerning this case, especially in Europe where there is widespread gossip concerning a supposed conspiracy, for many years.

The Director told Manchester that the statement that some of the information may be withheld by the Warren Commission naturally gave rise to further rumor. Manchester replied that he could understand the Chief Justice's statement in this regard inasmuch as not just any individual should be allowed to look at the classified material sent to the Commission by some agencies. The Director replied that the issue in point is such that excessive precautions of security is unwise. The Director explained that he had never been a great believer in wasteful precautions or going overboard regarding excessive security. He stated that an item is either classified or else it isn't classified. The Director gave examples of leaks in Government that have given several Presidents extreme cause and worry. He stated that the FBI is usually called upon to investigate these leaks, however, newspapermen naturally do not desire to reveal their sources. The Director stated that if newspapermen did reveal such sources that quite naturally the sources would dry up.

Manchester inquired of the Director as to whether the assassination case became one of major concern following the President's call at 7:25 p.m., November 22, 1963. The Director stated that as he had previously indicated, the FBI had already entered this case. He added, however, that after the President's call we went all out in doing such things as working around the clock, sending a Washington-based FBI official to Dallas and adding approximately 30 Agents to the Dallas personnel complement. The Director stated that we still have at least 50 men who are tied up in running down leads on this particular case throughout the FBI's service. He stated that this case will never be closed from an investigative point of view inasmuch as we will continually receive leads, many from mental cases, which necessarily have to be checked out.

- 5 -

DeLoach to Mohr 6-4-64
Re: William Manchester, Author of Kennedy Book
To Be Published in 1969
Appointment with Director, 10:10 a.m., 6-4-64

Manchester asked if the matter of a President being assassinated not being a Federal crime had ever been discussed fully by the Congress, or anyone else, according to the Director's knowledge. The Director replied that there had been no discussion to any extent. He stated the matter had just never been considered.

Manchester inquired as to whether the FBI had prior material on Oswald before the assassination. The Director replied that we did have some information regarding Oswald, however, it was quite flimsy in nature. The Director then explained at some length the background of Oswald. He told Manchester of the press releases that Oswald made in Moscow. He told Manchester of Oswald's employment in a factory in Minsk, Russia, and of the fact that Oswald had later returned to Moscow. The Director stated that he certainly did not understand why the Department of State had failed to have Oswald sign an affidavit forfeitting his American citizenship at the time Oswald returned to Moscow and visited the U. S. Embassy. Manchester spoke up and stated that the State Department claimed they had wanted to find out if Oswald had committed an extraditable crime in the Soviet Union, therefore, no signed affidavit was taken from him. The Director again deplored the failure to have such an affidavit executed.

The Director continued that we had interviewed Oswald within two or three days following his arrival in the United States. He explained that we, of course, desired to find out if Oswald had been recruited as an intelligence agent by the Soviet Union. The Director told Manchester that this did not appear to be true. He added that Oswald had classified himself as a Marxist rather than a communist. The Director added that Oswald had later been interviewed in New Orleans after getting into a street squabble with anti-Castroites over leaflets being handed out by Oswald. The Director told Manchester that Oswald could best be termed a "loner." He explained Oswald's communications with the Communist Party in the United States but added that Oswald had never joined the Party. The Director told of the incidents surrounding Oswald's attempt to kill General Walker in Dallas. He added that Oswald's wife, Marina, had advised us of this incident following the assassination. The Director summarized this part of the interview by indicating there appeared to be nothing in Oswald's background which would reflect that he was a man of violence and most certainly nothing which indicated that Oswald had any intentions of assassinating the President.

Manchester asked if the Director did not find it odd that Mrs. Oswald had failed to tell anyone about the attempted assassination of General Walker until after the murder of President Kennedy. The Director replied that he did not find this odd in view of the cold relationship between Oswald and his wife, the language barrier on the part of Mrs. Oswald and the fact that Mrs. Oswald did not have the natural instincts of an American woman but to the contrary had a different attitude altogether. He stated he placed no significance in Mrs. Oswald's failure to advise of this incident prior to the assassination.

- 6 -

DeLoach to Mohr 6-4-64
Re: William Manchester, Author of Kennedy Book
To Be Published in 1969
Appointment with Director, 10:10 a. m., 6-4-64

The Director told Manchester that it was extremely difficult to speculate on the motivations of Oswald to kill the President. The Director stated it was entirely possible Oswald may have wanted to kill Governor John Connally. He explained that Oswald had written communications to Governor Connally protesting his particular type of discharge from the U. S. Marine Corps. The Director added that President Kennedy was an intellectual liberal type. He stated that President Kennedy had been desirous of keeping peace with honor. He stated that President Kennedy desired peaceful co-existence --American style. The Director added that the President, although he had been firm in his dealings with Khrushchev, had a fairly good relationship with Khrushchev and the Soviet Union. The Director summed up by stating that Oswald could not have desired to kill the President because the President had dealt harshly, or spoken harshly, against the Communist Party and Chairman Khrushchev.

Manchester speculated that perhaps the communists, including Oswald, did not like the relationship between the late President and Khrushchev; therefore, the communists desired to do away with President Kennedy so that this obstacle to their desired philosophy could be removed. The Director replied that this was entirely possible; however, he wanted Manchester to clearly understand that Khrushchev was not a person to be trusted and that Chairman Khrushchev had a very cold and evil mind. The Director, at this point, gave examples of Khrushchev's understanding of the English language despite the fact that he had Troyanovsky, an excellent interpreter, with him at all times while on his visits to the United States. The Director told Manchester that he had always felt it better to kick individuals like Khrushchev on the shins once in a while rather than to boot-lick them. The Director explained that Khrushchev was basically an oriental and that individuals opposing orientals usually lost face in the oriental's opinion when fear or trepidation was shown.

Manchester inquired as to whether the Director's duties and responsibilities allowed him to participate personally in the funeral ceremonies. The Director replied in the negative. He stated he had been at his desk constantly. He added that he had issued instructions that FBI personnel participate officially in the ceremonies by assisting Secret Service as much as possible. The Director spoke of the many visiting foreign dignitaries and of the dangers involved in the march from the White House to St. Matthew's Cathedral. He told Manchester that over 40 Special Agents had been assigned to assist Secret Service, particularly at St. Matthew's Cathedral. He further told Manchester that the authority to protect the President was clearly a function of the Secret Service; however, since the assassination we have assisted when called upon. The Director briefly advised Manchester at this point of the immediate widespread ramifications of this case following the actual shooting. He told Manchester that leads had spread to Mexico as well as throughout the entire United States. Therefore, it has been necessary for him personally to remain at his desk so as to supervise this matter.

- 7 -

DeLoach to Mohr 6-4-64
Re: William Manchester, Author of Kennedy Book
To Be Published in 1969
Appointment with Director, 10:10 a.m., 6-4-64

At this point I reminded Manchester of his previous statement to me that he had to be at the White House at 11:15 a.m. Manchester thanked the Director twice upon his departure and stated that he was very appreciative of the Director's cooperation and considerable time taken from a busy schedule to be of assistance.

ACTION:

The Director may desire to send the Attorney General the attached letter indicating that he had seen Manchester.

- 8 -

APPENDIX 9

HELMS'S AFFIDAVITS IN HEINE V. RAUS

IN THE UNITED STATES DISTRICT COURT
FOR THE DISTRICT OF MARYLAND

EERIK HEINE, Plaintiff,	)	
v.	)	Civil Action No. 15952
JURI RAUS, Defendant.	)	

AFFIDAVIT

Richard Helms, Director of Central Intelligence, first being duly sworn, deposes and says that:

1. In Paragraph 2 of my Affidavit dated April 22, 1966, which I executed as Deputy Director of Central Intelligence, I stated in part: The defendant was instructed to warn members of Estonian emigre groups that Eerik Heine was a dispatched Soviet intelligence operative, a KGB agent.

2. The content of that statement means, I intended by that statement to convey, and I now so state: The defendant, Juri Raus, was instructed by the Central Intelligence Agency to warn members

4. During the periods of time specified in paragraphs 5, 6, and 7 of the complaint, the defendant, Juri Raus, was employed as a highway research engineer for the Office of Research and Development, Bureau of Public Roads, United States Department of Commerce.

5. During the same periods of time, the defendant was the National Commander of the Legion of Estonian Liberation, Inc., and was familiar with Estonian emigre activities.

6. For a number of reasons, including his past history and his position as National Commander of the Legion of Estonian Liberation, the defendant has been a source to this Agency of foreign intelligence information pertaining inter alia to Soviet Estonia and to Estonian emigre activities in foreign countries as well as in the United States.

7. The Central Intelligence Agency has employed the defendant from time to time -- concurrently with his duties on behalf of the Bureau of Public Roads -- to carry out specific assignments on behalf of the Agency. Defendant was so employed on those occasions specified in paragraphs 5, 6, and 7 of the complaint.

8. On those occasions specified in paragraphs 5, 6, and 7 of the complaint, the defendant was furnished information concerning the plaintiff by the Central Intelligence Agency and was instructed to disseminate such information to members of the Legion so as to protect the integrity of the Agency's foreign intelligence sources. Accordingly, when Juri Raus spoke concerning the plaintiff on the occasions about which complaint is made, he was acting within the scope and course of his employment by the Agency on behalf of the United States.

9. On May 29, 1963, prior to the occasions specified in paragraphs 5, 6 and 7 of the complaint, the defendant signed a Secrecy Agreement with the Agency, a copy of which is attached, which Agreement is still in full force and effect.

10. After a personal review of the Agency's activities pertaining to Eerik Heine, I have reached the judgment on behalf of the Agency that it would be contrary to the security interests of the United States for any further information pertaining to the use and employment of Juri Raus by the Agency in connection with Eerik Heine to be disclosed, other than the disclosures already made in the defendant's answer, my own affidavits, and the defendant's affidavits, which I have read.

11. Acting pursuant to the authority lodged in the Director of Central Intelligence by virtue of the provisions of Title 50, United States Code, Sections 403d and 403g, and the implementing Regulations promulgated thereunder, I have determined that it would be contrary to the national interest and would further compromise the proper protection of intelligence sources and methods to disclose further information in regard to those material matters which the plaintiff has sought to have revealed through his pleadings. I am herewith directing Juri Raus to make no further disclosures concerning his

- 3 -

employment by the Agency or relating to this matter without specific authorization by proper officials of the Central Intelligence Agency.

Richard Helms

Attachments as stated.

STATE OF VIRGINIA)
) ss.
COUNTY OF FAIRFAX)

Subscribed and Sworn to before me this 1st day of April, 1966.

Notary Public

My commission expires 24 September 1969.

(SEAL)

IN THE UNITED STATES DISTRICT COURT
FOR THE DISTRICT OF MARYLAND

EERIK HEINE,)
Plaintiff,)
v.)
)
JURI RAUS,) Civil Action No. 15952
)
Defendant.)

A F F I D A V I T

Richard Helms, Deputy Director of Central Intelligence, being first duly sworn, deposes and says that:

1. Under the Director's Delegation of Authority to the Deputy Director of Central Intelligence, dated 28 April 1965, a copy of which is attached, I have been delegated all authorities vested in the Director of Central Intelligence in his position as Director of Central Intelligence and head of the Central Intelligence Agency including those authorities set forth in Central Intelligence Agency Regulation HR 10-20, a copy of which is attached.

2. I have familiarized myself with the allegations contained in the complaint in the above-entitled case.

3. I have familiarized myself with the Central Intelligence Agency's participation in communicating information concerning Eerik Heine to representatives of the Estonian emigre community in the United States.

of Estonian emigre groups that Eerik Heine was a dispatched Soviet intelligence operative, a KGB agent.

SIGNED

Richard Helms

STATE OF VIRGINIA)
) ss.
COUNTY OF FAIRFAX)

Subscribed and sworn to before me this 7th day of October, 1966.

Edward R. Dougherty, Jr.
Notary Public

My commission expires 24 September 1969.

(SEAL)

ENDNOTES

EDITOR'S INTRODUCTION

1 The details of evidence are beyond the scope of this book. However, a few examples to illustrate the basic points may be found in Appendix 1. As Weisberg makes clear, the Warren Report was only able to arrive at its conclusions by misrepresenting, distorting, and ignoring its own evidence as contained in the twenty-six volumes of evidence and other files.

2 See Selected Bibliography for a list of Weisberg's published works.

3 These are now part of a permanent archive at Hood College in Frederick, MD (http://jfk.hood.edu).

4 These can also be found at the Hood College archive. See above.

5 A more detailed biography can be found in his unpublished manuscript, *Inside the JFK Assassination Industry*, which can be accessed at the permanent archive at Hood College. (http://jfk.hood.edu)

6 It should be noted that this work includes extensive research and writing about the assassination of Martin Luther King Jr. Weisberg served as an investigator for the legal team that attempted to get the accused assassin, James Earl Ray, the trial he never had. His book on the King case is *Frame Up: The Martin Luther King—James Earl Ray Case*. Outerbridge & Dienstfrey: New York, 1971.

7 "Strangelovian" refers to the award-winning 1964 film directed by Stanley Kubrick, *Dr. Strangelove or: How I Learned to Stop Worrying and Love the Bomb*. The screenplay was written by Kubrick, Peter George, and Terry Southern and based on the novel, *Red Alert*, by Peter George. It centers around, "An unhinged American general order(ing) a bombing attack on the Soviet Union, triggering a path to nuclear holocaust that a war room full of politicians and generals frantically try to stop." (IMDb) The Joint Chiefs of Staff in the Kennedy Administration contemplated something quite similar in the context of the Cuba Missile Crisis, as Weisberg brings out. We decided, however, to drop "Strangelovian" from the title not because it is not relevant, which it is, but because we believe most readers would not be familiar with the reference.

CHAPTER 1

1 An important milestone was the National Security Act of 1947 which created the National Security Council and the Central Intelligence Agency and reorganized the military.

2 "One of the most deadening mechanisms of control over the conduct of everyday life comes neither from the callous imposition of brute force nor from the ruthless exercise of censorship but from the quiet denial of knowledge." (Wrone, 1978: ix).

3 President John F. Kennedy Assassination Records Collection Act of 1992.

4 A. Hamilton and C. Rossiter, *The Federalist papers; Alexander Hamilton, James Madison, John Jay*. 25.

5 Schlesinger, Arthur. M. *A Thousand Days ; John F. Kennedy in the White House*. (Houghton Mifflin.,1965), 338.

6 Schlesinger, *A Thousand Days.*

7 It was not a "Cuban" missile crisis.

8 I researched it for the book about it which I had planned while trying to get my first book published in 1965. The working title was *Tiger to Ride: The Untold Story of the Cuba Missile Crisis*. I was not able to get to that writing. In recent years, international conferences of those who were involved on both sides that got little attention from the major media have since confirmed my contemporaneous analysis that led to the book's title: In placing those missiles in Cuba Khrushchev gave Kennedy his own tiger to ride.

9 "Shuttle Crew Plucks Satellite From Its Orbit," *The Washington Post*, September 16, 1994, 3.

10 Clearly, the situation today is quite different than it was as the Cold War was winding down. But of course, the Russian invasion of Ukraine has left the world in a much more perilous state.

CHAPTER 2

1 Kenneth O'Donnell and David Powers, *"Johnny, We Hardly Knew Ye"; Memories of John Fitzgerald Kennedy*, (Little Brown, 1972), 382.

2 John M. Newman, *JFK and Vietnam: Deception, Intrigue, and the Struggle for Power*, (Warner Books, 1992), 446.

3 Newman, *JFK and Vietnam,* 432–433.

4 Newman, *JFK and Vietnam*, 438 ff.

5 Newman, *JFK and Vietnam*, 446.

6 Newman, *JFK and Vietnam*, 447.

7 Newman's source for the Johnson quote is Stanley Karnow's book *Vietnam: A History*, p.326. Karnow, S. (1983). *Vietnam : a history*. The Viking Press.

8 Hunt, E. Howard, *Undercover: Memoirs of an American Secret Agent.* (Berkeley Publishing, 1974), 131.

9 O'Donnell and Powers, *"Johnny, We Hardly Knew Ye"*, 14.

10 O'Donnell and Powers, *"Johnny, We Hardly Knew Ye"*, 269.
11 O'Donnell and Powers, *"Johnny, We Hardly Knew Ye"*, 277.
12 O'Donnell and Powers, *"Johnny, We Hardly Knew Ye"*, 13.
13 O'Donnell and Powers, *"Johnny, We Hardly Knew Ye"*, 14–15.
14 O'Donnell and Powers, *"Johnny, We Hardly Knew Ye"*, 15.
15 O'Donnell and Powers, *"Johnny, We Hardly Knew Ye"*, 16.
16 O'Donnell and Powers, *"Johnny, We Hardly Knew Ye"*, 17.
17 O'Donnell and Powers, *"Johnny, We Hardly Knew Ye"*, 269.
18 O'Donnell and Powers, *"Johnny, We Hardly Knew Ye"*, 383.
19 Reeves, Richard, *President Kennedy: Profile of Power*, (Simon & Schuster, 1993), 259.
20 Reeves, *President Kennedy*, 260.
21 Walt Rostow was one of the more articulate of the hawks in government.
22 Reeves, *President Kennedy*, 260.
23 O'Donnell and Powers, *"Johnny, We Hardly Knew Ye"*, 18.

CHAPTER 3

1 This and other Weisberg manuscripts can be found in the Weisberg Archive at Hood College. www.jfk.hood.edu.
2 About a year after Weisberg completed the draft of this book, he received a copy of a book by Carlos Lechuga, former Cuban ambassador to the United Nations. (Lechuga, C. (1995). *In the Eye of the Storm: Castro, Khrushchev, Kennedy and the Missile Crisis* (M. Todd, Trans.). Ocean Press.) It presents the unique Cuban perspective on the crisis that nearly led to nuclear annihilation. Lechuga provides an account of his discussions with Attwood as well as the meetings between French journalist Jean Daniel and President Kennedy and Fidel Castro, all of which were efforts to explore better relations between the United States and Cuba. As the book's editor, Mirta Muñiz writes in his Preface, this initiative was brought to an abrupt halt by the assassination of President Kennedy. He goes on to say, "Carlos Lechuga suggests that these conversations in which he participated could have precipitated the assassination in order to block any thawing of relations between the two countries." As Weisberg writes, "we may never know."
3 Daniel, Jean, "When Castro Heard the News," *The New Republic*, December 7, 1963, 7–9.
4 This is also to say that some of these theories are unreasonable, like Texas oil interests' involvement in a conspiracy. Although the French equivalent of the CIA, then known as SDECE, did not originate the Texas-oil conspiracy theory, the fake book it turned out when New Orleans District Attorney Jim Garrison was getting extensive attention with his theory that the jury ruled against in less than an hour, did impress many. That book, originally titled, *L'Amerique Brule*, roughly, *America Burns*, was re-titled *Farewell America* at

Garrison's suggestion. It is so libelous it could not be published or imported into this country, but some copies did cross over from Canada.

5 "Operation Northwoods," drafted by the Joint Chiefs of Staff, was another. The previously classified documents on it were publicly released in 1997. They describe various proposals for false flag operations that would provide a pretext for a US invasion of Cuba, including the sinking of Cuban refugee boats at sea, blowing up American ships, engaging in terrorist acts against Cuban immigrants in the US, blaming it all on Cuba. President Kennedy rejected these proposals. (See Appendix 2).

6 O'Donnell and Powers, *"Johnny, We Hardly Knew Ye"*, 244-245.

7 The currently available version includes the employee name as "QDDALE."

8 O'Donnell and Powers, *"Johnny, We Hardly Knew Ye"*, 270.

9 O'Donnell and Powers, *"Johnny, We Hardly Knew Ye"*, 270-271.

10 O'Donnell and Powers, *"Johnny, We Hardly Knew Ye"*, 271.

11 O'Donnell and Powers, *"Johnny, We Hardly Knew Ye"*, p. 306.

12 O'Donnell and Powers, *"Johnny, We Hardly Knew Ye"*, p. 272.

13 O'Donnell and Powers, *"Johnny, We Hardly Knew Ye"*, p. 273.

14 O'Donnell and Powers, *"Johnny, We Hardly Knew Ye"*, p. 308–310.

CHAPTER 4

1 James G. Blight, Bruce J. Allyn and David A. Welch, et al., *Cuba On The Brink: Castro, the Missile Crisis, and the Soviet Collapse,* (Pantheon Books, 1993).

2 This was the premise for the analysis I had intended writing in *Tiger to Ride* These conferences demonstrated the essential correctness of my analysis.

3 O'Donnell and Powers, *"Johnny, We Hardly Knew Ye"*, 313.

4 Robert F. Kennedy, *Thirteen Days; A Memoir of the Cuban Missile Crisis,* (W. W. Norton, 1969), 14–15.

5 Kennedy, *Thirteen Days,* 36.

6 Kennedy, *Thirteen Days,* 85–86.

7 Kennedy, *Thirteen Days,* 86.

8 Kennedy, *Thirteen Days,* 48.

9 Kennedy, *Thirteen Days,* 55.

10 Blight, Allyn, and Welch, *Cuba On The Brink.*

11 Kennedy, *Thirteen Days,* 55.

12 O'Donnell and Powers, *"Johnny, We Hardly Knew Ye"*, 317.

13 O'Donnell and Powers, *"Johnny, We Hardly Knew Ye"*, 318.

14 Reeves, *President Kennedy,* 379.

15 Confirmed by Reeves, *President Kennedy,* 36.

16 O'Donnell and Powers, *"Johnny, We Hardly Knew Ye"*, 318–320.

17 O'Donnell and Powers, *"Johnny, We Hardly Knew Ye"*, 320.

18 O'Donnell and Powers, *"Johnny, We Hardly Knew Ye"*, 321.

19 O'Donnell and Powers, *"Johnny, We Hardly Knew Ye"*, 322.
20 O'Donnell and Powers, *"Johnny, We Hardly Knew Ye"*, 324.
21 O'Donnell and Powers, *"Johnny, We Hardly Knew Ye"*, 326–327.
22 O'Donnell and Powers, *"Johnny, We Hardly Knew Ye"*, 332.
23 O'Donnell and Powers, *"Johnny, We Hardly Knew Ye"*, 332–333.
24 O'Donnell and Powers, *"Johnny, We Hardly Knew Ye"*, 333.
25 O'Donnell and Powers, *"Johnny, We Hardly Knew Ye"*, 335.
26 O'Donnell and Powers, *"Johnny, We Hardly Knew Ye"*, 336.
27 O'Donnell and Powers, *"Johnny, We Hardly Knew Ye"*, 336–337.
28 Kennedy, *Thirteen Days,* 96.
29 Kennedy, *Thirteen Days,* 97.
30 Kennedy, *Thirteen Days,* 98.
31 O'Donnell and Powers, *"Johnny, We Hardly Knew Ye"*, 339–340.
32 O'Donnell and Powers, *"Johnny, We Hardly Knew Ye"*, 341.
33 Reeves, *President Kennedy,* 425.
34 Bill Bell, "Cool JFK in Tapes of Crisis in 1962," *New York Daily News*, July 28, 1994, 6.
35 Bell does make reference to a short section of the tape that was erased for national security reasons. The speaker on that section of the tape is "presumed to be General Maxwell Taylor," the Chairman of the Joint Chiefs of Staff.
36 Jon Marcus, "New Cuba Tapes Show Congressional Leadership Wanted an Invasion." *Associated Press*, December 21 1994.

CHAPTER 5

1 Kennedy, *Thirteen Days,* 35.
2 Kennedy, *Thirteen Days,* 68.
3 Kennedy, *Thirteen Days,* 77.
4 Kennedy, *Thirteen Days,*.63.
5 O'Donnell and Powers, *"Johnny, We Hardly Knew Ye"*, 357.
6 Elie Abel, *The Missile Crisis*, (Lippincott, 1965) 26.
7 Abel, *The Missile Crisis*, 29.
8 Abel, *The Missile Crisis*, 26–27.
9 Abel, *The Missile Crisis*, 23.
10 Abel, *The Missile Crisis*, 29.
11 Reeves, *President Kennedy,* 229–230.
12 Reeves, *President Kennedy*, 696.
13 "Right" is the government's word repeated by the *Post.* It is not a "right" bestowed by anything at all or by any authority, but rather a unilateral option.
14 R. Jeffrey Smith, "Clinton Decides to Retain Bush Nuclear Arms Policy," *The Washington Post,* September 22, 1994, a1.
15 Margaret Shapiro, "Russian missile center has electricity cut off," *The Washington Post*, September 22, 1994, a26.

16 David Wise, *The Politics of Lying: Government Deception, Secrecy, and Power.* (Random House, 1973), 104–105.

CHAPTER 6

1 It is important to note that the official determination not to investigate the crime itself does not necessarily implicate those who did the cover-up. I am confident that there are other reasons for the de facto conspiracy to cover up the crime.

2 Linda Hunt, *Secret Agenda: The United States Government, Nazi Scientists, and Project Paperclip, 1945 to 1990* (St. Martin's Press, 1991).

3 "C" is how Britain's chief of intelligence was known. "C" was Sir Stewart Graham Menzies. The book is *C: The Secret Life of Sir Stewart Graham Menzies, Spymaster to Winston Churchill* by Anthony Cave Brown.

4 Anthony Cave Brown, *"C": The Secret Life of Sir Stewart Graham Menzies, Spymaster to Winston Churchill.* (Macmillan 1987).

5 Walter Pincus, "According to Panel, CIA Should Lock Its Internal Watchdog in the Doghouse," *The Washington Post*, November 3, 1994 a23.

6 Pincus, "According to Panel," a23.

7 It was Brendan Sullivan of the Edward Bennett Williams law firm who made a national hero of the convicted felon Oliver North who, while on the Reagan White House staff, implemented policies that violated our Constitution and our laws in its childish concept of what intelligence is and what intelligence agencies do.

8 Arthur M. Schlesinger, *A Thousand Days; John F. Kennedy in the White House.* (Houghton Mifflin, 1965) 94. Averell Harriman was an elder statesman who held a high position in the State Department and Carl Kaysen was the former Harvard professor who was then McGeorge Bundy's deputy on the National Security Council.

9 In Harold Weisberg, *Whitewash: The Report on the Warren Report*, (By the Author, 1966), 180.

10 Harold Weisberg, *Never Again!: the Government Conspiracy in the JFK Assassination*, (Carroll & Graf, 1995).

11 That this was suppressed and the transcript was not published by that committee is merely one of the reasons I refer to it as "The House assassins committee." Under the tight control of its chief counsel and staff director Robert Blakey, it suppressed this fact of the greatest possible significance in any honest investigation.

CHAPTER 7

1 Weisberg, *Whitewash*, 24–25.

2 Weisberg, *Whitewash*, 30, printed in facsimile.

3 Harold Weisberg, *Oswald in New Orleans*, (Canyon Books, 1967) 85ff.

4 Weisberg, *Oswald in New Orleans*, 93–94, WC Hearings 8H 297–8. This is the Commission testimony of John E. Donovan who was the captain under whom Oswald worked in their special radar unit that sometimes was in the van that would be placed on the deck of a carrier.
5 The autopsy photographs and X-rays, essential to understanding the crime, were refused by the FBI in the preparation of its report on the assassination. And at the insistence of Chief Justice Warren, only a few of the Warren Commission staff had very limited access to it. In addition, the pathologists who conducted the autopsy were not given access to them in relation to their testimony before the commission.
6 False swearing to what is material is the felony of perjury.
7 The transcript of the press conference is available on the History Matters website https://www.history-matters.com/archive/jfk/arrb/master_med_set/md41/html/Image0.htm.
8 Weisberg, *Whitewash*, 161–162.
9 Harold Weisberg, *Post-Mortem*, (By the Author, 1969), 565–596.
10 Weisberg, *Post-Mortem*, 597.
11 Weisberg, *Post-Mortem*, 310.
12 Weisberg, *Post-Mortem*, 524.

CHAPTER 8

1 Weisberg, *Whitewash*, 121–122.
2 Warren Commission, *Investigation of the Assassination of President John F. Kennedy: Hearings Before the President's Commission on the Assassination of President John F. Kennedy*. (U.S. Government Printing Office 1964), 15H283-434, in Weisberg, *Whitewash* 122.
3 quoted in Weisberg, *Whitewash*, 122.
4 Weisberg, *Oswald in New Orleans*, 98.
5 This Memorandum to the Commission from Slawson and Coleman can be viewed in the Weisberg Archive at Hood College, http://jfk.hood.edu/Collection/Weisberg%20Subject%20Index%20Files/S%20Disk/Slawson%20W%20David/Item%2003.pdf.
6 Weisberg, *Post-Mortem*, 627–8.
7 Weisberg, *Whitewash*, 123.
8 Editor's Note: Weisberg notes here that his voluminous files were also open to anyone writing on the subject, along with the use of his copier.
9 Weisberg, *Whitewash*, 124–125, 127, 132.
10 Weisberg, *Whitewash*, 126, 130–131, 200.
11 Weisberg, *Post-Mortem*, 486. Under FOIA, I ultimately did obtain all the Commission's withheld executive session transcripts. All were classified TOP SECRET. There is not a thing in them that justified this classification or any classification at all. The only reason to keep them Secret was

to prevent embarrassment. The law is specific in stating that under it this is not justification for withholding anything. I published this January 22, 1964 executive session transcript in facsimile in *Post Mortem.* (1975:475ff) I published the transcript of the January 27 session, a follow-up on this one, also in facsimile in *Whitewash IV.* (By the Author, 1974), 36ff.

12 Weisberg, *Post-Mortem*, 485, 487.

13 Facsimile in Weisberg, *Post-Mortem*, 487.

14 Harold Weisberg and James Lesar, *Whitewash IV: JFK Assassination Transcript*, (By the Author, 1974), 62–63.

15 Weisberg and Lesar, *Whitewash IV*, 58.

16 Weisberg and Lesar, *Whitewash IV*, 124–130.

17 Weisberg and Lesar, *Whitewash IV*, 146.

18 Both Jaworski and Hobby had connections to the CIA. When he was appointed as Watergate Special Prosecutor, Jaworski "was and remained a director of the M.D. Anderson Fund, a CIA front, despite the CIA's involvement in the scandals." Jaworski managed to cover up the CIA's heavy involvement. Hobby, Jaworski's contact at the *Houston Post* "also had a CIA foundation front. Both were exposed in 1967." As a consequence, much of the CIA's involvement remained secret. Jaworski was still alive when I wrote of this in *Whitewash IV* but had not a word to say about it.

CHAPTER 9

1 Sidney Kaufman's field was movies. He produced the *Macbeth* that won an Emmy for NBC-TV, among his many accomplishments in that field. He served in both the Army and the Navy in World War II and was in the OSS with me.

2 John Sparrow, *After the Assassination: A Positive Appraisal of the Warren Report.* Chilmark Press. 1967. 77 pages.

3 The next publisher to whom I was referred predicted an even greater success. "With this book, your background and our public relations know-how," the editor who read it told me, "You will be the best-known private citizen in the country and we'll have the *Green Felt Jungle* of 1965." (I had been a reporter, an investigative reporter, a Senate investigator and editor, and I had been in intelligence, the OSS, in World War II. I go into this background in detail in the manuscript *Inside the JFK Assassination Industry.*) That was the excited prediction all the way up to the president, who also owned most of that publishing house. He had a legitimate reason for rejecting *Whitewash* as he did. He had published a fraudulent book, *Calories Don't Count.* Six men were already under federal indictment over that book. As his words were conveyed to me, "Were I to publish this book it would be the red flag under the charging bull. I do not want to be the seventh man indicted."

4 Harold Weisberg, *Photographic Whitewash: Suppressed Kennedy Assassination Pictures*, (By the Author, 1976 edition), 295ff.
5 Tim Weiner, "Director Of C.I.A. To Leave, Ending Troubled Tenure," *New York Times*, December 29, 1994, 1.
6 Wise, *The Politics of Lying*, 113–114.
7 Weisberg and Lesar, *Whitewash IV*, 72, 62–62.
8 House Select Committee on Assassination (HSCA), *Hearings*, (U.S. Government Printing Office, 1979), Volume IV, 55ff, 118ff.
9 David Wise, "Patrician for the CIA," *New York Times*, December 11,1994, BR9.
10 HSCA, *Hearings*, IV:5-250.
11 Senate Foreign Relations Committee, *Events Incident to the Summit Conference*. (U.S. Government Printing Office, 1960).
12 J William. Fullbright, "Speech in the U.S. Senate, *Congressional Record*, 1960, 14734.
13 Mary McGrory, "Rebel Without A Trace, *The Washington Post*, November 6, 1994, c01.
14 Walter Pincus, "Panel Head Presses Clinton, CIA to Close Gap." *Washington Post*, December 3, 1994, a11.
15 Christopher B. Daly, "Ex-Director Faults CIA Of Carter Era; Reports `Irrelevant,' Turner Tells Meeting," *Washington Post*, December 3, 1994, a11.

CHAPTER 10

1 More recently, other factors seem to have taken on greater importance in the vice presidential selection process, where the effort to achieve broader appeal involves focusing on gender, race, age, differing levels of governmental experience, etc. Historically, however, the ideological balancing seems to have been the most significant consideration.
2 Weisberg, *Whitewash*, 26, 30.
3 Weisberg and Lesar, *Whitewash IV*, 24–25.

CHAPTER 11

1 In a 2003 essay, Galbraith goes into greater detail on Kennedy's plans for ending U.S. involvement in the Vietnam war. (https://www.bostonreview.net/articles/galbraith-exit-strategy-vietnam/).
2 Khrushchev quoted in Heather A. Purcell and James K. Galbraith, "Did The U.S. Military Plan A Nuclear First Strike For 1963?" *The American Prospect*, Issue 19, 1994, 88.
3 Purcell and Galbraith, "Did the U.S. Military. . . ."
4 Purcell and Galbraith, "Did the U.S. Military. . . ."
5 Purcell and Galbraith, "Did the U.S. Military. . . ."

6 A subsequent investigation contradicted the CIA's claim that Olson killed himself. And Eric Olson's testimony to the House of Representatives Government Operations subcommittee on legislation and national security on Sept. 28, 1994 included the following: "a former agent who worked with an intelligence team headed by Dr. Sidney Gottlieb, one of two CIA agents responsible for secretly dosing Dr. (Frank) Olson with LSD, . . . has confirmed that members of that small group (of CIA agents) all believed that my father was murdered."

7 HSCA Report Volume II, "Testimony of John Hart," (U.S. Government Printing Office, 1978), 487ff.

8 Editors' Note: Unfortunately, Weisberg did not indicate the papers or the exact date, so the quotations cannot be properly cited. The GAO testimony itself can be found at the GAO website at https://www.gao.gov/assets/t-nsiad-94-266.pdf.

9 Pincus, "According to the Panel . . .,"1994 a7.

10 Oswald had been careful to initiate his defection without actually defecting, and as we have seen, he was not a "Red"—rather, he vehemently opposed the Communist Party USA, and was anti-Soviet, even when he was in the Soviet Union.

11 Weisberg, *Whitewash*, 163.

12 William Manchester, *The Death of a President: November 20-November 25*, (Harper & Row,1967).

CHAPTER 12

1 Because in the time permitted nobody in the world, not the country's best shots in tests for the Commission, could replicate the feat attributed to Oswald—a poor shot with a faulty weapon! This also is documented with official records in *Never Again!* and as it is relating to the Commission in the first chapter of my *Post Mortem*.

2 FBI, *Investigation of the Assassination of John F. Kennedy November 22, 1963,* (U.S. Government Printing Office, 1963), 1, (Warren Commission Document CD1).

3 Wise, *The Politics of Lying*, 134ff.

4 Wise, *The Politics of Lying*, 154.

5 Heine's first name is spelled "Erik" in some sources.

6 John Hanrahan, "CIA Chief Faces Quiz in Agent Slander Suit," *The Washington Post*, June 7, 1969, A7.

7 Wise, *The Politics of Lying*, 149–150.

8 Wise, *The Politics of Lying*, 53.

9 Wise, *The Politics of Lying*, 14.

10 Wise, *The Politics of Lying*, 15–16.

11 Wise, *The Politics of Lying*, 18.

12 Wise, *The Politics of Lying,* 96–97.
13 Wise, *The Politics of Lying.* 144–145.
14 Robert J. Donovan, *Eisenhower: The Inside Story.* Harper and Brothers. 1956.
15 Available in the Harold Weisberg Archive at Hood College at jfk.hood.edu.

CHAPTER 13

1 Editors' note: Drawing primarily on the work of Harold Weisberg, the editors wrote and presented a paper on this very theme entitled, "The JFK Assassination and the Failure of Institutions: The Sociological Significance of a Major Historical Event" at the annual meeting of the Society for the Study of Social Problems in Washington D.C. on August 18, 1995.
2 Robert G. Blakey and Richard N. Billings, *Fatal Hour: The Assassination of President Kennedy by Organized Crime,* (Berkley Books, 1992).
3 Civil Action 75-1996. Acting Director L. Patrick Gray and Assistant Director Edward Miller were indicted for approving illegal break-ins during the Nixon administration.
4 Weisberg, *Whitewash.*
5 Gerald L. Posner, *Case Closed: Lee Harvey Oswald and the Assassination of JFK,* (Random House, 1993).
6 Harold Weisberg, *Case Open: The Unanswered JFK Assassination Questions,* (Carroll & Graf, 1994). (Weisberg, 1994).
7 Michael L. Kurtz, *Crime of the Century: The Kennedy Assassination from a Historian's Perspective,* (University of Tennessee Press, 1982).
8 James H.Lesar, "Crime of the Century: The Kennedy Assassination from a Historian's Perspective," [Book Review], *Journal of American History,* 1983, 70, no. 2, 469.
9 David S. Lifton, *Best Evidence: Disguise and Deception in the Assassination of John F. Kennedy,* (Macmillan, 1980).
10 Harrison Edward Livingston and Robert J. Groden, *High Treason: The Assassination of President John F. Kennedy: What Really Happened,* (Conservatory Press, 1989); *High Treason 2: The Great Cover-Up of the Assassination of President John F. Kennedy,* (Carroll & Graf, 1992).
11 Harrison Edward Livingston, *Killing the Truth: Deceit and Deception in the JFK Case,* (Carroll & Graf, 1993).

CONCLUSION

1 Since Weisberg wrote this, three more impeachments have occurred: President Clinton once and President Trump twice. None resulted in conviction. Nixon resigned before a likely impeachment.
2 The cost of these bombers probably exceeded the entire national budget in the years of my youth.

3 Wise, *The Politics of Lying*, 342–343.
4 Wise, *The Politics of Lying*, 400.
5 Wise, *The Politics of Lying*, 305.
6 Wise, *The Politics of Lying*, 311.
7 Wise, *The Politics of Lying*, 354.
8 Wise, *The Politics of Lying*, 353–354.
9 Wise, *The Politics of Lying*, 353.
10 Thomas Paine, *Common Sense*.

AFTERWORD

1 Richard Rhodes, "The General and World War III." *The New Yorker*, June 19,1995, 47.
2 Rhodes, "The General . . ."
3 Rhodes, "The General . . ."
4 Rhodes, "The General . . ."
5 Richard Rhodes, *Dark Sun: The Making of the Hydrogen Bomb,* Simon & Schuster, 1995.
6 Rhodes, *Dark Sun,* Jacket.
7 Rhodes, *Dark Sun,* 575–576.
8 Dino A. Brugioni and Robert F. McCort, *Eyeball to Eyeball : The Inside Story of the Cuban Missile Crisis*, (Random House. 1991), 59–60.

APPENDIX 1

1 Warren Commission, *Hearings*, 6H377.
2 Sylvia Meagher, *Accessories After the Fact: The Warren Commission, the Authorities, and the Report,* (Vintage Press, 1976), 62–63.
3 FBI Memorandum from Belmont to Tolson. September 23, 1964. 62-109060. Archived by the Mary Farrell Foundation. https://www.maryferrell.org/php/showlist.php?docset=1196.
4 FBI Radiogram from Director to SAC Dallas. March 31, 1964, 62-109060-2783. Archived by the Mary Farrell Foundation. https://www.maryferrell.org/php/showlist.php?docset=1196.
5 Gerald D. McKnight, *Breach of Trust: How the Warren Commission Failed the Nation and Why*, University Press of Kansas, 2005), 399.
6 David R. Wrone, *The Zapruder Film: Reframing JFK's Assassination*, (University Press of Kansas, 2003), 166.
7 McKnight, *Breach of Trust*, 17–18; Weisberg, *Never Again!* 29–30.
8 FBI Message from SAC Dallas to Director, December 13, 1963, 62-109060-1899. Archived by the Mary Farrell Foundation. https://www.maryferrell.org/php/showlist.php?docset=1196. See also Wrone, *Zapruder Film*, 155.
9 Warren Commission, *Hearings,* 3H444.

10 Meagher, *Accessories After the Fact,* 107.
11 Meagher, *Accessories After the Fact,* 108.

INDEX

J

K

L

Z